The Obesity Epidemic

Although increasing obesity levels are currently big news, very few people have stopped to think carefully about what this trend actually means. For example, the scientific community has announced that the 'obesity epidemic' is both the natural consequence of 'modern Western lifestyles' as well as an urgent and unprecedented global health crisis for which nothing short of an all-out 'war on obesity' will do. As a result, experts from across the spectrum are now advocating profound changes to the ways we live. Everybody – including family doctors, parents, teachers, sporting clubs, big and small business and governments – has a role to play in the 'war on obesity'. But is talk of an obesity 'crisis' justified? Is it the product of measured scientific reasoning or age-old 'habits of mind'? Why is it happening now? And are there potential risks associated with talking about obesity as a 'crisis' or 'epidemic'?

The Obesity Epidemic proposes that contemporary obesity science and popular comment are a complex mix of highly uncertain knowledge, familiar (yet usually unstated) moral agendas and ideological assumptions. It argues that it is both unhelpful and unwise to talk about 'modern Western lifestyles' as if we all lived in the same way. The authors also challenge a long list of often repeated claims such as that physical activity levels are declining, that food consumption is going up and that televisions and computers are making children fat. They ask us to think about the political, moral and ideological questions which *do not* get asked when experts talk about an 'obesity epidemic' as if it were a problem for 'everyone everywhere'. Finally, they ask us to pause for a moment to consider what might be the unintended consequences of a 'war on obesity', particularly for children, women and those who find themselves classified as overweight or obese.

This is a controversial book about a critical theme in health and exercise studies. It provides much needed, thorough and reflective analysis of the current state of research and will transform debates about body weight, physical activity, food and health. It is essential reading for anyone interested in health and obesity issues, including teachers, scientists, health workers, doctors and policy makers.

Michael Gard is Senior Lecturer in physical education at Charles Sturt University, Australia.

Jan Wright is a Professor of Education and the Associate Dean (Research) in the Faculty of Education at the University of Wollongong, Australia.

The Obesity Epidemic
Science, morality and ideology

Michael Gard and Jan Wright

Routledge
Taylor & Francis Group

LONDON AND NEW YORK

First published 2005 by Routledge
2 Park Square, Milton Park, Abingdon, Oxon OX14 4RN

Simultaneously published in the USA and Canada
by Taylor & Francis Inc
270 Madison Ave, New York, NY 10016

Reprinted 2005, 2006

Transferred to Digital Printing 2007

Routledge is an imprint of the Taylor & Francis Group, an informa business

Typeset in Goudy by
Florence Production Ltd, Stoodleigh, Devon
Printed and bound in Great Britain by
TJI Digital, Padstow, Cornwall

British Library Cataloguing in Publication Data
A catalogue record for this book is available from the British Library

Library of Congress Cataloging in Publication Data
A catalog record for this book has been requested

ISBN 10: 0-415-31895-5 (hbk)
ISBN 10: 0-415-31896-3 (pbk)

ISBN 13: 978-0-415-31895-2 (hbk)
ISBN 13: 978-0-415-31896-9 (pbk)

Contents

For Lily

Illustrations

Figures

Tables

Acknowledgements

From Michael

The research that produced this book was supported by Charles Sturt University's Faculty of Education, School of Human Movement Studies and Office for Research and Graduate Studies. Thanks go to all my colleagues and friends at Charles Sturt University who, together, create such a warm working environment. In particular, I would like to acknowledge the support, insights and friendship of my Head of School, Frank Marino, who continues to be a steadying influence on all who have the good fortune to work with him. Thanks, as ever, to Bob Meyenn for his care, interest and support. Thanks also to Ramona Wesley and Tony O'Neill for their assistance in the final hectic weeks.

I am grateful to the Auckland College of Education for its financial support of my visit to New Zealand in 2003 during which I was able to present, discuss and develop this work. Special thanks to Bruce Ross for his scholarly input and to the Ovens family for their hospitality.

My parents, Beverly and Ralph, have patiently and lovingly watched over all my mistakes, stumbles and occasional triumphs. I hope this book brings them some small pleasure and reward for all they have done.

Throughout the ups and downs of writing of this book I was sustained by both the Gards and Lecouteurs and by my Bathurst family. They have all been indispensable in their own way.

Finally, this book would not have happened without the encouragement, hard work, friendship and inspiration of Sharon Pickering.

From Jan

My thanks to my family Nick, Kate and Tim for their patience and support and to Tina for her editorial support in the final versions of the manuscript.

Contributor biography

Bruce Ross has published on muscle cramp and motor unit recruitment, physical education history and philosophy and tertiary teaching from a Freirian perspective. Currently he teaches Bachelor of Physical Education students at the Auckland College of Education after twenty-eight years as a senior lecturer in work physiology at the University of Otago School of Physical Education.

1   Science and fatness

The first section of Steven Jay Gould's (1996) *Life's Grandeur* is called 'How shall we read and spot a trend?'. Gould's subjects here are nothing less than the meaning of life on earth and the cherished human idea of 'progress'. He begins by discussing people's tendency to use both the word and the metaphor of 'progress' whenever they talk about 'natural selection' and 'evolution', even though formal evolutionary theory suggests no such thing. For Gould, this is a mistake because, as with pre-Copernican and pre-Darwinian ways of thinking, it tries to locate humanity at the centre of creation, constructing it as the crowning achievement of life on earth. The idea of 'progress' also assigns to evolution a sense of inevitability, as if the only reason for there being life in the first place was to produce human kind. So even though we may think humans are the embodiment of 'progress', we should not forget that *Homo sapiens* is 'only a recent twiglet on an ancient and enormous genealogical bush' (Gould 1996: 41).

The idea of 'progress' is also an example of the way people retrospectively impose order on events so that we might understand (or think we understand) what has happened. After all, not only are random events and systems virtually impossible to predict or control, it is also extremely difficult to tell a good story about them. 'Progress' *is* a good story, something which no doubt partly explains its popularity and Gould shows how people as varied as footballers, artists, journalists and scientists often use the word 'evolution' as code for 'progress'. While we may be inclined to assume that footballers and journalists are more likely to fall into these unfortunate habits of mind than scientists, Gould's message is that this is also a trap – scientists, as much as any other group of people, often think in predetermined, pre-packaged ways which, rather than telling it 'like it is', interpret data so that they fit the story they wanted to tell all along.

Writers and scholars have often noticed that archetypal stories and ideas, such as the idea of 'progress', co-exist within cultures alongside their opposites. For example, the idea of essential human goodness exists, no doubt, partly as a consequence of the opposite idea that at their core humans are self-centred animals acting on base instincts. In the same way, the story of inevitable decline in human affairs is just as familiar as the one about inevitable progress. Gould (1996: 79) writes: 'Remember that our cultural legends include two canonical modes for trending: advances to something better as reasons for celebration, and declines to an abyss as sources of lamentation'.

At the risk of committing the same folly of 'trend spotting' that Gould warns against, the story of decline seems particularly prevalent in the current age. It is as if we now live in a time of perpetual crisis – everything from democracy to law and order and public transport is often said to be either in crisis or on the verge of one. But crises are not limited to institutions. Human beings, both their bodies and minds, are also under siege from threats of one kind or another. As a recent magazine article puts it:

> There seems to be a new one each week. In the last three months alone, we have had a swathe of them reported: shoplifting, methamphetamine, addiction, diabetes, meningitis, schizophrenia. Yes, we are in the midst of an epidemic of . . . epidemics.

The article goes on:

> The most serious, costly and deadly of these, say health experts, is obesity. We are told that our ballooning weight leads to disease and early death and is costing millions in health spending. Competing headlines make a catastrophe of the situation, as we 'declare war' on this 'ticking time bomb'. We are force-fed a monotonous mantra: we are fat and getting fatter, and we must lose weight.
>
> (Lockett 2003: 17)

The 'monotonous mantra' to which the article refers – the so-called 'obesity epidemic' – is the subject of this book. In our view, the time has come for a critical appraisal of the idea of an 'obesity epidemic' that allegedly afflicts a large proportion of the countries of the world and threatens a global health catastrophe. To take up Gould's point, while there appears to be a trend of some kind – the number of people who are classified as overweight and obese does seem to have increased – the way we 'read' or interpret this trend is subject to people's preconceived ideas and biases. For example, a central argument in this book is that people have latched on to the idea of an 'obesity epidemic' because it conforms to a familiar story about Western decadence and decline. The 'obesity epidemic', so the argument goes, is the product of an 'effortless' Western lifestyle which has become progressively hostile towards physical activity and dietary restraint. In other words, Westernized living makes you lazy, gluttonous and, eventually, fat. We will argue that this represents a serious misreading of Western life as it currently exists. However, it is a popular version of a familiar story which pre-dates by centuries the relatively recent spike in overweight and obesity statistics.

As we write, the 'obesity epidemic' as a bad news story is at fever pitch in both scholarly journals and popular reporting (Anderssen 2000; Brownell and Horgen 2004; Critser 2003; Dietz 2001; Kelly 2003; Klein 2004; Radford 2002; Strauss and Pollock 2001; Tabakoff 2002; New York Times 2001a; Wang 2001; Waters and Baur 2003). And just as Gould noticed that neither footballers nor scientists were immune from making the erroneous slide from the theory of evolution to the story of 'progress', this book will show that, scientific credentials or not, people find the story of Western decadence and decline irresistible when it comes to discussing obesity.

Tied up with the *causal* story of Western decadence and decline are claims about the *consequences* of the 'obesity epidemic'. To take just one recent example (Fox 2003: 1): obesity is claimed to be the world's 'number one health problem' with the potential to 'reduce life expectancy by 10 years or more'. We are concerned that discussion (both popular and scientific) about the consequences of increasing numbers of overweight and obese people may be just as misguided as talk about why it is happening. In this book we explore the possibility that the dire predictions and sheer intensity of 'obesity talk' has more to do with preconceived moral and ideological beliefs about fatness than a sober assessment of existing evidence.

The central argument of this book is that there are many questions that we should ask before putting our faith in the idea of an 'obesity epidemic' or our energies into trying to solve it. In order to make this argument, we will consider the 'obesity epidemic' from a variety of angles. We will examine what scientists and non-scientists say about it, especially its causes and solutions, and ask whether these things are true or even make sense. We will ask whether it is just possible that the problem of obesity has been significantly over-stated. We will examine the ways in which preconceived ideas and beliefs have shaped what people say about the 'obesity epidemic'. We will offer readers alternative ways of thinking about the phenomena of overweight and obesity from the ones which are currently dominant. And we will conclude this book by arguing that, rather than a global health crisis or an 'objective' scientific fact, the 'obesity epidemic' can be seen as a complex pot-pourri of science, morality and ideological assumptions about people and their lives which has ethically questionable effects.

Certainty and uncertainty

The scientific literature on overweight and obesity is now huge. As with any area of knowledge, decades of sustained scholarship and research have produced a proliferation of fields and sub-fields of specialization in which, as the adage goes, more and more is known about less and less. Viewed sympathetically, the current state of knowledge about overweight and obesity could be seen as an incomplete jigsaw for which the pieces are gradually being found and fitted together. From this viewpoint, the general causes and cures for what has been called the 'obesity epidemic' are basically known – modern Western societies have become more sedentary, people are consuming too much food, particularly high-fat food, which is cheap and widely available, and we must now eat more wisely and exercise more often. Many people researching and writing about overweight and obesity will readily admit that the specifics of this line of argument remain to be completely fleshed out. For example, the significance of a person's genetic inheritance in determining their propensity to gain weight remains controversial, as does the exact preventative effect of exercise on particular diseases. However, the overall picture, of an increasingly sedentary and overfed Western (and, increasingly, non-Western) populace is now widely accepted.

In this book we offer a different perspective. We argue that the current state of our scientific 'knowledge' about overweight and obesity is not so much incomplete as confused and replete with flawed and misleading assumptions. More controversially, we will argue that it is difficult to see how the scientific study of overweight and obesity is 'progressing' – leading to more useful, sophisticated, humane and ethically defensible knowledge – at all. Many of these problems seem simply to result from the reluctance of researchers to read outside of their own discipline. For example, many scholars who write for medical and scientific journals claim that reported increases in childhood obesity are partly the result of less time being devoted to physical education in schools, and then go on confidently to predict that more school physical education will lead to less overweight children. No link between school physical education and either the long-term health, body weight or physical activity levels of children has ever been established. Indeed, some physical education scholars have speculated about whether physical education, as it is often taught, is not more likely to *dissuade* children from being physically active (Tinning and Fitzclarence 1992).

However, there is more to the story than sheer academic insularity. Some of the problems with current knowledge about overweight and obesity appear to be more wilful and are the products of a determination to see the world in particular ways. For example, the overweight and obesity literature is dominated by the idea that Western society *in general* is more sedentary than in the past when almost no empirical evidence for this claim exists. In fact, there are many core ideas within the science of body weight and health and the mediating role played by exercise and diet which are simply assumed to be true.

Sometimes the most interesting thing about reading scientific research articles occurs when authors write in non-scientific ways. It is in these moments, when scientists 'loosen up' and move away from dry data description and analysis to a more speculative and even informal register, that the full significance of their work, not to mention the sheer intellectual skill which produced it, becomes apparent. But this change of register can be revealing in other ways. It can also signal the moment when the authors have turned their minds to the question of causation. As most scientists will readily admit, it is extremely uncommon that raw data alone explains what is going on. To do this, scientists are often forced to step outside of their data and to venture into fields of knowledge where they have much less formal training and expertise.

This situation occurs frequently when human beings are the subject of research. So even though scientific journals might report that the incidence of conditions such as clinical depression are rapidly increasing (some say we are in the midst of an 'epidemic' of mental illness), the reasons for this increase generate heated and absorbing scientific debates, in part because it forces scientists to think about the social and cultural worlds in which we live. Are modern, competitive, commercialized societies becoming increasingly 'toxic' or is it simply that the social stigma of mental illness is declining, resulting in more people seeking clinical help? Or is it something else? Whichever the case, those whose job it is to produce statistics about mental illness or treat the mentally ill must inevitably move outside of their area of specialization when people ask them 'why?'. This is by no means a bad thing. Scientists and physicians, like everyone else, have a right to contribute to discussion about complex problems, particularly those, like mental illness, which appear to have both biological and social dimensions.

The study of obesity is another case in point. Measuring a person's body weight and classifying them as overweight or obese tells us nothing about how and why they got to this point. This is an even bigger challenge when we are discussing large populations and yet the reasons given for the so-called 'obesity epidemic' have mostly been made up of the speculations of the scientific community, albeit speculations delivered with an air of certainty. So as well as being a critical assessment of the knowledge claims of 'obesity epidemic' researchers and commentators, this book is also about certainty and uncertainty – the ways in which sheer speculation comes to be thought of as 'fact', both in scholarly literature and the popular media.

People who talk about the 'obesity epidemic' often adopt a tone of absolute conviction. Both the extent of the problem and its causes are held to be self-evident. But as we will show, whatever we might say about the science of body weight, health, exercise and diet, the one thing we cannot say is that these are fields in which consensus is common. In fact, they are fields in which experts are constantly coming together in an attempt to formulate consensus statements precisely because it is so hard to achieve. What is interesting, then, is the way people who talk and write about obesity and its causes, in fields such as medicine, exercise science and public health, in the midst of great uncertainty, manage to speak with such unified certainty about the obesity crisis.

In this book we will suggest that when people talk about the 'obesity epidemic', the scientific uncertainties which exist tend to be papered over by unsubstantiated assumptions. It is as if empirical confusion and uncertainty has created the perfect environment for rampant speculation. This is an interesting state of affairs, not least because, as university teachers, we are constantly reminding undergraduate students to provide evidence for their beliefs and, where evidence is lacking, to reconsider their views. We point out the dangers of speaking in blithely uninformed ways about concepts and phenomena that have been thoroughly researched by others. We tell our students that this advice is not intended to discourage them from thinking creatively, but rather to show that crude generalizations are no substitute for careful, time-consuming and sometimes tedious scholarship. But at the level of public and scientific discussion, generalizations are, if anything, the lifeblood of 'obesity epidemic' thinking. Take the following example.

In 1999, the journal *Medicine and Science in Sports and Exercise* published a supplementary issue devoted to overweight and obesity. The issue, which we refer to a number of times in this book, presented the findings of the then recently held American College of Sports Medicine Consensus Conference on physical activity in Indianapolis. As the word 'consensus' suggests, the purpose of the conference and supplementary issue of the journal was to assess the state of scientific knowledge about the relationship between physical activity, overweight and obesity, and human health. In their introductory article, the leading obesity researchers Claude Bouchard and Steven Blair describe what they saw as the growing worldwide problem of obesity and concluded:

> The tools available to reverse this unhealthy trend are remarkably simple in appearance as they center on the promotion of eating regular and healthy meals, avoiding high caloric density snacks, drinking water instead of energy-containing beverages, keeping dietary fat at about 30% of calories, cutting

down on TV viewing time, walking more, participating more in sports and other energy-consuming leisure activities, and other similar measures. However, it will be a daunting task to change the course of nations that have progressively become quite comfortable with an effortless lifestyle in which individual consumption is almost unlimited.

(Bouchard and Blair 1999: S500)

In this passage two well-known obesity scientists are 'caught in the act' of speculation, although their tone of certainty may have the effect of obscuring the fact that they are speculating. While Bouchard is well known for his work on the genetics of physical activity and body weight and Blair is an exercise physiologist who works with obese people, they appear to have joined forces here to comment, perhaps even pass judgement, on society at large. As well as apparently claiming that people today generally eat too much unhealthy food, watch too much television and partake in too little exercise (all highly debatable claims in themselves), they then cast themselves in the roles of social commentators, even moral philosophers, arguing that nations have become 'progressively . . . comfortable with an effortless lifestyle'. The use of the word 'progressively' is significant here because it suggests that people have become *more* 'comfortable' and life *more* 'effortless' than in previous times, claims which have certainly never been addressed, let alone substantiated, in the work of either author or, indeed, of other researchers working in the same fields. They then turn part social-psychologist, claiming that changing people's behaviour will be a 'daunting task', presumably because Bouchard and Blair believe that people are generally unwilling to change their lives in ways that would make them less 'effortless'. Dare we even suggest that, as well as being debatable, their claim that we live in societies where 'consumption is almost unlimited' sounds a little like the pronouncement of an economist? Whether or not this is fair, the point of interest to us here is the air of matter-of-fact certainty with which these claims are made.

Why is all this important? As we have already suggested, the idea that the world is in the grip of an 'obesity epidemic' is currently ubiquitous. Scientists, doctors, politicians, teachers, health professionals, journalists and others say that the 'obesity epidemic' represents nothing less than a looming global health catastrophe. Perhaps not surprisingly, very few of those who have announced the 'obesity epidemic's' arrival have been satisfied with being mere messengers. Most have also been unable to resist the temptation of claiming to know why it is occurring and what we need to do about it.

Despite this array of different voices, a remarkably similar story about why it is happening has emerged. The 'obesity epidemic', we are told, is the consequence of modern 'Western life'. Children, in particular, have been singled out as an especially problematic lot. Experts of one kind or another regularly describe today's children as not only fatter than previous generations, but also less active, less athletically skilled, less interested in physical activity, less self-disciplined (and therefore more likely to choose the 'easy' or 'soft' option, be it with respect to physical activity or food) and more addicted to technology.

The 'obesity epidemic' is, in short, a modern-day story of sloth and gluttony – Western life has produced a never-ending array of temptations which we have not had the self-discipline or moral fibre to resist. The field of public health, in particular, has long complained about the difficulties associated with getting people to change their exercise and eating behaviours, usually framing the problem as one in which basically recalcitrant populations refuse to do what is good for them. No doubt some readers will have noticed in the above passage that all of Bouchard and Blair's 'remarkably simple' solutions all relate to the behaviour of individual citizens and say nothing about the actions of governments, corporations and other institutions. Even so, having described the solution to the problem of obesity as 'remarkably simple', Bouchard and Blair apparently believe it is *still* too 'daunting' a task for most people.

Whether or not we have correctly interpreted the intention of Bouchard and Blair's words, their characterization of the 'obesity epidemic', its causes and solutions, is representative of popular and scientific comment. And for us, each coming to the issues of overweight and obesity with different life experiences and areas of expertise, the question of whether this characterization is true, fair or even helpful was the primary motivation for writing this book.

To put our argument simply, the 'obesity epidemic' story of sloth and gluttony is one which has a number of ingredients. The first is certainty in the face of uncertainty. There is a great deal we do not know about overweight and obesity and their effect on human health, and there are a number of different ways of interpreting current overweight and obesity levels. However, at present, only one story is told. Where there are gaps in empirical knowledge, people, including scientists, often fill these gaps with assumptions and generalizations. This is not to ignore the fact that the *existence* of comparatively solid empirical findings may not be enough to stop some people from generalizing. However, the existence of uncertainty probably encourages many who would not otherwise do so.

Second, the assumptions which are used to fill these gaps appear to be supported by entrenched and widely held popular beliefs. For example, the assumption that technology per se has a corrupting influence, particularly on children, and that it corrupts both our bodies and our minds, is virulent in 'obesity epidemic' thinking. This is a belief that persists despite an obvious lack of empirical support.

Third, the 'obesity epidemic' relies, in part, on a particular form of morality. It is a morality that sees the problem as a product of individual failing and weakness. In terms of the overall critique of 'obesity epidemic' thinking that we offer in this book, this is an important point. Some readers will be aware that many contributors to the scientific literature claim that overweight and obesity have 'exploded' in Western countries over the last twenty to thirty years. Does this mean that at some point during the 1970s or 1980s huge numbers of people around the world suddenly went into moral decline? Despite what would appear (at least to us) to be the obvious implausibility of this argument, we will show that this is exactly the argument put forward by some commentators. On the whole, those who make this kind of argument are not obesity scientists and researchers. By the same token, the science of overweight and obesity is strongly influenced by a usually (although not always) unstated moral agenda. As such, it is easily interpreted and used by others to construct dubious moral arguments about why the 'obesity epidemic' has happened.

An intellectually critical approach to the so-called 'obesity epidemic' is important for two reasons, one straightforward and one more subtle. First, there is the danger that the language of 'epidemic' exaggerates the situation with which we are faced. Regardless of what some might say about the formal definition of 'epidemic', it is a word that conjures visions of a looming disaster that threatens to engulf us all. It also suggests that obesity is a disease (itself a contentious idea) that is catching and could claim any one of us. Faced with an 'epidemic', all manner of drastic measures are likely to be advocated and enacted by policy makers and others in positions of authority. If the label 'epidemic' *is* unwarranted, then it is possible that many of these measures will be unwise, unnecessary and wasteful of scarce resources, while others may turn out to be counter-productive or even harmful in unforeseen ways. In short, the first danger that this book addresses is that talk of an 'obesity epidemic' has the potential to do more harm than good.

The second danger is related to the first but concerns the knowledge people draw on when they talk about the 'obesity epidemic'. As we have already seen, there is a tendency to rely on widely held assumptions about people and the societies in which they live in order to explain what is going on. As with many assumptions, there is the danger that these may be ill-informed and unhelpful. If they are, then what people say about *why* we are living through an 'obesity epidemic' (leaving to one side whether we really are) may lead to a misdiagnosis of our current situation and, once again, to dubious and unfortunate courses of action – or, as people who work with computers sometimes put it, 'garbage-in, garbage-out'. Therefore, the second danger that this book addresses is the possible consequences when people (including scientists, journalists and other authors) offer misguided explanations for the 'obesity epidemic'.

These two concerns, the first about the use of the term 'epidemic' and the second about the way people attempt to explain its causes, will be addressed throughout this book. However, drawing these two concerns together, there is a more serious and perhaps more controversial argument at the heart of this book.

In *The Skinny on Fat* (1999), the science writer Shawna Vogel attempts to provide readers with an up-to-date summary of the state of scientific knowledge about overweight and obesity. In particular, she is concerned that much of what people think and do about their body weight is driven by a combination of ignorance, guilt and irrationality, all of which mean that they are generally unable to manage their weight. For Vogel, the solution to this malaise is 'science' and 'scientific' ways of thinking. What we need, she argues, is a way of thinking about our bodies which is

> more mechanistic and less freighted with guilt ... One of the goals of this book is to give readers a way of thinking about their bodies they may not have considered before – a more scientific way of seeing things.
>
> (Vogel 1999: 4)

The book's conclusion strikes an optimistic note:

> Now scientific research on weight is taking us into an entirely new terrain. In the ongoing effort to both understand our bodies and gain some control of them, there is reason to hope that the frustration is nearing an end.
>
> (Vogel 1999: 214)

In this book we articulate a point of view that is diametrically opposed to the one put forward by Vogel. Our argument is that thinking 'scientifically' or 'mechanistically' about the human body has not led, and is unlikely to lead, to more satisfactory ways of thinking about overweight and obesity. There are at least three reasons for this.

First, the science of overweight and obesity, health and the mediating role of exercise and diet are severely mired in controversy and contradiction. For example, it is reasonably safe to accept the scientific claim that some regular exercise is good for one's health and, on balance, probably helps to limit weight gain. But, as we will suggest in Chapter 4, these are claims that are at least hundreds and probably thousands of years old and it is not at all clear how modern science has advanced our knowledge in this area. Beyond these basic and very old propositions, scientific consensus is extraordinarily elusive. It is certainly difficult to see how the average educated reader, having thoroughly familiarized themselves with the scientific literature, would finish with firm conclusions other than those we might see as common sense.

Second, it seems optimistic in the extreme to suggest that the populace is on the verge of dispensing with their superstitions, fears and prejudices about body weight in favour of a more 'mechanistic' or 'scientific' way of thinking. As we will show in Chapter 4, a string of scientists over the years have declared that more scientific knowledge about body weight would produce less moral stigmatization of fatness. While fewer in number, there have been those who take the opposite view: that more scientific knowledge has *increased* stigmatization because, it is claimed, we have learned more about the health dangers of fatness. Both arguments are mistaken and derive from an overestimation of the importance of science in this particular area of human affairs. Instead, the moral significance of fatness is largely, although not completely, a separate matter from the state of scientific knowledge. For example, the assertion that overweight and obesity have a genetic component could be understood as reducing stigmatization – because it suggests body weight is partly a matter of inheritance rather than personal choice – or increasing it. In his book, *The Fat of the Land*, Michael Fumento (1997a) argues that, since there is no evidence that genetics alone cause obesity, those who invoke genetics are just making excuses for their lack of self-control.

What scientists say about overweight and obesity is important because the public picks up pieces of scientific information, usually from media reports and commentaries and incorporates them into their existing beliefs about the world. While Vogel may dream of a day when people are freed from their 'superstitions' and 'irrational' beliefs, our contention is that people already incorporate science into their thinking and may even do so now more than at any other time in history. Science is not separate from people's superstitions. Rather, it is already an important component of them. In fact, what is interesting about scientific knowledge on overweight and obesity on the one hand, and popular beliefs on the other, is not so much their differences but their similarities (see Chapters 2, 3 and 5).

Third, it is not at all clear *how* a more 'mechanistic' or 'scientific' view of overweight and obesity would be a good thing. As we have said, our argument is that the 'scientific' view of overweight and obesity, as exemplified by Bouchard and Blair, is anything but ideologically neutral or, in Vogel's words, 'less freighted with guilt'. Indeed, Bouchard and Blair's words seem heavy with moral censure. In addition, a 'mechanistic' view of the human body invites us into a world where the social, economic and cultural factors that shape people's food and exercise behaviours and attitudes are either obscured or ignored. Viewing the body as a machine is unlikely to tell us much about how people live and why they live the way they do. Judging by the scientific literature, a 'mechanistic' view of the human body seems to demand that we think of body weight as determined simply by the difference between the number of calories we consume and the number of calories we expend. This way of thinking about the body may help us to understand the body weight of a single person or a small group of people. However, it is not at all clear how this way of thinking helps us come to terms with what is claimed to be a global health catastrophe. We would argue that, in this context, very different ways of thinking are needed.

Some clarifications and qualifications

More often than not, when people talk about the 'obesity epidemic' they are including people who are actually not obese at all, but rather overweight, a distinction we will discuss in more detail later in this book. Therefore, although a little long-winded, throughout this book we will use the term 'overweight and obesity' except when we are referring explicitly to the separate technical categories of overweight or obese. At the same time, the terms overweight and obesity have their own histories and only came into technical scientific usage during the twentieth century. Therefore, we will use the word 'fatness' when discussing pre-twentieth-century contexts or when referring to the general idea of excess of body fat.

Our choice of the terms 'morality' and 'ideology' in the title of this book is not without potential pitfalls. We are aware that the meanings of both have been the subject of debate and more sustained commentary than we offer here. However, we will use them in what we hope is a straightforward, even vernacular sense. We take 'morality' to be an idea or set of ideas which separate 'right' and 'wrong', particularly in terms of how people behave. Therefore, for us a 'moral argument' is one which deems certain behaviour right or wrong based on some more general and pre-existing premise. 'Ideology', on the other hand, is taken to be a way of understanding the world, particularly the human world, how it works and how and why it changes. A simple example of this is the classic opposition between, on the one hand, the idea (or ideology) that the world is primarily shaped by the autonomous actions of individuals and, on the other, that individuals are largely shaped by the structures, conventions and rules of society.

Regarding the word 'science', we take an equally pragmatic and non-technical approach. When we refer to 'scientists' and the 'science of overweight and obesity', we are alluding to the academic fields that study overweight and obesity, but particularly the fields of medicine, exercise science and epidemiology. We are well aware that opinion within these fields is not monolithic and we highlight some of the disagreements which exist in Chapters 3, 5 and 6. However, a core assertion in this book is that the idea of an 'obesity epidemic' is now rampant across a range of academic fields and that the existence of an 'obesity epidemic' is said to be based on evidence and rational thinking. That is, it is said to be a 'scientific' phenomena.

Some readers will be aware that there has been a vigorous academic debate in recent years – sometimes called 'the science wars' – about the extent to which science has been a force for good or ill in the world. Some defenders of science have misunderstood the critiques of others as an attack on the entire enterprise of science. But as the philosopher Mary Midgley points out: 'We don't now need to tell each other that science is good any more than we need to say that freedom is good or democracy is good. As ideals, these things are established in our society' (Midgley 2003: 5).

We are certainly not advocating an anti-science agenda in this book. Instead, we are calling into question the role played by scientists in the construction of the so-called 'obesity epidemic' as well as suggesting that a 'mechanistic' science of the body, where body weight is understood simply in terms of energy-in and energy-out, may actually be an unhelpful and misleading way of thinking about population levels of overweight and obesity. We have come to the conclusion that the science of overweight and obesity, as it is currently practised, has greatly contributed to the confused and 'superstitious' ways Western societies think about body weight. But we want to stress that this state of confusion is actually 'business as usual', the normal state of human affairs. People have been incorporating science into their thinking and language for centuries and this has never – and will never – produce a population quite as 'rational' and 'scientific' as some in the scientific community would wish. People have also been concerned about their body weight for many decades, partly because they have listened to things that scientists have to say. What is different about the current moment is that this confusion has produced something called an 'epidemic'.

We also want to point out that this book should in no way be read as downplaying the health dangers of extreme obesity. What we *will* question is the way people who are classified as 'overweight' and those who are moderately obese are included in statistics, which are then used to claim that we are on the verge of a health catastrophe. If it is the case that extreme, life-threatening obesity is increasing, the reasons for this are not clear. We certainly do not see how appealing to 'Western lifestyles' or the general social 'environment' contribute to an understanding of the plight of the morbidly obese. In any case, what is at issue in this book is not whether severe obesity is a problem, but whether the world is in the middle of an obesity crisis.

About the authors

It is not common for books of this kind to spend time talking about the authors. However, in this case our background is central to the concerns of this book, its motivation and its arguments.

Jan, Bruce (who contributed Chapter 5) and Michael are all university physical educators and are involved in the training of physical education teachers. As some readers will be aware, undergraduate training in physical education is eclectic. It includes foundational study in anatomy, physiology and exercise physiology as well as introductions to other scientific disciplines that consider the movement of human bodies such as motor learning and biomechanics. Students usually also get smatterings of sociology, history, psychology, sports coaching, health studies, pedagogy (educational theory) and some practical training in sports, gymnastics and dance. For those that care to look, this loose assortment of knowledge traditions presents students with a series of tensions and contradictions. For example, is the physical education practitioner a coach or a teacher? Should s/he be concerned with enhancing the athletic performance of more gifted children or with promoting basic skills and positive attitudes towards physical activity among *all* students? Should they be concerned primarily with the health and physical performance of human bodies, or do they have a role to play in developing the intellectual, social and cultural lives of students? Do we need to think of the human body as an autonomous machine or as located within social and cultural contexts that shape people's health and access to physical activity? At a deeper level, there are questions about what kind of knowledge counts as 'truth', scientific or non-scientific? And although it is always risky to leap to generalizations, our experience is that undergraduate physical education programmes around the world rarely ask students to think about the concept of truth or to problematize their beliefs about what kinds of knowledge are most valuable or relevant to the work of physical education teachers. In fact, these tensions and contradictions go largely unaddressed.

But, as writers in the philosophy of science have pointed out, people *do* have opinions and beliefs about what kinds of knowledge are most important, and physical education undergraduates are no exception. And while these opinions and beliefs are by no means uniform across the world, it is clear that science, particularly biomedical science, has assumed a dominant position in the training of physical education teachers (Abernethy *et al.* 1997; Green 1998; McKay *et al.* 1990; Pronger 1995; Swan 1993). As teachers, researchers and teacher educators, we have seen first hand the tightening grip of the sciences, or at least scientific ways of thinking, on the hearts and minds of students, school teachers and fellow academics and researchers. So although one might answer the questions posed in the previous paragraph by saying that there is no reason why physical education teachers cannot be both coach and teacher, scientist and educator, health professional and social activist, at present and in each case it is the former which holds sway over the latter.

These are not abstract academic concerns. The answers that students and trainee teachers come to about these questions directly affect the experiences of children in schools. For example, it was not such a long time ago that Australian physical education teachers spent a great deal of class time on 'fitness' and 'fitness testing'. In general, the physical education profession came to the conclusion, based on research and personal experience, that this approach to our subject was neither enjoyable nor likely to inspire a lifelong commitment to physical activity among young people.

However, the emergence of the 'obesity epidemic' has given rise to renewed calls for fitness and fatness testing of school students as well as more 'vigorous' physical education lessons, which will (it is assumed) promote fitness and reduce obesity. These calls have come almost entirely from outside the physical education profession, often from politicians and the scientific and medical communities.

There is now a real danger that we will repeat the mistakes of the past and that our current preoccupation with obesity will result in worse, not better, experiences for children in schools. As we will show in Chapter 9, however, this is not only an issue for physical education. Some of those writing in medical and other scientific journals are advocating that a whole range of other professions be enlisted into the 'war on obesity'.

In this context, the danger of reductive ways of thinking and hasty conclusions rather than careful and sophisticated analyses is ever present. If we train our focus narrowly on the graphs and tables which purport to show the numbers of people classified as overweight or obese then, given certain pre-existing ways of thinking about fatness, we may come to the conclusion that we have a crisis on our hands. But what happens if we widen our focus, listen to multiple voices, read across disciplines and, in particular, think about health generally instead of preoccupying ourselves with body measurements?

In all of this, our position as physical educators is not insignificant. It is possible that some readers will dismiss the arguments put forward in this book simply on the grounds that we are not, ourselves, scientists and, therefore, not sufficiently trained to comment upon, let alone criticise, the science of overweight and obesity. The quality of the analyses presented here is for others to assess. However, our own feeling is that our training as physical educators means that we bring a multi-disciplinary perspective to this work and that this is an asset rather than a liability.

Structure of this book

In the following chapter we analyse predominantly print-based mass-media comment about the 'obesity epidemic'. In compiling this chapter we wanted to provide a sense of the urgency and alarm with which the matter has been discussed as well as a summary of the widely circulating understandings about why it is happening. What emerges is the extent to which, rather than being opposed, scientific and popular ideas intermingle to produce the public face of the 'obesity epidemic'. We chose to concentrate on print rather than electronic media for no particular reason other than the relative ease of collecting and storing printed matter. Television, radio and Internet comment has been equally ubiquitous and an adequate survey of electronic media would have required more space than is available here while not significantly altering the general picture.

This chapter also acts as a backdrop for the following four chapters, which consider the science of the 'obesity epidemic' more explicitly. In Chapter 3 we assess the current state of the science of obesity. While the previous chapter pointed to some of the moral and ideological imperatives at work, this chapter shows that the scientific foundations of 'obesity epidemic' thinking are far less certain than commonly assumed. This is significant because a whole range of medical, political, health and educational initiatives, based on what is taken to be the self-evident 'truth' about overweight and obesity, is often proposed by obesity scientists. We argue that before agreeing to these often startling and drastic measures, we should at least attempt to evaluate the evidence on which they are based. More fundamentally, Chapter 3 also raises doubts about the entire enterprise of studying human body weight, health and physical activity in a rigidly

mechanistic fashion: has the science of overweight and obesity produced knowledge that is 'true' or useful? Here we focus on two examples: research into
physical activity and health, which assumes that body weight is a straightforward
product of energy-in and energy-out; and the role of technology in childhood
overweight and obesity.

In Chapter 4 we digress briefly to show how strikingly similar present-day scientific assumptions about body weight, health, food and physical activity are to those
of centuries past. We do this for a number of reasons, but two are worth mentioning
here. First, some historical perspective adds to the sneaking and discomforting
conclusion that contemporary science is not advancing our understanding of overweight and obesity in any substantial way. Second, there is an often repeated
scientific assertion that as scientific knowledge accrues, the moral stigma of excess
body weight will recede. Our conclusion, one that we return to throughout this
book, is that not only does the state of scientific knowledge not ameliorate social
stigma, but it may also even set the scene for more sophisticated and supposedly
well-informed personal and institutional forms of stigmatization.

This discussion about obesity science is extended by Bruce Ross in Chapter 5.
Here, Ross looks at the scientific credentials of the body mass index (BMI) and
the categories of 'overweight' and 'obese'. Most discussions of the 'obesity epidemic'
begin with the claim that more and more people have a BMI which classifies
them as 'overweight' or 'obese' but it is rare that the assumptions that underpin
these categories are discussed outside of the specialist literature. Putting to one
side the question of how useful the BMI is, Ross then assesses the epidemiological
case that being 'overweight' or 'obese' is bad for health and attempts to answer
one of the trickiest of all scientific questions: exactly how dangerous is it to be
overweight or moderately obese? As difficult as it is, this is a crucial question
because 'overweight' and 'obese' are often described as being *states of disease* and
it is this connection – between the BMI and disease – which makes the idea that
we are in the middle of an 'epidemic' possible.

At this point, some readers may be concerned that the critique we offer is
narrowly academic and confined to the practice of obesity science. However, as
Chapter 6 shows, when scientists turn to explaining the cause of the 'obesity
epidemic', they step out of the realm of science and draw on often conservative
and age-old ideas about social and moral decline. Despite an almost complete
dearth of compelling evidence, obesity scientists regularly propose wide-ranging
measures to 'cure' this decline, from what children should learn at school,
how parents should manage their childrens' lives, to the ways buildings should
be constructed. In short, there appear to be few areas of our lives which obesity
scientists would leave untouched in the 'war on obesity'.

Having moved from the popular to the scientific domains, in Chapter 7 we
move back in the direction of the popular to examine 'obesity science for the
people' – the name we give to the many general audience books that have appeared
in the last decade and which purport to shed light on the 'obesity epidemic'. In
each case, the authors of these books claim to be the 'true' voice of science.
However, the 'scientific' explanations proposed by these authors turn out to be
yet more moralistic and ideological musings on the decline of modern Western
life. There are, in our view, few answers here either and there is certainly no

'pure' reading of the scientific literature which, contrary to what these authors claim, all 'fair-minded' people ought to be able to see. Above all, these books bring us face to face with the realization that science is not going to save us.

Having argued in previous chapters that science and its popular interpretations command most of the public consciousness about the 'obesity epidemic', in Chapters 8 and 9 we look to other ways of making sense of obesity and over-weight. First, in Chapter 8 we consider feminist writers who, from the early days of second wave feminism, have provided an alternative position on weight and fat to that of science. This position, in the first instance, challenges the simplistic notion of the body as a machine and, secondly, locates body weight and fatness as social and cultural issues. In this chapter we also provide a space for the highly marginalized point of view of fat people themselves, as they speak out in research and in the contexts of various forms of fat activism.

In Chapter 9, we look to sociological work on the body to challenge more directly the hold science has on the ideological space of the 'obesity epidemic', and to the sociology of health to question the assumptions made in the epidemi-ological literature about the relationship between social factors and overweight and obesity. Here we also consider the *effects* of 'obesity epidemic' thinking in terms of what kinds of policies it promotes and what kinds of interventions and practices it allows in families, health work and schools.

If this book is about anything, it is about the contemporary political contexts in which decisions about health research and policy are made. Therefore, in the final chapter we bring together the central concerns of this book. First, it is clear to us that some forms of knowledge are distinctly more powerful in shaping health agendas than others and, in the case of obesity science, it is apparent that this power does not necessarily spring from a solid, uncontroversial and sophisticated knowledge base. Second, in order to challenge the power of dominant scientific and popular ideas about the 'obesity epidemic' we need to look at their harmful effects and consider other ways of thinking about bodies, weight and health. With these two concerns in mind, we offer resources for thinking differently and for considering the ethical dimensions of the 'obesity epidemic' as social phenomena.

Thinking differently about the 'obesity epidemic' is important for many reasons but perhaps the most important is that it may help us to see ourselves and our societies in a new light. While we might hope that decisions about health agendas and the resources devoted to addressing them are made according to available evidence, this is not always the case. Certain ideas, such as the ideas that the best way to study health is scientifically and that the best way to study health scientifically is to think of the body as a machine, often have more power than other ideas. This power may have very little to do with the extent to which these ideas provide answers, as is the case with the science of overweight and obesity, but may derive from their age, because they have worked well in other contexts or because the people who subscribe to them are themselves powerful. Looking at the moral and ideological content of these ideas, however, may lead us to conclude that they are not quite as scientific as they are usually held to be. This is not a pessimistic conclusion. It is a reminder that the most important ques-tions are usually not scientific, but moral and ideological and, therefore, that we are all qualified to join the discussion and voice an opinion.

2   The war on obesity

While this book is very much concerned with the things that scientists say about overweight, obesity and the so-called 'obesity epidemic', this is by no means our only focus. Scientists, like all of us, make mistakes and this fact alone hardly constitutes a compelling reason for writing a book. What is so striking about the current situation is the extent to which the 'obesity epidemic', including its central *scientific* ideas and knowledge claims, has infiltrated everyday talk.

Few readers will have escaped the avalanche of public comment about overweight and obesity in the last few years. A quick Internet search of newspaper articles shows that during 1990 the word 'obesity' appeared only twice in the headlines or lead paragraphs of three leading Australian newspapers. In 1999 this number was fourteen and in the twelve months to September 2003 it was seventy-three. In the UK's *The Times* the word 'obesity' appeared in ten articles in 1985, fifty-five in 1995, eighty-one in 2000 and in 205 articles in the twelve months prior to September 2003. While hardly significant in themselves, these numbers hint at the possibility that Western countries are entering a new phase of the 'war on obesity'; a war that has bubbled along quietly for at least a century but which appears to be rapidly building in intensity.

In this chapter we look at the 'obesity epidemic' through the window of the mass-media. We have chosen to do this for two reasons. First, we want to provide a broad overview of what the 'obesity epidemic' is, or at least what it is claimed to be, including the nature of the problem and its origins. This is what we might call the 'obesity epidemic's' intellectual content. We readily concede that people obtain information about matters of public interest from a variety of sources and that the sources we present here are by no means exhaustive. For what it is worth though, our own conversations with family, friends, colleagues and students strongly suggest that the mass-media version of the 'obesity epidemic' accords closely with what many people actually believe.

But as well as considering its content, our second reason for looking at the mass-media account of the 'obesity epidemic' is, in a sense, to take its 'temperature'. The 'obesity epidemic' is not just big news. It is also a subject that has generated an almost visceral reaction among some commentators and, as we will see, an apparently irresistible desire to lash out and blame someone. Nothing and no one completely escapes responsibility for the waistlines of Western populations; body weight appears to be one of those topics which can be seized upon by people of virtually any ideological persuasion. We want therefore to draw the attention of readers not just to *what* is said but *how* it is said. It is in the tone of 'obesity epidemic' talk that its moral and ideological dimensions come more sharply into view.

What follows in this chapter, then, should be seen as part contextualization and part explanation for the state of the science of overweight and obesity, which we discuss in later chapters. After all, there is no reason to think that scientists are any less influenced by ideas circulating in the wider culture than anyone else. And because culture is dynamic – constantly circulating and feeding off itself – the mass-media acts as a window on Western culture, helping us to see the results of the recent intensification of interest in overweight and obesity among 'experts' in the field.

'Everyone everywhere'

While there are many ways to interpret the overweight and obesity statistics published in scientific journals, mass-media reporting is of one mind – they are a disaster and warn of a looming global health catastrophe. The situation is described as an 'obesity epidemic' or an 'obesity crisis' in ways which suggest the terms are largely interchangeable. Quoting 'US scientists', the UK's the *Guardian* describes obesity as nothing less than a threat to 'world health' (Radford 2002: 8). An Australian expert is reported saying that it is 'a time bomb' about which '[m]ost doctors and health professionals are tearing their hair out' (Teutsch 2002a: 10). Where the problem is said to be at its most acute – the US – it is claimed that obesity kills 300,000 people each year, a number which the media constantly recycles. Under the headline 'Obesity alarm', the *New York Times* reports:

> The surgeon general, Dr. David Satcher, warned that obesity may soon over-take tobacco as the chief cause of preventable deaths in the United States. About 60 percent of adults in this country are overweight or obese, as are nearly 13 percent of children, and some 300,000 Americans die annually from illnesses caused or worsened by obesity. He called for major steps to be taken by schools, communities and industry.
>
> (*New York Times* 2001a: 2)

Elsewhere, under the headline 'U.S. warning of death toll from obesity' (*New York Times* 2001b: 26), the US Surgeon General is quoted as saying that: 'The toll of obesity has been rising and threatens to wipe out progress fighting cancer, heart disease and other ailments'. As for childhood obesity, the situation is equally dire. Madeleine Nash, writing in *Time* magazine, warns:

> The surge of obesity among children, in short, presages a global explosion of illnesses that will drain economies, create enormous suffering and cause millions of premature deaths. 'This is a true health-care crisis,' says Robert Lustig, a pediatric endocrinologist at the University of California, San Francisco, far bigger than severe acute respiratory syndrome (SARS) and ultimately, he thinks, even bigger than AIDS.
>
> (Nash 2003: 56–7)

At this point we would simply note the way the term 'global' is used so freely in connection with the 'obesity epidemic', a rhetorical flourish which is difficult to square with the persistence of hunger and malnourishment in the world.

Tona Kunz (2003), writing for the *Chicago Daily Herald*, describes the problem of childhood obesity as a 'ticking time bomb' and quotes a health expert who describes obese children themselves as so many 'ticking time bombs'. Later in the article the author mentions research from the University of California at San Diego which claims that the quality of life for obese children is as bad as children undergoing chemotherapy.

Not only does the mass-media appear to be of one mind about the seriousness of the current situation, it seems that no prediction about the future is too apocalyptic. From *Marie Claire* magazine (Johnson 2001: 233) we learn that: 'By 2025, experts predict that nearly every Australian will be overweight or obese'. Oddly enough, despite the fact that we regularly read about the US's pre-eminent position atop the obesity tree, in other reporting it is claimed that it will not be until 2050 that its population reaches the 100 per cent overweight or obese mark (e.g. Cooke 2003; Miller 2003). In 2003, Canada's the *Hamilton Spectator* (Morrison 2003: 1) ran with the extended headline: 'Obesity a growing threat to our children: Kids and their parents may be lining up for heart bypass surgery at the same time'. The report opens with:

> A Canadian doctor paints a horrific picture of the consequences of childhood obesity in the not-too-distant future. 'I don't think it's inconceivable that we're going to see fathers and sons, mothers and daughters, lining up together for bypass surgery,' said Dr Mark Tremblay, author of a new study on physical activity and childhood obesity. He said this scenario is within the realm of possibility, given the couch-potato lifestyles of Canadian children, with the television clicker within as easy reach as potato chips.
>
> (Morrison 2003: 1)

According to Cassie McCullagh (2003: 16), writing for Australia's *Illawarra Mercury*, a former president of the Australian Medical Association claimed that 'today's children risked being labelled "Generation O"', and that a recent press release from Dr Simon Clarke of Sydney's Westmead hospital declared that 'this generation may well die before their parents'.

Although these kinds of predictions have been made repeatedly over the last five years, we are not aware of any concession that they are strategically alarmist: that is, examples of hyperbole designed to shock people into changing their behaviour. Indeed, claims that obesity will seriously damage Western economies, that generations of parents will soon be burying their morbidly overweight children or that within a few decades entire Western societies will be classified as overweight or obese are consistently made without the usual qualifications and equivocations for which academics and other experts are so famous. Instead, the uncertainty that, in our view, surrounds many of these claims is nowhere to be seen and often it is the experts themselves (not journalists or politicians) who appear to provide the mass-media with their most confidently apocalyptic predictions.

While the socio-demographic dimensions of overweight and obesity are mentioned occasionally, the mass-media coverage of the 'obesity epidemic' has tended to portray it as affecting 'everyone everywhere'. Writing for the *New York Times*, Natalie Angier puts it this way:

> Make no mistake: the dreaded obesity epidemic that is everywhere in the news is not restricted to any race, creed, ethnicity or slice of the socioeconomic supersized pie. As recent studies reveal, virtually every group known to demography is getting fatter. The poor are getting fatter and the well-to-do are getting fatter. The old are getting fatter, baby boomers and Generation Xers are getting fatter, children too young to have a category are really getting fatter.
>
> (Angier 2000: 1)

The idea that the US is the fattest nation in the world appears to be widespread and generally accepted. A 2001 edition of the *Sydney Morning Herald* (10th January, 2001: 7) carried the headline 'Americans too well rounded to feel the pinch', a reference to a US researcher's complaint that his skinfold callipers were fast becoming useless as more and more of his research participants presented him with skinfolds which are simply too big to measure.

At the same time, apart for some comment about the populations of small Pacific islands such as Western Samoa and Nauru (e.g. Engel 2002), the print-media of other countries appears to be engaged in a strange kind of race for second prize behind the US. In the lead up to the 2000 Olympic Games, a headline in Australia's *Sunday Advertiser* (2000: 7) announced 'Aussie silver for obesity' and quoted a prominent researcher who claimed that Australian obesity levels trailed only the US.

The importance of the 'everyone everywhere' version of the 'obesity epidemic' cannot be overestimated. Because it does not differentiate between particular social groups, it creates the perfect context in which people can talk vaguely about the 'environment' or 'society', 'Western societies' or 'modern lifestyles' or simply 'we'. For example, Jenny Tabakoff's opinion column for the *Sydney Morning Herald* (headlined 'Slam the brakes on fast food before health problems get any worse') begins with:

> Western societies have a substance-abuse problem that is filling hospital beds and causing premature deaths. Worse, it is affecting children. Governments, however, are doing nothing to combat it ... As a society, it is becoming increasingly obvious that we are helpless to combat the rising tide of fast food.
>
> (Tabakoff 2002: 11)

In *Sport Health* magazine, Ester Guerzoni writes:

> In the last twenty years, technology has greatly reduced the amount of 'incidental' energy we expend at work, home and during our leisure time. We drive to the local shop, we catch elevators and escalators, we hire gardeners and house cleaners, we choose three hours of Doom II to a game of basket ball. We've chosen the no pain ... period.
>
> (Guerzoni 1996: 11)

For Tim Radford in the *Guardian*:

> The global pandemic of fat could not be explained by any genetic changes: it had occurred too fast. At bottom, societies were eating foods with higher densities of calories and fat, and becoming more sedentary.
>
> (Radford 2002: 8)

The use of the word 'global' is notable here again and, as ever, no attempt is made to justify its use. In the *Weekend Australian* David Crawford from the Australian Society for the Study of Obesity is quoted as follows:

> We know that we are gaining weight because of lifestyle changes, we're doing less physical activity and our eating patterns have changed. It is not due to genetics. We need to get people to change their habits, reduce their snacking and make lifestyle changes.
>
> (Pirani 2002: 21)

The word 'epidemic' is part and parcel of the 'everyone everywhere' thesis. It is constantly used in media reporting to conjure images of a rampant disease spreading indiscriminately through the population. In an 'epidemic' we are all potentially vulnerable and we must all take measures to ensure we do not fall victim.

The 'everyone everywhere' 'obesity epidemic' has generally been explained in the mass-media using a mixture of scientific jargon and a kind of common sense logic. Notwithstanding a recent flurry of interest in genetic accounts of overweight and obesity, there has been a striking uniformity in this explanation. Mike Safe (2000), writing in *The Australian*, offers an exemplary case in point and for this reason is worth quoting at length.

In this article Safe relies heavily on the high-profile Australian epidemiologist and health activist, Garry Egger. First, Egger is quoted as saying that obesity is a disease just like any other:

> Egger points out that the United Nations' World Health Organisation has declared obesity to be the fourth major disease of the new century, alongside AIDS, cancer and heart disease. 'With an epidemic, and that's what this is, you have to look at what's called the epidemiological triangle – the host, that's the person who gets fat; the vector, what makes them fat; the environment, the conditions under which they live. It's no different to an infectious disease like malaria – the host is the person bitten by the mosquito; the vector is the mosquito; the environment is the swamp where the mosquito breeds. You'll never deal with malaria by just saying always use repellent and sleep under a net. That doesn't get rid of the problem. What you do is drain the swamp and spray for mosquitos. Obesity might be a behavioural epidemic, not an infectious one,' he says, 'but the principles are the same.'
>
> (Safe 2000: 17)

There is, however, one difference between malaria and obesity according to Egger:

Egger says the problem with obesity is that it's nice to get, unlike malaria. 'It's comfortable to sit on your arse and eat yourself fat . . . Everything humanity has been aimed at is about comfort. If you say let's change that – take away the cars and remote controls, walk up stairs and forget escalators – well it just won't happen.'

(Safe 2000: 18)

Egger, like many others, claims to know what is causing the 'obesity epidemic':

Interestingly, Egger believes that the nutrition message has gotten through, but we are now slaves to technology. 'It's not Ronald McDonald who's causing the problem, it's Bill Gates. Emails are more fattening than hamburgers in this technological environment. Nobody considers the downside of tech-nology. We all look at these improvements as being absolutely and irrevocably positive. All technology is designed to reduce effort in one way or another. But when you reduce effort, people get fat.' He points out every 25 steps burns a calorie but we're walking a lot fewer of them.

(Safe 2000: 18)

It is not our intention in this chapter to provide a detailed critique of any of the quoted points of view. This will come in later chapters. At this stage we would ask readers to consider the words attributed to Egger in this article. What are we to make of comments such as 'It's comfortable to sit on your arse and eat yourself fat' and 'Everything humanity has been aimed at is about comfort'? And what of the assertion that 'Emails are more fattening than hamburgers'? For now, we would simply ask, are they true and what judgements about people or, as Egger puts it, 'humanity', are being made here? As an epidemiologist he says that we need to consider the person and the environment, but a description of anybody's 'environment' is not what we get. Instead, we are presented with relentless gener-alizing about how people live and their reasons for doing so. Overweight and obese people are presented as sitting on their 'arse' and eating themselves 'fat' while, inexplicably, in the next paragraph food intake is apparently ruled out of the equation – the problem is that people are now compliant and passive 'slaves' to technology. This is not just a contradiction, although it certainly is that. It is also a style of explanation driven by moral imperatives – 'everything' about 'humanity' is aimed at 'comfort'. It would seem that doing something about the 'obesity epidemic' presents us with no less a challenge than changing human nature itself.

Some readers may object to the questions posed here – surely the words of experts are constantly being twisted and 'dumbed down' for publication in news-papers? However, this would only be a justified criticism so long as it could be shown that what experts say when they are relatively free to speak and write for themselves (such as when they write for scientific journals) is at odds with the things they are reported to have said in the mass-media. In Chapters 4 and 6 we will see how similar the pronouncements of obesity scientists in academic journals are to those of the mass-media.

Couch potatoes and tubby tots

There is an image, which we have already encountered, that has virtually become the 'brand' of the 'obesity epidemic'. Sometimes the image is captured with photographs, sometimes with words. The image, repeated with small variations all over the Western world, depicts a (usually male) child who would convention- ally be considered overweight. Sometimes the child is lying on a couch. On top of a nearby table is a pizza box with one or two remaining slices and a half- finished soft-drink bottle. Sometimes there are other kinds of food instead of pizza – ice cream, chips or popcorn. Sometimes the child is captured just as he is putting food in his mouth. Often, the child is watching television, eyes glazed, as if in some kind of trance. In his various manifestations, he is, of course, the 'couch potato'.

Photos of 'couch potatoes' are ubiquitous in reporting about childhood over- weight and obesity. With slight variations, they accompany headlines such as 'Schools rear crop of couch potatoes' (Campbell 2000), 'Generation XXL' (Cowley 2000) and 'High blood pressure and only aged seven' (Teutsch 2002a). The term 'couch potato' is now not only widely used but also, it seems, understood. Even the British Heart Foundation's (2000) public information brochure *Couch Kids: The Growing Epidemic* featured their own version of the 'couch potato' on the cover. Inside, the brochure reports:

> UK children are getting fatter. This is not just because some may be eating more (many studies have shown that on average children are eating less) but because physical activity has radically decreased ... The majority of studies on children and adolescents indicate low levels of physical activity with many children not doing enough to promote cardiovascular health.
>
> (British Heart Foundation 2000: 2–3)

And later:

> A major problem working against our children's activity levels is that free time, traditionally spent on active play, is increasingly being spent on sedentary interests such as watching TV and playing computer games. As children grow older, the amount of time spent on such activities increases from ten hours per week in two to seven year olds to 17 hours per week in 13 to 15 year olds. Throughout, girls tend to spend slightly longer than boys on sedentary activities.
>
> (British Heart Foundation 2000: 5)

These passages, as well as the visual and verbal imagery of the 'couch potato', are significant because they sum up what appear to be widely held understandings of the 'obesity epidemic'. In short, the 'couch potato' reminds us that we are fat because we are lazy. Children, so the story goes, have become addicted to tech- nology and an unlimited supply of high-fat food. Children choose to use technology because it requires less effort and to eat high-fat food because they (and we) are, by nature, gluttons. But it is not just its substance – *what* it claims to be true –

which is notable about this explanation of the 'obesity epidemic' among children. What is also striking is its tone of absolute certainty. In fact, the reason for the 'obesity epidemic' is regularly described as 'obvious'. Underpinning the sense of certainty appears to be a moralistic view of the present and a nostalgic view of the past. The result, once again, is a steady flow of generalizations about how people live today and how things have changed. The following report from Australia's the *Sun-Herald* neatly captures the apparent ease with which people are able explain what is going on:

> 'The kitchen never shuts in many houses. Gone are the days when children asked for things, and parents seem to have difficulty saying no. Children are also less active,' said Martha Lourey Bird, a Weight Watchers spokeswoman and academic with a background in childhood obesity. 'Christmas day is a classic example,' she said. 'Before we would be outdoors, playing with our new toys all afternoon. Now, kids are more likely to be indoors, playing on the computer.'
>
> (Teutsch 2002a: 10–11)

In a similar vein is this passage from Sian Powell's (2000: 6) article, headlined 'One in four Australian children overweight. Slower, stiffer, heavier – they are the cotton-wool generation' (see Figure 2.1), for the *Weekend Australian*:

> Driven to school, picked up from school, kept off the dangerous streets and away from the dangerous parks, they are the cotton-wool generation and, often the only physical exercise they get is when their parents have time to supervise. A child these days doesn't break an arm falling off his billycart, he develops a bad case of Nintendo thumb – a recognised medical problem. The average Australian child aged 5–13 spends between two and three hours a day watching television, lying supine, soaking up advertisements for high fat junk food. These are the real telly tubbies. If we follow in American foot-steps, as we so often do, TV viewing will increase, to slowly soak up almost all the leisure hours of children.
>
> (Powell 2000: 6)

Once again, the image of the 'couch potato' is to the fore, although here s/he is more of a 'couch sponge' as s/he lies 'supine', passively 'soaking up' television advertisements. As the stereotypes flow, notice also that 'average' children are gathered up in this none-too-flattering portrait of modern children; the 'couch potato' is not simply a worrying minority, s/he is the 'average' child. Amid all of this, there appear to be few who are prepared to draw breath and consider the different ways different children live. Indeed, the opposite seems the case. In the world of the 'obesity epidemic' there are two kinds of children – those who are obese and those who are about to become obese. We are even told that we should be just as worried about babies and infants getting fat. 'Warning: too tubby tots face lifetime of obesity' is how England's the *Observer* (Hill 2002: 9) reported scientific findings about the links between infant and adult obesity. The journalist, Amelia Hill, writes:

Figure 2.1 'Why Australian children are getting slower, stiffer, fatter', taken from the *Weekend Australian*, 27–8 May, 2000. © Copyright. Reproduced with the permission of News Ltd.

Babies who put on too much weight during the first four months of their lives could be condemned to a lifetime of obesity, according to the largest-ever study into infant weight gain. While the bouncing baby has long been a cause for celebration, the findings suggest it should now be the subject of concern and regarded as a key to the epidemic of childhood obesity that is spreading the nation.

(Hill 2002: 9)

In 'War on obesity begins in infancy' the *Ottawa Citizen* reports on initiatives to get the very young moving:

Childhood obesity is such a worry that even babies as young as six months are enrolled in classes to encourage physical activity. From infant massage, sensory stimulation and gym 'n' swim, they can move on to crawling activities, and then climb, run and kick their way into formal sports. Even the Teletubbies have turned the spotlight on their chubby teletummies. Dipsy, Po, La-la and Tinky-Winky will jump, march and dance in their first fitness special, called Go! Exercise with the Teletubbies goes to air March 20 on PBS.

(Young 2001: 1)

It would surely not be unreasonable to conclude from these kinds of reports that *all* parents and *all* children are now expected to be part of the 'war on obesity'. It is not just a minority of children who are classified as overweight and obese who are at risk – obesity is now a disease that can strike anywhere, anytime and we must all be vigilant. As Anna Patty, writing in Australia's the *Daily Telegraph* reports:

Sports dietician Karen Inge said children without weight problems could not afford to neglect their diets. 'Even if you are normal weight you need to concentrate on what you eat because it will have an impact on your future health and well-being. Parents really need to set a positive example to their children by not only offering a greater range of healthier foods, but eating them themselves'.

(Patty 2000: 19)

Children, obesity and sport

The medical and scientific communities have not been alone in their concern about the body weight and 'lifestyles' of 'Western' children. The representatives of elite and junior sport have also become regular contributors to print-media comment on the subject and, while not always for identical reasons, their vision of the future is no less cataclysmic. Headlines such as 'Schools rear crop of couch potatoes' (Campbell 2000: 6) in the UK and 'Aussie kids can't jump ... as far as they used to' (Teutsch 2002b: 10) in Australia catch the mood of the moment: kids today are fatter, more sedentary and less athletically skilled than children of previous generations. Almost without exception, these headlines are accompanied by stories about the release of a research report of some kind and the comments of an expert in the field

For example, Peter Corrigan's (2000: 19) 'Lottery lunacy and schools for scandal' reports on a Sport England study:

> A sample of more than 3,300 children aged 5 to 16 found that on average they spent 7.5 hours on sport and exercise, both in and out of school, in the previous week, compared with 11.4 hours watching television and 4.4 hours playing video games.
>
> (Corrigan 2000: 19)

Corrigan then explains why we should see these statistics as significant by providing a synopsis of the prevailing causative narrative which goes something like:

1   children play less sport than they should;
2   children spend more time watching television and playing computer games than they should;
3   because they play less sport than they should we can conclude that they are less active than they should be;
4   they are spending less time in physical education and therefore not developing sufficient sporting skill;
5   the lack of sporting skill perpetuates this vicious cycle because it is the childrens' lack of skill and, therefore, confidence which deters them from playing sport; and
6   all of these things lead to fat, unfit and unhealthy children.

Corrigan writes:

> As a result [of the small amount of time spent doing physical education], many kids are not learning the basic skills that would enable them to develop or enjoy sporting involvement or even to keep fit, leaving them at risk of serious health problems in later life. Sport England's chairman, Trevor Brooking, said that children leaving primary school now were technically the worst generation he had ever seen in terms of fitness and familiarity with the basic knowledge of how to play games.
>
> (Corrigan 2000: 19)

Given the prevailing atmosphere in which children are constantly being portrayed as slower, fatter, lazier and less athletically skilled, it is quite possible that some readers of this column would not have viewed the claim that today's children are 'technically the worst generation' in living memory as particularly contentious, even though no supporting evidence for the claim is offered.

Along similar lines, the *Independent*'s Judith Judd (2000) quotes Nigel Hook from England's Central Council of Physical Recreation:

> There must be a compulsory two hours' PE a week in primary schools. At present, the average is only 70 minutes. We are storing up a disaster with young people becoming disaffected with sport and building up poor lifestyles.
>
> (Judd 2000: 3)

Another case in point is 'Literacy 2, sport 0' (Crace 2000: 4) from the UK's the *Guardian*. The author, John Crace, begins with:

> The fat cats of the junk food industry will be feeling just a little fatter this morning. A report published by Sport England confirms what many of us have suspected for years. Our tuberous schools really are turning the nation's children into couch potatoes. In the five years since the previous survey, the proportion of six- to eight-year-olds spending two hours or more per week taking part in PE declined from 32% to 11%. The figures for nine- and 10-year-olds make similarly bleak reading: a decline from 46% to 21%.
>
> (Crace 2000: 4)

Notice here that the author is unable to resist the temptation to connect issues that appear unrelated. Why people who sell 'junk food' should be buoyed by news that English children are doing less physical education is, at least to us, a complete mystery and no clarification is offered in the article. Without claiming to be able to read the mind of the journalist, however, the reason for making this connection seems obvious and is, in a sense, spelled out in the article itself: both are consistent with the image of the 'couch potato' that he invokes. In other words, as with so much of what is said and written about the 'obesity epidemic', this is an example of the way a particular ideology comes to be constructed and widely accepted. In fact, we wonder whether it is going too far to suggest that the idea of the 'couch potato' has become an ideology in itself – an idea so pervasive that people find it difficult to think about children, food and physical activity without reference to it.

In addressing the question why we should be concerned about the number of hours of physical education that English children do, Crace turns to the former England soccer player, Trevor Brooking:

> Throughout his England career, Trevor Brooking was known as the gentleman footballer, the player who never stood out of line, but in his current role as chairman of Sport England he is sufficiently worried by the findings to have no intention of allowing governmental apparatchiks to spin the implications of the report with a more favourable gloss. 'Children are at their most impressionable between the ages of five and 10,' he says, 'and they aren't being given the time or opportunity to find out whether they enjoy sport or are good at it. PE teachers at secondary schools tell me that they are now working on basic skills with 11- and 12-year-olds that used to be expected of six-year-olds. We're running the risk of losing our next generation of sportsmen and women.'
>
> (Crace 2000: 4)

Brooking is then quoted as claiming that the problems of 'youngsters becoming involved in drugs and other anti-social behaviour patterns' is linked to their lack of involvement in sport. Crace himself blames the alleged demise of English physical education on the crowded school curriculum, too much emphasis on more sedentary school subjects ('The other prime culprits are the government's literacy and numeracy strategies' (2000: 4)) and other extra-curricular activities. He concludes:

> Believe it or not, the government likes to take credit for some of these extra-curricular activities. The curriculum, we are told, should be viewed more fluidly to include activities outside the classroom and classroom hours. So that presumably includes sleeping, which appears to be our youngsters most popular pursuit.
>
> (Crace 2000: 4)

It is a truism that there is a human tendency for each generation to despair about the generation that follows it. It is certainly difficult to see how current generations of Western children could be more of a disappointment to the adults who write about them than they presently are.

Obesity and nostalgia

A slightly more subtle aspect of the 'obesity epidemic' concerns what appears to be the different ways 'obesity talk' has resonated in different Western countries. For example, in both Australia and England there has been an overwhelming sense that something important has been lost, although the thing that has been lost varies. Without attempting to analyse the significance of these differences, one general point is worth keeping in mind. The ideas that modern life, particularly modern urban and city life, creates 'weak' minds and 'soft' bodies and leads to a steady moral and physical decline are not new. It has been an explicit or implicit driving force behind what Goldstein (1992) has called 'the health movement' for at least 150 years. So, when we hear and read comment to the effect that modern Western populations 'ain't what they used to be', it is important to at least register the point that Western populations have *never* been what they used to be (this point is discussed in more detail in Chapter 4). There have always been people eager to point out that we are pale imitations of our forebears. Whether or not these comparisons are valid or justified are questions we return to in later chapters.

In England, the 'obesity epidemic' has tended to be interpreted through the lens of the alleged decline of English sport. Depending on who is writing or talking, the 'obesity epidemic' is seen either as the cause or the effect of the nation's transition from international sporting superpower to relative mediocrity. Why people should interpret the 'obesity epidemic' in this way is no doubt a complex matter, but it is probably tied up with the enduring (though by no means universally accepted) idea that Britain invented modern sport and gave it to the rest of the world, a view articulated by *The Times*' John Bryant:

> There was a time when Britain gave the world lessons in sport. In the confident high-noon of Victorian England, the middle classes gave sports the rules that were to catapult them around the world. Tennis, football, rugby, modern track and field were all nurtured in this great British cradle, and the place of sport in British education was envied and imitated everywhere. But since

those heady days, sport has been almost wiped out in our state schools, the sporting ethos kicked ragged by the selling-off of more than 5,000 playing-fields. . . . Today, children deprived of their playing-fields are routinely driven walkable distances to school where any form of physical activity is being squeezed out of existence. Their only contact with sport is reading about it or watching it on television.

(Bryant 2000: 37)

There is another layer, that of social class, which needs to be factored in here. While sport has remained an integral part of the curriculum of wealthy English public schools right to the present day, some, like Bryant, have argued that English stateschools have de-emphasized sport and physical education, both for financial reasons and, it is said, because of the increasingly crowded curriculum. Certainly, the sale of playing fields by stateschools in order to raise funds has been a 'hot' political issue for some time.

In 'Heading for the top?', the *Sunday Times'* Sian Griffiths (2002: 10) manages to link all of these threads together – school sport, elite sport, social class and the perils of city living and obesity. She writes:

We [England] play more sports than any other country bar Germany – 112 at last count – yet sport for many schoolchildren is a shambles; underfunded disorganised, way down on the list of teachers' priorities. A British Medical Journal study last May revealed that one in five nine-year-olds is overweight and one in 10 is obese. But playing fields are still being sold off. Since 1998, 104 applications to sell off school playing fields have been approved and only two rejected. In some inner-city primaries children are forbidden to play football at break-times, so cramped are their grim tarmac playgrounds.

(Griffiths 2002: 10)

Notice here the way the statistics about childhood obesity are simply dropped into the middle of a discussion of school sport. While the links between these issues may have seemed self-evident to the journalist, they are not explained in the article. Griffiths goes on:

The idea of a healthy mind in a healthy body – that regular exercise can boost academic results and improve behaviour, especially for boys – has been out of favour in state schools, although private schools swear by the benefits of a bracing game of rugby or lacrosse. Many boarding schools reserve most afternoons for games. Stephen Smith, chairman of the Headmaster's and Headmistresses Conference sports subcommittee, and head of the Bedford Modern school says: 'There is plenty of evidence that what independent schools say is right – that sport is linked to the development of the whole person, it's to do with discipline, targets, health – and can improve academic performance'.

(Griffiths 2002: 10)

Once again, a whole set of habits of mind, what we have called ideologies, are used explicitly or are at least implied here: that high academic achievement is the same as having a 'healthy mind', that physical exercise not only leads to a 'healthy mind' but also 'good behaviour' and 'self-discipline', that boys need and are more inclined towards physical activity than girls, that sport is 'healthy' and that the generally superior academic results of private schools are in part due to the time they devote to sport. While readers may or may not agree with these propositions, the instructive point is the apparent ease with which overweight and obesity are linked with this diverse list of social and moral domains. Obesity is never just itself.

A striking example of the assumed link between overweight and obesity and elite sporting success is '£150m bid to get couch potatoes into school gym' (Goodbody 2000: 10) from *The Times*. The journalist reports:

> The government launched a £150 million pound plan yesterday which it hopes will help young 'couch potatoes' to become world-class athletes ... The joint move by the culture and education departments makes sport in schools a priority and the basis for the international success and the health of the nation. David Blunkett, the education Secretary, said: 'We have a challenge on our hands, not least because the ethos of couch potatoes is something that we will have to overcome.'
>
> (Goodbody 2000: 10)

Although media anxiety about an obesity 'crisis' (Kelly 2003) has been no less acute in Australia, it has been much more difficult to link the 'obesity epidemic' to elite sporting performance. Australia's success in international sport has, if anything, steadily increased in recent decades at precisely the same time as the population's waistlines are said to have expanded. Rather, talk of an 'obesity epidemic' has piqued nostalgia for the 'bronzed Aussie': the archetypal beach-going, suntanned, Australian whose (presumably) physically active outdoor life kept him or her fit and healthy. Angela Evans' (2001: 15) article 'Stopping Australians getting fatter & slacker? It will be no mean feet!' for *Sport Health* magazine asks:

> So where is the quintessential bronzed, lean, young Aussie hiding? ... So what about the once seemingly ubiquitous lean physique which in previous generations characterised Australians apart from our plumper first world neighbours in the United States?
>
> (Evans 2001: 15)

The front page of the *Sydney Morning Herald*'s health and fitness lift-out 'Fit' (1st March, 2001) features the image of a woman, smiling broadly while she stands knee deep in the surf, small white-water waves crashing around her apparently fat-free thighs. Everything about the image evokes nostalgia for the 1950s, from the hairstyle to the one-piece patterned swimsuit and the blue and white beach ball she is holding. The accompanying caption reads 'Body of evidence: How a trim, taut, terrific nation let itself go'.

Bruce Montgomery's (1999: 4) report on overweight and obesity for the *Weekend Australian* appears under the extended headline: 'Our ancestors would barely recognise us. Australians are growing taller. And much, much fatter. The future is not a good look.' The accompanying illustration (see Figure 2.2) depicts a familiar

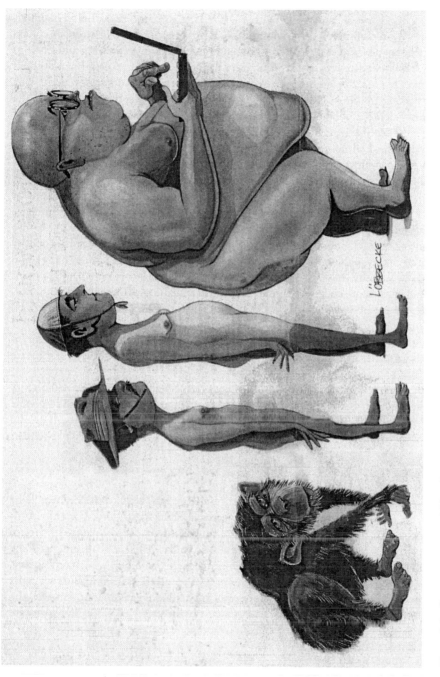

Figure 2.2 'Our ancestors would barely recognise us', taken from the *Weekend Australian*, 8–9 May, 1999. © Copyright. Reproduced w th the permission of News Ltd.

'evolution of species' style collection of four figures: from left to right they are a chimpanzee on all fours, a very thin (presumably) First World War soldier in his trademark Australian 'slouch' hat, an only slightly less thin surf life-saver and, finally, a hugely obese male figure with bald head, glasses and hand-held computer.

However, in common with England there has been considerable attention given to the level of physical skill (e.g. running, jumping, throwing, catching and hitting) among children. Reports on surveys into the skill level of Australian children announce 'Students caught out on sports' skill' (Raethel 1996) and 'Students lack basic sporting abilities' (Raethel 1998). Once again, while there appears to be some disagreement about whether the 'obesity epidemic' is the cause or effect of the alleged decline in childrens' skill levels, nobody appears to doubt that they are linked. And while commentators in Australia have not been able to blame obesity for poor international sporting results, as they have in England, in late 2003 a flurry of newspaper articles appeared suggesting that elite Australian sport was on the verge of a 'crisis' because of rising childhood obesity (e.g. Conway 2003; Hurrell 2003). No attempt to provide evidence for a link between elite sporting success and childhood obesity is made in these articles.

While acknowledging these international differences in discussion of the 'obesity epidemic', we would argue that there are still powerful overarching moral and ideological agendas at stake. There appears to be broad agreement that humans are (or at least have become) a generally weak-willed lot who, given the chance, will choose inactivity over activity and 'unhealthy' food over 'healthy' food. To make matters worse, we all find ourselves in an environment that panders to our allegedly slothful nature. This 'environment' is overwhelmingly talked about in generalized terms so that it is 'Western societies' and 'modern lifestyles' that are to blame. 'Everyone everywhere' is at risk.

So far, we have seen examples of mass-media coverage of overweight and obesity and the concerns of the medical and scientific communities and the spokespeople for elite and junior sport. We now want to briefly look at the ways in which the 'obesity epidemic' has been incorporated into other moral and ideological agendas.

Darwinian fat

It was probably inevitable that the 'obesity epidemic's' 'why' question would be doused in science's latest 'universal acid' – neo-Darwinian theory. For the uninitiated, the idea that virtually any aspect of human life can be explained in terms of Darwinian natural selection has for the last thirty years or so been spreading through the academic world and has infiltrated fields as diverse as neurobiology, psychology, ethics, sociology, philosophy and even aesthetics. Think of virtually any aspect of human life – the concept of beauty, people's behaviour at work, the food they eat, the art they like, their sexual predilections or taste in real estate – and you can be reasonably sure that someone somewhere has proposed a Darwinian explanation for it.

Writing in *The Australian*, Tony McMichael (2002: 9) explains the basics of the 'Darwinian fat' thesis in his article 'Not knowing what makes us tick has made us sick'. In passing, it is worth drawing attention to McMichael's use of the word 'sick' here. As we saw earlier, the idea that overweight and obesity are themselves 'diseases' or 'sicknesses', and that increasing overweight and obesity constitute an 'epidemic', have become commonplace. Indeed, the very concept of an 'obesity epidemic' rests on being able to see increasing overweight and obesity as a 'disease'. This then gives license to people to describe Western populations (us) as 'sick', regardless of what one might actually think about one's current state of health.

McMichael's argument is that it is not good enough to simply blame the environment for our 'sickness'; it is not until we understand our evolutionary past that we will really have a handle on overweight and obesity. It is, he argues, knowledge about our prehistoric ancestors (the '2 million years of the Homo genus') and the fact that we 'come from a long line of meat eaters dating back at least to the beginnings of the Pleistocene period' that holds our best hope for understanding the present: 'we would be less perplexed if we recognised the evolutionary basis of human biological functioning in relation to foods' (2002: 9). He even suggests that, armed with this knowledge, we might choose to eat kangaroo meat rather than beef or mutton. He concludes:

> Yes, recent dietary changes may have contributed to obesity in Australia (now the second-fattest developed nation). But consider, also, our daily energy expenditure – now that we obtain food from supermarkets, not fields; drive to work, not walk or cycle; and push buttons at work, not levers. Our children watch television rather than run around. Hunter-gatherers and early farmers expended considerable energy to produce a meal.
>
> (McMichael 2002: 9)

Proponents of neo-Darwinian theory, particularly evolutionary psychologists, are fond of claiming that the knowledge produced by their theories will improve society. For example, having studied the sexual habits of ducks and scorpions in captivity, the American evolutionary psychologists Thornhill and Palmer (2000) argue that their research provides both an intellectual and moral compass for how we should deal with human rape. Echoing McMichael, their argument is that we must first acknowledge that rape is a behaviour that exists today because, for millennia, it has conferred evolutionary advantages on those who do it. Only then will we be able to draft appropriate rape laws and have mature conversations about the subject. McMichael does not explain how understanding the evolutionary explanation of overweight and obesity will help us solve the current crisis, although one assumes his solution would be for us to live in ways that are more similar to our prehistoric ancestors.

A key intellectual ally of neo-Darwinian explanations of human life has been the science of genetics. The news that overweight and obesity may be the result of genetics rather than environment has received considerable media attention. For example, in 2002, an election year, the government of the Australian state of New South Wales convened a major 'childhood obesity summit' at which experts from a variety of fields presented their views. The 'summit' concluded by advocating a range of community- and school-based initiatives to combat overweight and obesity, largely by changing children's exercise and eating habits. At the same time, the state's premier, Bob Carr, became unusually vocal on the issue and made much of his government's commitment to reducing childhood obesity.

Shortly after the 'summit', and under the headline 'Premier's obesity solution "rubbish"', *The Australian*'s Deborah Hope reported that:

> Scientists from Sydney's prestigious Garvan Institute have slammed Bob Carr's campaign against childhood obesity as misrepresenting a genetic problem and offering a solution that is 'scientific rubbish'. The scientists, experts in diabetes and obesity, say the debate is dominated by 'thought police' ignoring evidence that fat children result from genes, not just lifestyle. 'Childhood obesity is a genetic problem,' David James said. 'If you tell the average Joe in the street the problem will be fixed by shutting down school canteens and building a couple more bike tracks they are going to be disappointed. It is a misrepresentation.'
>
> (Hope 2002: 3)

Whether or not overweight or obesity are inherited conditions is not simply a scientific question and the critics of neo-Darwinian theory are not limited to its many academic adversaries. The idea that some people are more genetically predisposed to greater fatness than others has clearly struck some commentators as just another poor excuse for sloth and gluttony. Tom Robinson's (2003) sarcastic 'Rest easy, couch potato, and blame it on your genes' for the *Virginian-Pilot and the Ledger Star* is typical of those none-too-impressed by the genetic argument.

What is interesting about print-media discussion about the genetics of overweight and obesity is the polarized positions that are articulated. Even though knowledge about the mechanism and the size of the contribution of genetics to overweight and obesity is currently very sketchy, this does not appear to inhibit commentators from expressing a definitive, and often blatantly self-righteous, view on the matter.

Bad people and bad families

As we saw in the previous chapter, Shawna Vogel bases her book *The Skinny on Fat* (1999) on the premise that more scientific knowledge can lead to less moralistic views about overweight and obesity. There is precious little evidence of this in the print-media. Writing in the *Sydney Morning Herald*, Paul Sheehan (2003) uses American research that casts doubt on the contribution that diet changes have made to the 'obesity epidemic' to argue that: 'Reality bites – if you're fat, you're lazy, too.' That overweight and obesity are moral failings is not open to debate for Sheehan. What is at issue here is *which* moral failing is to blame: if it is not gluttony then it must be sloth.

Elsewhere, other warriors of the political right have leapt on the 'obesity epidemic' with undisguised enthusiasm. In Australia, Angela Shanahan has blamed increased overweight and obesity on the decline of 'family values', a cause she writes about continually in her regular columns. In 'Why fat is a family issue' (2002: 97) she claims that: 'All over the Western world, and increasingly in wealthy Asian societies, obesity has become the single greatest health concern for children'. Shanahan's solution to the fattening of Australians is for parents (actually mothers) to buy only 'real food', 'turn off the TV and sit at the table for dinner. Talk to your children, and make dinner time a central, defining ritual of life in every way – a healthier family life.' While Shanahan articulates a very particular and highly nostalgic vision of how Western people should live their lives, our interest here is in the way she incorporates the 'obesity epidemic' into her pre-existing world-view. Shanahan, like so many other commentators, journalists and (as we will see) scientists, seems able only to start at the end: that is, to arrive at apparently firm conclusions about the causes and solutions of the 'obesity epidemic', which are simply re-statements of familiar ideological commitments.

Striking a similar note is 'Parent and child fitness bond broken. We're too busy to be role models' by Brad Crouch (2002: 17) for South Australia's *Sunday Mail*. Quoting experts, the article blames 'modern life', the ubiquitous but largely ill-defined villain-of-the-peace. In this case, the critique of 'modern life' takes the following novel form:

> The parent-child role model link to a healthy lifestyle has been shattered by modern life. New research shows the once-strong bond between physically active parents and their children has been eroded to a point it is no longer significant. Longer work hours, less time with children and changed family structures are partly to blame, University of South Australia research shows. However, modern gyms also share the blame with health centres catering to adult fitness further cutting into shared play time.
>
> (Crouch 2002: 17)

From a different quarter come those who hold global corporations responsible. Leading the charge has been American nutritionist Marion Nestle. Her books and numerous newspaper columns (e.g. Nestle 2000, 2002) lay the blame for both the 'obesity epidemic' and problems with the US food safety system at the feet of the food industry, particularly its mega-corporations and their allegedly close relationship with legislators. For Nestle, these problems are the result of naked self-interest. Because the US produces too much food, competition is fierce and profit margins are narrow. Food producers, she argues, are resistant to both public health messages, which encourage people to eat less food, and to tougher food safety regulations.

But just as some popular writers appear uncomfortable with genetic explanations for overweight and obesity because they let people 'off the hook', Nestle's attempts to shift the focus of attention to corporations has, for similar reasons, not always been welcomed. In his review of Nestle's book *Food Politics* and Eric Schlosser's *Fast Food Nation* (see Chapter 7 for more discussion of these books), Ewin Hannan for *The Age* reminds readers that it is lazy individuals, not corporations, who are to blame:

> By producing books that cast light on the methods of the fast-food giants, publishers serve the public interest. But demonising Big Food also gives comfort to a generation that stubbornly refuses to acknowledge the underlying reason for its expanding waistline. After all, we are what we eat.
>
> (Hannan 2003: 8)

Seeing obesity everywhere

The 2000 final of the UEFA Cup, a competition between some of the leading male soccer clubs of Europe, pitted England's Arsenal against Galatasaray of Turkey.

The game was broadcast live in England by the BBC with commentators Martin Tyler providing descriptions of play, and the ex-England player, Trevor Brooking (whom we met earlier in this chapter) offering expert comments.

The game was tight and finished 0–0 at the end of normal time. Another 30 minutes of extra time failed to split the teams. The players then prepared for the obligatory penalty shoot-out, the notoriously nerve-jangling tie-break system in which players from either side alternately try to score from 12 yards out with only the opposing goalkeeper to beat.

With the penalty shoot-out tied at 2–2, Davor Suker stepped forward to take Arsenal's third penalty. He missed. The next Galatasaray player scored. Arsenal's next penalty taker, Nicolas Anelka, also missed which left the next Galatasaray player needing to score to claim the trophy for the Turkish club. He made no mistake and the English team was beaten. Arsenal, a heavyweight European club with its multinational roster of players had been humbled by the unfancied Turks made up of predominantly home-grown talent.

Brooking could not help himself. Although working as a broadcaster and (presumably) far away from his work with England's junior sporting talent he immediately blamed Arsenal's defeat on the sorry physical state of English youth. 'Although to be fair', said Tyler, 'the two Arsenal penalty misses were by a Croat [Suker] and a Frenchman [Anelka].' The commentary box fell silent.

Although some print-media commentators emphasize exercise, and others food or genetics, the central message is remarkably unified: we are in the middle of an obesity-driven health crisis. The culprit is 'modern life' and 'everyone everywhere' is at risk. 'Modern life' has made food more easily accessible and exercise harder to fit in. Although this is a highly generalized diagnosis, some specific causative factors are commonly proposed. They include televisions and computers, fast food restaurants, our evolutionary past, declining levels of physical education, declining 'family values' and a general human tendency toward laziness.

Out of all of this, an interesting situation emerges. While the basic propositions that overweight and obesity are bad and too many people are too fat remain constant, the way in which 'modern life' has created this situation causes people to return to their respective moral and ideological 'comfort zones'. These 'comfort zones' are habitual ways of talking and thinking into which the 'obesity epidemic' is inserted. They cause people to look at the same phenomenon – in this case rising overweight and obesity statistics – but to see very different things, which perhaps explains why someone might look at highly paid Croatian and French professional footballers and see obese English school children. And they explain why some see technology or large corporations or modern approaches to parenting or genetics or human nature as the root cause of the crisis we are supposedly in.

This inevitably raises the question of who is speaking the truth. As we saw in this chapter, obesity experts have become an indispensable component of print-media coverage of the 'obesity epidemic', no doubt because their contributions give newspaper and magazine articles an increased air of credibility, no matter what assertion is being made. But in order to find the truth, some people turn to the research literature.

3   The ghost of a machine

At this point it may be tempting to think that the occasional excesses that media coverage inevitably entails are one thing, but that the science of the 'obesity epidemic' is quite another. However, it is not difficult to find examples from the scientific literature in which the current situation is similarly described in cataclysmic terms. Seidell (2000), for example, claims that there may be one billion overweight and obese people in the world: that is, one billion people who are sufficiently fat to be classified as 'diseased' on account of their body weight alone. The situation is regularly described as an obesity 'crisis' (Beebe 2002; Deckelbaum and Williams 2001; Ebbeling *et al.* 2002; Klein 2004), requiring a 'war on obesity' (Friedman 2003; Klein 1999).

As we saw in the quote from Bouchard and Blair (1999) in Chapter 1, the diagnosis of too much food and not enough physical activity is generally taken to be self-evident in the scientific literature. In fact, it seems that many researchers in this area have moved past asking why the 'obesity epidemic' is happening to the development of strategies to reduce the number of calories people consume and to increase the calories they expend (e.g. Hill and Peters 1998; Peters *et al.* 2002). Chakravarthy and Booth (2003: 731) claim that by 'watching less TV, eating fewer higher-calorie fast foods, and being more physically active . . . the current rising physical inactivity and obesity epidemics can be thwarted'.

At the risk of oversimplification, this assessment seems to be saying that 'we know that overweight and obesity are serious diseases, we know what causes them, and, in broad terms, we know what to do about them'. Over the course of this and the following three chapters, we offer an alternative perspective. We survey the scientific literature and argue that there are, in fact, many aspects of both the causes and consequences of overweight and obesity, which are poorly understood. We ask, if it is the case that the causes and consequences of overweight and obesity are unclear; how is it possible to speak about a present crisis and a future calamity with the air of certainty which characterizes much of the scientific literature? Is it possible that the apparent uniformity of the view that too much food and not enough physical activity has produced a global health crisis has more to do with cultural attitudes towards fatness than the weight of scientific evidence? Chakravarthy and Booth (2003: 731) describe the current sedentary and obesity-promoting lives which (they allege) Westerners increasingly live as 'sedentary death syndrome'. Elsewhere, however, Bouchard and Blair claim that:

the body of knowledge on physical activity and relevant obesity outcomes is extremely limited. There are few randomized clinical trials that have lasted 1 year or more, with reasonable statistical power, adequate monitoring of intervention protocols, high levels of compliance, and proper measurement of the outcome variables. The net result is a general lack of a solid research database regarding the role of physical activity in the prevention and treatment of overweight and obesity as well as their comorbidities.

(Bouchard and Blair 1999: S498)

It is this juxtaposition of certainty and uncertainty, of impending doom and a scarcity of corroborating evidence that is the focus of this chapter. In short, what do we really know about overweight and obesity?

However, our argument goes beyond questioning whether a credible scientific case exists for the idea of an obesity 'crisis'. We also question the value of treating the study of overweight and obesity as a science at all. In other words, we ask: is it possible that the scientific method itself is ill-suited to the task of understanding overweight and obesity and to helping us respond constructively to overweight and obesity when and where they happen?

One consequence of conceiving the study of health and human body weight as a 'science' seems to be that particular ways of thinking become pervasive, if not dominant. In the remainder of this chapter we take a detailed look at these ways of thinking and some examples of the kinds of knowledge this thinking produces. At all times, two questions will guide our discussion. First, has the scientific approach to overweight and obesity produced a consistent and reliable foundation of knowledge on which to base confident statements about the 'obesity epidemic'? Second, does the scientific approach to overweight and obesity produce *useful* knowledge? These are important questions because, as we have seen, scientists of one form or another have played an important role in making the case for the 'obesity epidemic' in the public sphere.

Energy-in/energy-out

The science of overweight and obesity rests on the assumption that the body is like a machine. In this view, the body is predictable and obeys laws that are more or less universal across time and space. For example, the idea that the body is governed by scientifically verifiable laws drives research designed to find out what kinds of physical activity best promote weight loss and general health.

According to the 'body as machine' model, increased body weight in an individual person or a population can only be explained by what is generally called 'energy imbalance', where dietary intake (food) exceeds energy expenditure (physical activity). According to Hill and Peters:

obesity can arise only when energy intake exceeds energy expenditure. Our current environment is characterized by an essentially unlimited supply of convenient, relatively inexpensive, highly palatable, energy-dense foods, coupled with a lifestyle requiring only low levels of physical activity for subsistence. Such an environment promotes high energy intake and low energy expenditure.

(Hill and Peters 1998: 1371)

In fact, the idea of energy imbalance simply restates the physical law of the conservation of energy, which holds that energy is never lost. So when we eat, the energy we consume does not disappear but is converted into some other form, such as body fat, or is utilized when we exercise and turned into mechanical and heat energy.

For the 'body as machine' model to work, it must be possible to make robust generalizations about the impact of both a given amount of dietary intake and a given amount of physical activity on a person's body weight. For example, scientists who write about overweight and obesity are fond of calculating the energy cost of a given amount of physical activity and then arguing that if this amount of activity were added to, or subtracted from, a person's lifestyle, say everyday, then this would lead to a precise level of weight loss or gain. Take this short passage from the *Journal of the American Dietetic Association*:

Even small energy deficits achieved consistently can have a profound effect on weight loss. For example, if an individual engages in moderately brisk walking (4 mph pace) for 45 minutes 4 times a week for a year, and does not increase caloric consumption, an energy deficit resulting in weight loss (depending on the person's body weight) of approximately 18 lb will result.

(Rippe and Hess 1998: S33)

Bouchard provides another neat example of this logic:

For instance, a nonresting daily energy expenditure depressed by about 300 kcal will generate chronic positive energy balance and translate into a surplus of calories consumed of more than 100,000 kcal over a year. This would undoubtedly result in a body weight gain that may be as high as 50 percent of the total yearly caloric surplus caused by a sedentary lifestyle. If one assumes that one kg of body mass is, on the average, the equivalent of about 7,000 kcal, then a reduction of the daily level of habitual physical activity by 300 kcal would be associated with a body weight gain of 6 to 8 kg over a year.

(Bouchard 2000: 6–7)

Putting to one side Bouchard's curious juxtaposition of certainty ('this would *undoubtedly* result . . .') and uncertainty ('in a body weight gain that *may* be as high as . . .'), the dominant theme from both of these examples is the machine-like *predictability* of the body's response to food and physical activity. In the following passage, which appears shortly after the one above, Bouchard uses this style of thinking to provide a short list of possible explanations for the 'obesity epidemic'. In the process, he demonstrates how a metaphor about one thing – the body is like a machine – can affect the way someone thinks about another thing – what are the important things we need to consider if we want to understand the 'obesity epidemic'?

The increase in the last decades of the prevalence of overweight and obesity can be theoretically explained by one or a combination of the following three scenarios. The first scenario posits that the increase results from the fact that a large proportion of the population is consuming more calories than individuals of past generations with no change in habitual daily energy expenditure. The second scenario suggests that the cause of the increase can be found in a decrease in daily energy expenditure with no change in caloric intake. Finally, the third scenario proposes that caloric intake per capita has actually declined compared to previous generations, but daily energy expenditure has, on the average, decreased even more.

(Bouchard 2000: 11)

It would perhaps be churlish on our part to suggest that Bouchard has overlooked a fourth scenario, one in which average physical activity levels have gone up but food intake has gone up even more. Nonetheless, it is at least worth noting that the possibility that people are doing more physical activity today than in previous generations is apparently so ludicrous as to be unthinkable, and therefore not even worth including on Bouchard's list of *theoretical* possibilities.

Grundy *et al.* (1999) provide another example of this style of thinking. In their summary of the physical activity and obesity literature, the authors are faced with data that suggests people may, on average, be eating less at the same time as overweight and obesity rates are going up. They deal with this problem in the following way:

Some studies reported secular decreases in energy intake concurrently with increases in body weight, both in children and adults; these decreases infer a corresponding even greater decrease in energy expenditure, which would be a requirement for weight gain.

(Grundy *et al.* 1999: S504)

In attempting to explain why Australian girls from wealthier families appear to be leaner than girls from less affluent families, Booth *et al.* offer the following:

The possible causes of lower BMI among high SES girls are that higher SES girls may consume less energy, may have higher energy expenditure (are more physically active) or may engage in weight control strategies to a greater extent than other girls.

(Booth *et al.* 1999: 461)

Initially, there are three straightforward but important points to make about this style of thinking. The first, to which we have already alluded, is that it assumes that human body weight is subject to a rigid law that relates inputs and outputs. This law can be expressed as:

$$a - b = c$$

where a is energy consumed, b is energy expended and c is the resulting change in body weight. According to this law, if a and b are the same then body weight will remain constant. If they are not the same then body weight will change. Most obesity researchers accept that, in reality, the situation is more complicated, a point we will return to later in this chapter. However, as the passages quoted above suggest, this law underpins almost the entire field of obesity studies. In fact, it is difficult to see how a science of body weight could be possible without it.

The second point to make about the 'body as machine' model is that it does not leave much room for other factors that shape people's actions around food and physical activity. Because it assumes that all human bodies adhere to the same mechanical law, it is not so good at handling human differences such as cultural values, socio-economic class, ethnicity, gender, geographical location and age. Moving our lens out even wider, this model also tends not to have much to say about the decisions of governments, the workings of capitalism or the actions of large institutions such as corporations. This is not to say that the idea of the 'body as machine' stops anyone from thinking about these things and, indeed, some obesity scientists have attempted to do exactly this. For example, Nestle (2002) and Brownell and Horgen (2004) have argued that the economics of the production, marketing and selling of food are playing an increasingly important role in American overweight and obesity (see Chapter 7 for further discussion of these arguments). The question to be asked, however, is whether the 'body as machine' model makes it easier or more difficult to think about factors other than the amount of food people eat and the amount of physical activity they do? In other words, is the machine model a necessary first step that helps us to fill in important details before moving to other wider issues, or is it a distraction that causes researchers to get bogged down in unimportant detail and to pursue ultimately futile lines of research?

The third point is perhaps more contentious. Despite its scientific pedigree, the 'body as machine' model remains a largely theoretical proposition only. In fact, it is hard to find human beings in their 'natural setting' whose bodies conform to it. As Sobal and Stunkard point out:

> Carefully controlled laboratory studies have found exquisitely precise relationships between changes in energy balance and changes in body weight (Garrow 1978). These studies, however, have been short-term laboratory investigations. When one ventures outside the laboratory to longer term attempts to understand the origins of obesity, the picture becomes less clear. A major problem in population studies of this type is the apparent lack of relationship between food intake and body weight of adults (Keen, Thomas & Jarrett 1982, Keen, Thomas, Jarrett & Fuller 1979, Kromhout 1983), adolescents (Bingham, McNeil & Cummings 1981, Hampton, Huenemann, Shapiro & Mitchell 1967), and infants (Vobecky, Vobecky, Shapcott & Demers 1983), even when the effects of physical activity are controlled. This problem has frequently been ascribed to the underreporting of food intake by some obese persons. But even when food intake and energy expenditure are carefully monitored in field studies, the relationship between energy intake and body weight is weak (Edholm, Fletcher, Widdowson & McCance 1955).

(Sobal and Stunkard 1989: 265)[1]

Significant new data to support the efficacy of the 'body as machine' model have not appeared since these comments were published. In the supplementary 1999 edition of the journal of *Medicine and Science in Sports and Exercise* mentioned in Chapter 1, many of the contributing authors found a distinct lack of direct evidence supporting the idea that physical activity affects body weight in predictable ways. In their overview paper, Hill and Melanson summed up the state of knowledge as follows:

> Although we lack a definitive prospective study to show that a low level of physical activity is a risk for obesity development and that a high level of physical activity is protective against obesity, an overwhelming amount of indirect evidence suggests this is the case. The amount of physical activity that protects against obesity is not known, but some have suggested that a physical activity of 1.75 (daily energy expenditure of 1.75 times the metabolic rate) should be our target. We need more information in order to provide guidance to the public on this issue.
>
> (Hill and Melanson 1999: S516-17)

We are struck here by the comment that the 'amount of physical activity that protects against obesity is not known'. It suggests that the authors believe that a generalizable answer to this problem is waiting to be discovered and they even speculate about a possible answer. By 'indirect evidence' the authors mean large cross-sectional (that is, 'snapshot' style studies which assess groups of people at a given moment in time) and longitudinal population studies (sometimes called 'prospective' studies because they select people and then collect data about them over a given period of time, sometimes as long as a few decades). These studies rely heavily on self-report data (usually people's recollections and estimates of how much food they eat and physical activity they do) and can only ever offer correlational – not causational – conclusions about the relationship between physical activity and body weight. In her review of research into the extent to which physical activity prevents obesity, DiPietro concludes:

> Unfortunately, there is a paucity of longitudinal data that examine the role of physical activity on weight gain among the general population . . . The hypothesis that physical activity effects body weight inversely is logical, but observational population-based data on the longitudinal relationship between these two variables are somewhat confusing. Cross sectional associations between physical activity or fitness and body weight are stronger than those seen longitudinally, and although there is evidence of a relation to *attenuated weight gain*, it is not clear that increased physical activity actually prevents or reverses age-related weight gain at the population level.
>
> (DiPietro 1999: S543, emphasis in original)

Grundy *et al.* (1999: S504), reviewing similar research, also found that: 'No RCT [randomized controlled trials] are available that address whether sedentary life habits and inactivity contribute to the development of obesity in populations'.

In her review of research into the use of physical activity to treat, as opposed to prevent obesity, Wing (1999) found that studies which simply added a given amount of exercise to a person's weekly routine produced very 'modest' and, in some cases, no weight reduction. This is a difficult finding to square with the formulations quoted previously which claimed that a given amount of exercise will *inevitably* lead to a *precise* amount of weight loss. Wing also writes:

> The premise of behavioural weight loss programs has been that it is the total calorie expenditure that affects weight loss, not the intensity. However, there do not appear to be any long-term randomized trials that have specifically tested this hypothesis.
>
> (Wing 1999: S551)

It is important to note here that the issue of exercise intensity, as opposed to quantity, is an interesting complicating factor. For example, the uninformed lay-observer might ask, if the energy-in/energy-out law $(a - b = c)$ holds, then why should exercise intensity matter? Surely the only important issue is the number of calories expended, regardless of how this is achieved. Although researchers have given considerable thought to whether exercise intensity does matter (e.g. LeMura and Maziekas 2002; Pollock 1992), this naive question remains an awkward and unresolved challenge to the idea that human body weight is governed by predictable, universal and mechanistic laws.

A similar situation emerges if we look at childhood overweight and obesity. Over the decades studies have emerged to suggest that overweight and obese children are less active (e.g. Bullen *et al.* 1964; Johnson *et al.* 1956), just as active (Bradfield *et al.* 1971; Maxfield and Konishi 1966) and more active (Waxman and Stunkard 1980) than other children. Wolf *et al.* (1993) found no association between activity levels and childhood overweight and obesity while Grund *et al.* (2001: 1245) argue that 'the relationship between childhood obesity and energy expenditure or physical activity is far from clear'. Fogelholm *et al.* (1999: 1262) claim: 'It is still controversial whether inactivity promotes obesity in children.' Schutz and Maffeis' review of the literature finds that:

> Although hard evidence is lacking for reduced levels of energy expenditure as powerful etiologic factors in the development of obesity in children, most hypotheses do accept that the PAL [physical activity level] has an important role in children's weight regulation (Obarzanek et al. 1994).
>
> (Schutz and Maffeis 2002: 99)

Schutz and Maffeis' final comment that most researchers continue to accept that physical activity plays an important role in 'weight regulation' despite a dearth of evidence is interesting because it suggests that conclusive evidence may not be a particularly important factor in deciding what scientists hold to be true. In fact, as with the passages quoted above, there is a recurring refrain in the overweight and obesity literature in which the relationship between food, physical activity and body weight is described as 'obvious' despite a scarcity of evidence to that effect. As Hill and Peters put it:

> Will consumption of a low-fat, low-energy density diet prevent obesity in
> sedentary individuals, and will regular physical activity protect even those
> people eating a high fat, high-energy density diet? The answers to these ques-
> tions seem obvious, but there is little direct empirical evidence to prove the
> effectiveness of these strategies.
>
> (Hill and Peters 1998: 1373)

Schutz and Maffeis also point out that some *cross-sectional* (not longitudinal)
studies have found a correlation between overweight and physical activity levels
among children. But these data only suggest that overweight and obese children
are less likely to be physically active than non-overweight children, not that physical inactivity *causes* increased body weight. They also point out that some
cross-sectional studies do not even find a correlation. In any case, it remains true
that the idea that physical inactivity causes overweight and obesity in both adults
and children rests heavily on correlational self-report data.

The findings of numerous original studies (e.g. Donnelly *et al.* 1994; Sweeney
et al. 1993; Weinstock *et al.* 1998) have not supported a link between body weight
and physical activity and/or food intake. A number of reviews of research (e.g.
Dubbert *et al.* 2002; Goran *et al.* 1999; Westerterp 1999b) have found the
relationship between body weight and physical activity to be inconsistent, unclear
or controversial. The extent to which exercise induces weight and/or fat loss in
controlled studies is regularly described in the scientific literature as 'minimal'
(Brochu *et al.* 2000: 99), 'small', 'disappointing', 'modest' (e.g. literature reviews
by Ballor and Keesey 1991; Robinson 1999; Wilmore 1983) and in some circumstances non-existent (Shephard 1989). On the question of whether the health
benefits of exercise are independent of fat loss, Shephard writes:

> Those who argue that fat loss is the main source of the health benefit asso-
> ciated with regular exercise thus face the important theoretical difficulty that
> although long-term health benefits can be demonstrated, body fat does not
> change very much, particularly in the most vulnerable, severely obese segment
> of the population.
>
> (Shephard 1994: 93)

Epstein and Goldfield's review article concerning the role of physical activity
in treating childhood overweight and obesity is similarly inconclusive:

> This review highlights the limited number of randomized controlled studies
> investigating the efficacy of exercise in the treatment of pediatric obesity.
> The small number of controlled outcome studies in combination with the use
> of different dependent variables across studies limits the strength of conclu-
> sions that can be drawn. The only area in which there are sufficient studies
> to make quantitative data-based conclusions for body composition changes is
> in the comparison of diet versus diet plus exercise . . . There are too few
> studies comparing exercise versus no exercise, or comparing different exercise
> programs to make firm conclusions. In addition, there are very limited data
> on long-term effects of exercise, and any conclusions would be premature.
>
> (Epstein and Goldfield 1999: S556–7)

Whether or not excessive food intake causes overweight and obesity is also controversial. The idea that overeating causes fatness has a long history and yet it is an idea which researchers are *still* trying to prove. That it remains a controversial idea is amply demonstrated by the number (and the titles) of articles on the subject, particularly with respect to children. In their article, 'Is childhood obesity associated with high-fat foods and low physical activity?', Muecke *et al.* write:

> Childhood obesity has been described as 'one of the most complex and least understood clinical syndromes in pediatric medicine.' Convention suggests obesity results from overeating and inadequate physical activity. A recent survey of pediatricians revealed excessive calorie consumption was cited most frequently as a major cause of this disorder. Though some studies support the contention that overweight children over consume food, others contradicted this widely-accepted notion. Comparisons of obese adolescents to normal peers have demonstrated comparable energy intake and nutrient distribution. In adults, investigators using HANES I data concluded that 'neither the caloric intake nor the caloric intake adjusted for physical activity level and age was higher in the obese subjects.'
>
> (Muecke *et al.* 1992: 19)

On the same subject Hanley *et al.* claim:

> The cause of pediatric obesity has not been elucidated completely, although it is suspected that a complex interaction of genetic, environmental, and behavioral factors is responsible. Although the notion that obesity is caused by excess energy intake is not generally supported in the scientific literature, recent research suggests that aspects of diet composition, including high fat and low carbohydrate intakes, may play a role in overweight. Findings on the role of energy expenditure are also inconclusive, although low physical activity rates were associated with obesity and television viewing was shown to be a significant risk factor for pediatric obesity, both cross-sectionally and prospectively.
>
> (Hanley *et al.* 2000: 693–4)

More recently, Rolland-Cachera and Bellisle (2002) have argued that a positive relationship between the amount of dietary energy children consume and how much they weigh is difficult to find in the literature. Their review includes studies of childhood and teenage overweight and obesity from the US, France, Australia, Britain and Spain, and finds almost no evidence to support the proposition that overweight and obese children consume more calories than other children. In fact, they point out that data exist which suggest that overweight and obese children may consume less energy, particularly (but not only) when energy intake is expressed as a proportion of body weight.

Regarding the general population the situation is equally unclear. Writing twenty years ago, Wooley and Wooley (1984) argued that it was an open question whether overeating caused overweight and obesity, noting that it was certainly possible for very high body weights to be maintained on very low caloric intake. Blundell and

King (1999) describe the relationship between food intake, physical activity and 'energy balance' – the situation in which a person's body weight does not change – as 'poorly understood'. This is a particularly difficult position to square with the mechanistic theory of energy balance articulated by the obesity scientists quoted earlier in this chapter. Writing in the *Journal of the American Medical Association* about the tendency of the medical profession to see overweight and obese people as incurably gluttonous, Frank claims

> There is no reason to believe that patients' behaviour causes this disease. Even in 1760, Flemyng noted 'that not all corpulent persons are great eaters or thin persons spare feeders ... Tho' a voracious appetite be one cause of corpulency, it is not the only cause; and very often not even the conditio sine qua non thereof.' For over two centuries, thoughtful physicians have realized that overeating and obesity are not necessarily the same. Yet during all the years of my education (and for all the nonmedical world around me), there was an assumption that people are fat because they eat too much; they are punished for their willful misconduct. There is remarkably little evidence that patients become fat because they overeat.
>
> (Frank 1993: 2133)

As a result of these empirical difficulties, many studies have tried to tease out the respective contributions of both diet and physical activity to body weight, but particularly weight loss. These have given consistently confusing results. For example, some studies (e.g. Heymsfield *et al.* 1989) suggest that sedentary people who restrict their caloric intake may lose the same amount as people who add regular physical activity to the same caloric regimen. In passing, it is worth remembering this kind of research would not be necessary if the human body conformed to the energy-in/energy-out law.

In the next section we consider some possible reasons why the energy-in/energy-out law resists empirical confirmation. But before doing so, it is worth reflecting on where the preceding discussion leaves us. We certainly are not suggesting that the laws of physics are mysteriously suspended when it comes to human body weight. On whether the energy-in/energy-out law produces 'true' knowledge about body weight, the most defensible position would appear to be an open and undecided mind. More importantly, however, whether this model helps us to understand human body weight and why it changes – that is, is it a *useful* model? – would also seem very much open to question.

For example, once human body weight is framed as a matter of the balance between energy-in and energy-out, it is not unreasonable that the general public, in an earnest attempt to 'do the right thing', might try to reduce the former or increase the latter. There is ample evidence that many young people, particularly young females, are trying to do exactly this, despite (as we saw in the previous chapter) the tendency of some scientists and commentators to see young people as little more than junk food and technology addicts. We are aware of two studies that have investigated what happens when young people try to limit their energy-in. Both of these quite recent prospective studies (Field *et al.* 2003; Stice *et al.* 1999) suggest that children and adolescents who reported dieting to lose weight, either frequently or infrequently, had put on significantly more weight by the end of the research period (four years and three years respectively) than those who reported never dieting. In Field *et al.* (2003) boys and girls who reported dieting showed similar results. In addition, the dieters not only got fatter but reported doing more physical activity. It is also worth remembering that researchers consistently describe the long-term success of scientifically controlled weight loss programmes, where the energy-in and/or energy-out of individuals are modified as, at best, 'disappointing' and, at worst, 'dismal' (e.g. Frank 1993; Stunkard and Penick 1979). With particular emphasis on school-aged children, Robinson (1999: 1561) writes: 'Unfortunately, most prevention programs that specifically attempt to reduce fat and energy intake and increase physical activity have been ineffective at changing body fatness'. Swinburn and Egger (2002), also note that community-level interventions designed to directly modify energy-in and energy-out have rarely produced significant reductions in overweight and obesity. Taken together, these results are not conclusive proof of anything, but they should at least make us wonder about the usefulness of the science of obesity's preoccupation with the 'energy balance' – food and physical activity – of individuals.

Defending the model

In Thomas Kuhn's landmark work *The Structure of Scientific Revolutions* (1970), the author describes the way existing scientific paradigms are defended by its adherents until such time as the paradigm's weaknesses become intolerably obvious. At present, the energy-in/energy-out law of human body weight does not appear to be on the verge of revolutionary collapse. However, its adherents have proposed a range of reasons for the enduring empirical uncertainties, which, in our opinion, rather than shoring up the model, actually cast doubt on its long-term viability.

The first set of reasons is methodological and is widely acknowledged in the literature (e.g. Bauman and Owen 1999; Jebb and Moore 1999; Lee and Paffenbarger 1996; Melby *et al.* 2000). Put simply, nobody has yet devised a way of accurately measuring how much people eat and how much energy they expend in the course of their day-to-day lives. Researchers have mostly had to rely on the memory of research participants, both adults and children, either through diaries, questionnaires or interviews. Information collected using these methods is often called 'self-report' data and, as such, is inherently imprecise. For example, people may recall eating a bowl of ice cream but there is no way of knowing exactly how much ice cream and few people would agree to participating in a study that asked them to weigh everything they ate. Even if they did agree, imprecision would almost certainly remain a problem. Studies using more elaborate electronic devices to measure these two variables have appeared in recent years but these devices tend to be expensive, unreliable or cumbersome. In addition, trying to measure even a small group of people's energy-in and energy-out precisely is a very time-consuming, labour-intensive and technically demanding exercise, as in the so-called 'doubly labelled water' technique, which is now considered by some to be the 'gold standard' for measuring energy expenditure (Westerterp 1999a). It is therefore not surprising that most researchers rely on self-report data. However, this *does* mean that researchers who try to reconcile people's body weight with their food intake and energy expenditure are almost always dealing with imprecise data.

The fact that this research is conducted with human beings also presents another set of difficulties for the 'body as machine' model. People's memories are obviously fallible, but they may, for whatever reason, also give less than honest answers to researchers' questions. People who begin exercise programmes designed to help them lose weight may compensate by eating more although the extent to which increased physical activity leads to increased food intake is unclear (for a discussion of this issue, see Blundell and King 1999). Unless they were aware of this compensation, people might report that they were eating normally, thus obscuring the precise relationship between their body weight and energy consumption and expenditure.

The third set of possibilities is that there are biological differences between different people, or even within individuals across time, which mean that food and physical activity affect their body weight in differing ways. In recent times, obesity researchers have tended to concede that these differences exist, often calling them 'genetic' factors, despite the fact that few obesity researchers are geneticists.

The question of the genetic contribution to human body weight is a fascinating one for a number of reasons. As Chang and Christakis (2002) point out, medical researchers began asserting that human body weight had a heritable component as early as the 1940s, long before the current explosion of knowledge in molecular biology. But even today, scientists are prepared to make confident pronouncements about the genetic contribution to human body weight in the face of substantial and lingering uncertainty. Some describe the genetic contribution as 'mild' (Bouchard 2000; Damcott *et al.* 2003) while others see it as a 'strong' factor (Stunkard 1991). Maes *et al.* (1997) have claimed that research on twins reveals that 'genetic factors' explain between 50 per cent and 90 per cent of BMI variation between individuals. In a twins study published in the *New England Journal of Medicine*, Stunkard *et al.* (1990: 1483) wrote: 'We conclude that genetic influences on body-mass index are substantial, whereas the childhood environment has little or no influence'.

These contradictory claims have been made at a time when, although interest in genetics is intense, the idea that there is a straightforward genetic explanation for *anything* other than a narrow range of medical conditions remains controversial. In fact, there are those who argue that the idea of a gene or genes *for* any complex behaviour or human characteristic scarcely even makes sense (in particular, see Lewontin 2000; Morange 2002; Rogers 1999). This is because, firstly, genes themselves are generally only a small part of larger biological apparatuses and processes and, secondly, in most cases it is difficult to tease out where the influence of genes stops and the impact of other factors, such as culture, begins. The geneticist Steve Jones has written that: 'Fat parents have fat children, in the main, not because stoutness is in the genes, but because they feed their offspring with a diet like their own' (Jones 1999: 112). Given the equivocal and contested state of current knowledge, the claims of some obesity scientists that the amount of physical activity a person does is 29 per cent genetically determined or that between 10 per cent and 20 per cent of people's food preference is under genetic control (see chapter one of Vogel 1999) would seem extraordinarily brave.

It is apparent that speculative claims of this kind are derived from the percentage of statistical variation between research participants which scientists have not been able to explain by other means. Put another way, when researchers have found that human bodies do not conform to the energy-in/energy-out law, they have attributed the degree of non-conformity to genetics. For example, Salbe and Ravussin write:

> Many studies have shown that dietary fat intake is a major determinant of body fat, and fat intake is significantly associated with an increase in body mass index in women. However, there is considerable evidence showing that fat intake has actually been decreasing as the prevalence of obesity has been rising, which suggests that differences among individuals in fat metabolism may offer protection from or susceptibility to obesity; it is likely that these differences are under genetic control.
>
> (Salbe and Ravussin 2000: 73)

In the following short passage, the prominent obesity researcher F. Xavier Pi-Sunyer articulates the same line of reasoning with respect to Type II diabetes:

> Although the relationship of obesity and Type II diabetes mellitus is not wholly clear, two facts are incontrovertible. Excess body fat leads to increasing insulin resistance, and insulin resistance predisposes to diabetes. Why, however, some individuals may be obese for years without developing diabetes, whereas others develop it rapidly, *must depend on their genetic make-up*. Until more is known about the genes responsible for insulin resistance and for Type II diabetes, the exact mechanisms involved will not be clarified.
>
> (Pi-Sunyer 1999: S602, emphasis added)

The obvious point to make about these examples is that is difficult to understand how these authors can be so certain that further genetic research will explain the differences between people when they do not presently know how, or to what extent, genetics is a factor. In other words, the genetic explanation has become something of a 'black box' that acts as a kind of connection of convenience between two chosen variables – energy-in and energy-out – and a particular outcome – body weight. As Shim puts it:

> The concept of the *black box* (Latour 1987, Latour and Woolgar 1986) originates from cybernetics, where it is used in diagrams as a quick way of alluding to some complex process or piece of machinery: in its place, one draws a box and indicates only the input and the output, thereby side-stepping the need to detail the contents of the box itself. This metaphor captures critical aspects of the character of technoscientific facts such as the multifactorial model: hidden inside 'is an entire social history of actions and decisions, experiments and arguments, claims and counterclaims – often enough, a disorderly history of contingency, controversy, and uncertainty' (Epstein 1996: 28).
>
> (Shim 2002: 135, emphasis in original)

With the concept of the 'black box' in mind, our energy-in/energy-out law

$$a - b = c$$

could now be written as:

$$(a - b) \times k = c$$

Here, a is still energy-in, b is still energy-out, and c is still the resultant change in body weight. But now the difference between a and b is multiplied by the unknown variable k, our genetic 'black box'. We do not know the value of k and, in fact, it is imperative that we do not know, since if we did know it might turn out that the left side of the equation fails to equal the right side. If this were the case, we might decide to abandon the model.

In general, obesity scientists discount the significance of genetics (see Chapter 6) when trying to explain the 'obesity epidemic', arguing that human genetic material changes far too slowly for it to be playing a role in an epidemic barely three decades old. However, the *idea* of a genetic contribution to human body weight (if not solid empirical knowledge about such a contribution) performs an important role in holding the 'body as machine' model together. This is an intellectually precarious position to be in because it means that obesity scientists have to argue that genetics is both important – in determining an individual's body weight – and unimportant – in determining the *population's* body weight – at the same time. We return to this problem in Chapter 6.

For the moment it is worth reiterating that the science of human body weight is presently replete with uncertainties and rests on the far from empirically watertight 'body as machine' model. It is interesting to note that, almost without exception, scientific research papers that deal with the measurement of energy consumption and expenditure make some mention of the need for further research to develop more accurate instruments (e.g. Blair *et al.* 1992). However, this search for the perfect instrument is driven by a desire to prove a law ($a - b = c$) that the research community *already* believes in. A reasonable question might be to ask how we will be better off if/when the perfect instrument is found? Will it do anything more than tell us what we already knew? Put another way, if we already 'know' that overweight and obesity are the result of energy-in exceeding energy-out, what practical, public health benefits will flow from being able to calculate this imbalance to the nearest one-hundredth of a calorie? A more radical (although impossible to verify) reading of the situation might be to suggest that calls for more research derive not from a desire to prove the model but, in fact, are produced, even multiplied, by the flaws inherent in the model itself.

A healthy machine?

The central question being asked in this chapter is: where does a particular way of thinking, one that is rigidly mechanical, take us? Does it help us to understand human body weight and, more urgently, does it help us to arrive at reasonable conclusions and sound courses of action with respect to the so-called 'obesity epidemic'? In Chapter 2 we saw how mass-media discussion of the 'obesity epidemic' is characterized by certainty. Journalists and the scientists they talk to appear to be certain that we are faced with a looming health catastrophe and that over-weight and obesity are caused by too much food and not enough physical activity. However, in the light of the literature we have presented so far in this chapter, we would submit that this certainty is unjustified. In fact, we would put forward the working hypothesis that people's (including scientists') pre-existing beliefs about the 'obesity epidemic' are somewhat out of step with much of the existing scientific data. As we have tried to show, there is no shortage of scientists who, when asked to look closely at relatively narrow and tightly defined empirical questions – such as, does an increase in energy expenditure prevent or ameliorate weight gain? – will concede that there are no certain answers to these questions. In the remainder of this chapter we consider two more important examples from the field of obesity studies which, in our view, demonstrate both the futility and dangers of mechanistic thinking: the relationship between physical activity and health and the role of television viewing in childhood overweight and obesity. In each case, cherished assumptions, rather than the existing data, appear to be central to the conclusions scientists reach.

Physical activity and health

The significant difficulties that researchers have had concerning body weight are dwarfed by the problems associated with establishing whether food and physical activity have a direct, measurable and consistent effect on health. These are important 'obesity epidemic' issues because dietary restraint and physical activity remain the mainstay of anti-obesity public health campaigns. As Klein (1999: 1061) puts it: 'The difficult process of implementing lifelong modifications in eating and physical activity behaviors is the cornerstone of obesity therapy'. Moreover, medical researchers, often with more than a hint of exasperation, charge the general public with being insufficiently active (in particular, see Colditz 1999; Fentem 1994; Lee and Paffenbarger 1996; Savage and Scott 1998). A mechanistic approach to the human body assumes that if we look hard enough, laws – or at least patterns – concerning health, food and physical activity will emerge and that these patterns can then be communicated to the public so that they might lead 'healthier' lives. Indeed, researchers working in this area often assert that finding these laws or patterns will help us to combat the 'obesity epidemic' (Blair and Connelly 1996; Lee and Paffenbarger 1996; Schoeller 2003).

That physical activity is good for health is an ancient idea and, as we will see in the next chapter, has been held as self-evident by 'experts' for centuries. None-theless, twentieth-century researchers generally asserted that *scientific* evidence for this idea was lacking, a point borne out by the numerous large-scale longitudinal studies that were (and are still being) conducted in order to test it. These studies, such as the well-known Harvard Alumni Health Study (e.g. Lee *et al.* 1995; Sesso *et al.* 2001), have tracked very large groups of people over decades and generally found that more active individuals have somewhat superior health outcomes. The size of these studies is important because it gives researchers greater power to find statistically significant differences between the health outcomes of different groups of people, such as between regular exercisers and non-exercisers. However, there are a number of drawbacks with this kind of research. For example, because they rely on people's inevitably flawed recollections about the physical activity they do, these studies can say nothing very precise about the kind or amount of physical activity that might have led to improved health outcomes. This imprecision flows directly out of the large sample sizes of these studies since it is simply impractical to collect detailed information from such large numbers of people. Also, despite the efforts of some to argue otherwise, these studies can only offer correlational findings: physically active people may have fewer heart attacks but this may or may not be the result of physical activity. Indeed, the physiological (that is, mechanical) reason or reasons why physical activity might improve medical health remain largely unknown (Sesso *et al.* 2000). Some studies have attempted to hold various confounding variables constant, such as tobacco use and socioeconomic status, in order to strengthen the case for direct causation. However, this technique can never rule out the possibility that other confounding variables (that the researchers have simply not thought of) are at work, an extremely common occurrence throughout the history of experimental science.

If we accept the general premise that some regular physical activity is beneficial for human health, what else do we know? What kind of physical activity should we do? And for how long? At what age should we start? How strenuous should the activity be? As it turns out, these are questions that have proved extremely difficult to answer and, as Jebb and Moore (1999) note, exercise-for-health guidelines tend to vary widely from country to country, a point that might at least make us wonder about the science on which they are based.

An interesting case in point relates to the health benefits of physical activity for children. Twisk's (2001) review of physical activity guidelines for children and adolescents considers what he sees as the three theoretical pathways by which youth physical activity might affect long-term health. They are:

1   *youth physical activity → youth health = adult health*

In this formulation, youth physical activity improves youth health, which has long-term health benefits. On this proposition he concludes:

> In summary, it can be stated that there is only marginal evidence of a relationship between physical activity during youth and health status during youth, and there is hardly any evidence of a particular shape of that relationship. Indeed, it looks that there are different shapes of relationships for different health outcomes. In other words, in the scientific literature there is only marginal evidence for the guidelines proposed by the expert committees.
>
> (Twisk 2001: 623, emphasis in original)

2   *youth physical activity → adult physical activity = adult health*

This is perhaps the most popularly held idea about the relationship between youth physical activity and long-term health. This proposition asserts that if young people are active when they are young they are more likely to develop physically active 'habits', which last through their lives and, finally, lead to long-term health benefits. According to Twisk, this simplistic scenario is not supported by existing research:

> in conclusion, there is only marginal evidence that physical activity/inactivity during childhood and adolescence is related to physical activity/inactivity during adulthood. If a person is very active during youth, it will not imply that that individual will be very active during adulthood. The same is probably true for a person who is inactive during youth. Furthermore, there is no indication of a certain shape of the possible relationship or a certain threshold value from which guidelines for physical activity for children and adolescents can be obtained.
>
> (Twisk 2001: 624)

3   *youth physical activity = adult health*

This best case scenario for those who advocate youth physical activity would be proven if a *direct* relationship between youth physical activity and long-term health could be shown. On this Twisk writes:

> Studies investigating the direct relationship between physical activity during youth and adult health status provide the best information on which the rationale for physical activity guidelines should be based. However, such a study is difficult to obtain. The ideal study to answer the question of whether high levels of physical activity during childhood and adolescence lower the risk of developing chronic diseases later in life is a randomised controlled trial with a lifetime follow-up in which a large group of children and adolescents is assigned to either a sedentary or an active lifestyle; a study which will (probably) never take place.
>
> (Twisk 2001: 620)

Twisk argues that the Harvard Alumni Study is probably the closest we have to such a study. This research grouped its student participants into three categories: athletes; those who did sports for more than five hours a week; and those who did sport for less than five hours a week. Twisk summarizes the results as follows:

> The 3 groups did not differ regarding the occurrence of cardiovascular disease later in life. Student athletes who discontinued their activity levels after college encountered a cardiovascular disease incidence similar to the risk of alumni classmates who never had been athletes. In fact, individuals who became physically active later in life had the same health benefits as individuals who were active throughout the observation period. Therefore, this study provides no evidence for a direct relationship between physical activity during youth and health status in adulthood.
>
> (Twisk 2001: 620)

Twisk's overarching conclusion is to question the value of basing physical activity guidelines for youth on their alleged health benefits. He claims that health benefits are unlikely to motivate young people to be active and, in addition, long-term health benefits of physical activity are not supported by evidence.

Surveying the relevant literature Sleap *et al.* (2000) claim that there is no evidence that children's health is influenced by how physically active they are. Boreham and Riddoch reach a similar conclusion when reviewing the research into the benefits of physical exercise for children and adolescents. They write: 'Although we feel instinctively that physical activity ought to be beneficial to the health of children, there is surprisingly little empirical evidence to support this notion' (Boreham and Riddoch 2003: 17). They also consider the health benefits of exercise for adults across the lifespan. Here they point out that, although research suggests some health indicators such as blood pressure and fitness are improved by exercise, whether exercise leads to a longer lifetime of better health is unclear. They suggest that different forms of exercise *may* be beneficial during different stages of life but that: 'It is important to emphasise at the outset that most of what can be written on this topic remains speculative. No study exists which has recorded adequate birth-to-death information relating physical activity to health' (Boreham and Riddoch 2003: 14).

Rissanen and Fogelholm (1999) found that research into the role of physical activity in preventing or treating a range of diseases associated with overweight and obesity (apart from cardiovascular disease) is equivocal. They describe the evidence as either mixed or lacking with respect to cancers of the colon, breast, uterus and prostate; gallstones; osteoarthritis; back pain; sleep apnoea; reproductive abnormalities; and impaired health-related quality of life. According to the authors, the *strongest* evidence supporting the health benefits of physical activity related to breast cancer:

> Given the biological plausibility and the strength of the evidence from the literature, prevention of obesity and weight gain in adulthood and regular physical exercise could be expected to help reduce the risk of postmenopausal breast cancer in obese women. However, public health recommendations cannot be made on the basis of the existing evidence.
>
> (Rissanen and Fogelholm 1999: S635)

and colon cancer:

> The evidence of a strong inverse relationship between physical activity and risk of colon cancer seems unequivocal enough to justify the public health message that modest increases in physical activity of the population will help reduce the incidence of colon cancer.
>
> (Rissanen and Fogelholm 1999: S640)

It is also apparent that scientific opinion about the effect of physical activity on other illnesses such as other forms of cancer or osteoporosis varies considerably. In the case of osteoporosis, there are those who doubt that physical activity plays a preventative role (e.g. Blair and Brodney 1999) and those who are more confident (Colditz 1999; Janz 2002). There are even others who suggest that osteoporosis is improved by heavier body weight (Seidell *et al.* 1989) or that too much physical activity can increase osteoporosis risk (Kazis and Iglesias 2003; Papanek 2003), positions which are difficult to square with those who, like Colditz (1999), argue that osteoporotic disease would go down if people exercised more and lost weight.

It is significant that Twisk's (2001), Boreham and Riddoch's (2003) and Rissanen and Fogelholm's (1999) summaries of the literature are consistently non-committal and/or conservative about the amount of physical activity needed to achieve health benefits. The scientific literature is replete with articles that claim to summarize the health benefits of physical activity (e.g. Blair *et al.* 1992; Dinger 1998; Fentem 1994) but which offer little or no detail about what Vogel (1999: 122) describes as the 'question that many have asked but few have been able to answer. Just how hard do you have to exercise to get health benefits?'.

Some readers will be aware that over the last fifteen years or so health authorities around the Western world have drifted towards more conservative guidelines concerning health and physical activity dosage. For example, previous recommendations in favour of continuous, extended bouts of vigorous exercise have been replaced by the suggestion that healthful exercise can be accumulated through short, discontinuous bouts and need not be of high intensity. At present the so-called 'consensus' position in the literature is that people should accumulate thirty minutes of moderate intensity exercise on most days of the week in order to reduce their risk of chronic diseases such as heart disease and diabetes (Saris *et al.* 2003).

Researchers have proposed a number of reasons for this shift in thinking. Some suggest that self-report data has tended to underestimate the amount of low and moderate intensity exercise people do. For example, while people may find it easy to remember that they play tennis twice a week, it is usually more difficult to estimate how many flights of stairs they climbed and how far they walked during the same period. Therefore, it is argued that this under-reporting of lower intensity physical activity has meant that its contribution to health has also been under underestimated. Another reason proposed is that much of the research in this area has been conducted on young and relatively healthy populations. It is argued that these populations require a relatively high amount of exercise for health risk factors (such as body fat, blood pressure, cholesterol levels) to be significantly altered, particularly since young people tend to be more active than older people already. Some research suggests that other populations, such as the old and the already unhealthy, accrue significant improvement on some health indices after quite modest physical activity programmes (Shephard 1997; Wannamethee *et al.* 1998).

At this point, obesity experts on all sides of the physical activity dosage debate can be found. For example, Jebb and Moore (1999) suggest that we currently have insufficient information on which to base firm conclusions. There are those who are sceptical of the value of low and moderate intensity physical activity (Lee and Paffenbarger 1996; Morris 1996; Sesso *et al.* 2000). There are others who argue that the greatest amount of health benefits are derived when people change from being completely sedentary to being moderately active (Blair and Connelly 1996; Hu *et al.* 2003; Shephard 1999). Proponents of this view tend to maintain that much smaller health benefits are accrued by people who do more intense physical activity; more may be better but not much better. Slattery (1996) proposes that different amounts and kinds of physical activity may have different effects on different diseases, a highly troubling conclusion for those intent on telling the general public how much physical activity they should do. Highlighting the methodological difficulties associated with trying to address the physical activity dosage question, she writes:

> it is not clear if specific biological mechanisms exist whereby intensity of activity is related to disease beyond that of moderate activity, or if the associations between disease and vigorous activity reflect better recall of vigorous activities than of moderate activities.
>
> (Slattery 1996: 209)

Noting that relatively few young people die of the diseases most closely associated with sedentary living and overweight and obesity, Nicholl *et al.* (1994) and Coleman (1998) suggest that the health benefits of exercise are the same for people who exercise throughout their whole lives and those who take up exercise in middle-age after years of sedentary living. In fact, they argue that the health care costs incurred by young people as a result of exercising outweigh the long-term health care savings of this physical activity. On a purely cost–benefit basis they advocate sedentary living for young people and moderate physical activity among the middle-aged and elderly. The situation is complicated still further by debates about whether it is physical activity per se or the weight loss caused by physical activity that brings about better health (Saris *et al.* 2003; Shephard 1994).

Thus, the scientific literature linking body weight, physical activity and health presents us with a long list of unanswered questions. For example, what kinds and amounts of physical activity bring about weight loss and what kinds and amounts bring about better health? Are the answers to these questions the same or different? If they are different, should one's goal be weight loss or health? If, as some suggest, general health is significantly improved by moderate amounts of physical activity, why should we worry about body weight? What do Saris *et al.* (2003: 101) actually mean when they ask 'how much physical activity is enough to prevent unhealthy weight gain?'. What is the difference between physical activity for 'general health' and physical activity to prevent 'unhealthy weight gain'? We would observe that what these questions indicate is that the meaning of 'health' is actually an extremely complex matter, but this complexity is not something that the search for laws and patterns can easily accommodate. After all, not only does this research appear to assume that these laws or patterns exist, it is also driven by the hope we might be able to produce physical activity public health guidelines that are both easy to understand and scientifically sound. But what if these two goals – truth and simplicity – turned out to be completely at odds with each other?

There is a tendency among some obesity scientists to lament the state of the general public's knowledge about physical activity and health. For example, in the *British Medical Journal*, Fentem (1994: 1261) writes: 'According to the Allied Dunbar national fitness survey, three quarters of the general public (adults over 16 years of age) understand that exercise confers important health benefits but not what that means'. Quite why we should be concerned about this situation is not at all clear. As the next chapter will show, conjecture about the health benefits of physical activity has a long history. Contributors to medical journals in the nineteenth and early twentieth century suggested a variety of approaches to physical activity in order to treat overweight and obesity and improve health and often reported success. A century later, research into physical activity, body weight and biomedical health continues, suggesting that there are still those who believe generalizable and empirically verifiable answers are still possible. In particular, despite inconsistent, controversial, contradictory and (of late) conservative scientific findings, there are still researchers who are prepared to occupy one or other side of a quite polarized debate about physical activity dosage.

The difference between the situation a hundred years ago and today is that we now have a century's worth of inconclusive findings to consider and significant research funds being devoted to finding these elusive answers. This situation persists despite the widely acknowledged methodological difficulties preventing robust conclusions about physical activity dosage. We would submit that it is not that the answers to these questions are within our grasp or are ever likely to be resolved (our assessment of the evidence suggests the opposite) that drives this field of research, but rather the fact that body weight and physical activity itself have been 'medicalized'. For complex historical reasons, we now see physical activity as a kind of medicine for diseases we call 'overweight and obesity'. Large sections of the scientific community and general public have been converted to this point of view and it is for *this* reason that people can talk of physical activity 'dosage' and, what is more, patiently wait for science to produce the answers.

Rather than the general public being ignorant about the health benefits of physical activity, as Fentem implies, would it be too provocative to suggest that it is the scientific community's knowledge that lags behind that of the general public? If it is true that the general public understands quite well that physical activity confers some *non-specific* health benefits and that people are generally non-committal about the specifics of this relationship, this would seem an entirely defensible reading of the existing scientific data. What is most telling about this situation is that most members of the general public will have arrived at this conclusion without ever opening a scientific journal.

None of this is to suggest that anyone, least of all us, should have the last word on what is important research and what is not, nor to suggest that the scientific study of health and physical activity has produced nothing of value. Confirming what people already hold to be true, that physical activity plays some role in health, is an important finding. However, it is not at all clear where debates about physical activity dosage, resting on the assumption that there are laws to be found, have taken us. This research has not yielded clear or enduring health recommendations for how people should use physical activity and we would make precisely the same point about research into body weight, physical activity and food as discussed earlier.

Television, physical activity and overweight

Our second example of the problems that arise when mechanistic assumptions drive research into overweight and obesity concerns children's television viewing. In this case the mechanistic mode of thinking is slightly different, although equally dependent on the idea of a simple relationship between variables as in $a = b = c$.

The amount of time children spend watching television, and the relationship between this time and overweight and obesity, has attracted the attention of a large number of researchers and respectable size literature now exists. At present, an assumption that more time spent watching television means less time being physically active and a greater likelihood of becoming overweight or obese guides this literature. This assumption can be expressed in the following formula:

$$T_1 = T_2 - T_3$$

where T_1 is the amount of time in a day children spend being physically active, T_2 is the total non-sleeping time at children's disposal and T_3 is the time they are inactive or 'sedentary'. This is not a falsifiable formula since activity of any kind can be arbitrarily classified as 'physically active' or 'sedentary'. In other words, there are no readily imaginable circumstances under which this formula would not be true. There will be times when the activity in question may be on the border between 'active' and 'sedentary' but classification is an issue that faces all researchers and this is not a concern here.

The important part of this model is its 'zero sum' nature. It begins by assuming that there is a limited amount of time available for children to be physically active (T_2) and that the more time devoted to 'sedentary' pursuits (T_3), such as television viewing, means less time left over to be active (T_1). By definition, more of T_3 means less of T_1. This model often goes by the name of physical activity 'displacement' (Robinson 1999). The idea that television viewing 'displaces' physical activity, and contributes to people being more 'sedentary' than they should be, is widespread in the scientific literature (e.g. Dennison *et al.* 2004; Hill and Peters 1998; Jebb and Moore 1999; Saris *et al.* 2003). We have already seen examples of this way of thinking in Chapter 2 where we encountered the apparently widespread tendency among journalists and obesity experts to associate television watching and computer usage with physical inactivity and obesity. In particular, epidemiologist Garry Egger was reported blaming the 'obesity epidemic' on technology rather than fast food. In the following passage, Dietz includes the idea of displacement of physical activity by television among his primary causes for the 'obesity epidemic':

> the amount of physical activity that children engage in has been reduced by an increase in the use of cars, an increase in the amount of time spent watching television, and a decrease in the opportunities in many communities for physical activity on the way to or in school.
>
> (Dietz 2001: 314)

With this as a starting point an entire research community has sprung up around the problem of trying to prove that television viewing plays a role in the development of childhood overweight and obesity. This has meant trying to establish a reasonably lengthy chain of causation in which television viewing leads to greater inactivity and, further, that the component of inactivity caused by television viewing causally contributes to overweight and obesity. It is also hypothesized in the literature that television causes children to consume more high-fat snack foods, a point we will return to shortly. However, despite the proliferation of research papers on the topic, the results have been far from conclusive and, as with other areas of research discussed in this chapter, establishing causation has not proved a straightforward matter. On the question of whether there is a relationship between children's television viewing and their activity levels and/or body weight, some studies suggest (often weak) statistically significant correlations (Dennison *et al.* 2002; Durant *et al.* 1994; Hanley *et al.* 2000; Pate *et al.* 1997; Proctor *et al.* 2003; Tucker 1986) while others do not (Neumark-Sztainer *et al.* 2003; Rehor and Cottam 2000; Robinson *et al.* 1993; Taras *et al.* 1989; Waller *et al.* 2003; Wolf *et al.* 1993). In the case of Tucker (1986) and Durant *et al.* (1994), a correlation was reported between television viewing and lower fitness and activity levels respectively, but not with overweight. Robinson *et al.* (1993) found a weak correlation between television viewing and activity levels but no correlation with body fat or change in body fat over time. Shannon *et al.* (1991) found a correlation between fatness and television viewing among children from less affluent American school districts but not among children from more affluent districts. A prospective study of adults by Crawford *et al.* (1999) found a general correlation between BMI and television viewing for women but not for men. They also found that:

> There were no significant relationships between change in BMI and number of hours of TV viewing at baseline, average number of hours of TV viewing over the three year follow-up, or change in number of hours of TV viewing from baseline to three years. These findings suggest the link between obesity and TV viewing is complex, and that TV viewing may not be the simple marker of sedentariness we may have hoped.
>
> (Crawford *et al.* 1999: 437)

Reviewing this literature, Grund *et al.* (2001: 1246) argue that studies have yielded inconsistent and contradictory results and that: '[W]e concluded that the association between TV watching and overweight is unclear in children.' Their study of German children found that television viewing was correlated with fatness but not with aerobic or muscular fitness, poor diet, levels of physical activity or daily energy expenditure. Similarly, Wake *et al.* write:

> A link between television viewing and prevalence of overweight in adults has been well documented, although whether this relationship is causal is still unclear. Studies in children, mainly cross-sectional, have produced mixed results; most, but not all, have found small but significant relationships between child body mass index (BMI) and television viewing. Cohort studies of this issue are few and their support for a causal relationship mixed.
>
> (Wake *et al.* 2003: 130)

Wake *et al.*'s study of five- to thirteen-year-old Australian children found a weak association between television viewing and BMI (television accounted for 1 per cent of the variation in BMI scores) and no association between computer and video game usage and BMI. Moreover, when statistical adjustments were made for other contributing factors such as parental BMI and educational levels, the statistical association between television viewing and BMI disappeared.

In a study of the behaviours of 2,494 children from the US and the UK, Marshall *et al.* (2002: 401) found that: 'Physical activity and sedentary behaviour [including computer/Internet usage, video and television watching] are not two sides of the same coin.' In other words, more of one does not mean less of the other. In their review of the literature they write:

> The mechanisms by which sedentary behaviours contribute to negative health outcomes, particularly overweight and obesity, are not well understood. One hypothesis is that involvement in sedentary behaviour limits the time available for participation in health-enhancing physical activity. Most data do not support this hypothesis and cross sectional and prospective data between TV viewing and adiposity show inconsistent and weak associations. Sedentary behaviour appears able to coexist with physical activity, with each having a unique set of determinants.
>
> (Marshall *et al.* 2002: 402)

With respect to the data from their own study, they conclude:

> There were no instances of negative correlations between physical activity and sedentary behaviour which is consistent with several previous studies. Thus, it seems that physical activity does not interfere with behaviours such as reading or homework, or vice-versa. Overall these findings argue against the assumption that physical activity and sedentary behaviour share an inverse and causal relationship.
>
> (Marshall *et al.* 2002: 413)

It is also quite common for studies to report that the groups of children who watched (or reported watching) the most television (often boys) were also the most active (again according to self-report data) (e.g. Hernández *et al.* 1999; Lowry *et al.* 2002; Trost *et al.* 1996). Lowry *et al.* (2002) found differing results among American school children across gender and racial groupings (White, Black and Hispanic), from no correlation at all between television viewing and physical activity levels (White males, Black females, Hispanic females, Hispanic males), to negative (White females) and positive (Black males) correlations. They also found the correlation between television viewing and body weight to be non-existent (Black females, Black males, Hispanic males) and positive (White females, White males, Hispanic females). In addition, while an association between television viewing and overweight was found for the racial group who watched the least amount of television (Whites), no such association for the groups (Black and Hispanic) who watched the most television was found (34.2 per cent of Whites, 73.7 per cent of Blacks and 52.2 per cent of Hispanics watched more than two hours a day).

Our interpretation of the results of this study – and the literature in general – is that the relationship between television and overweight is at best extremely complicated or at worst tenuous. However, Lowry *et al.* (2002) move seamlessly from these results to claiming causation and urging parents to limit the amount of time children watch television:

Efforts to reduce TV viewing among youth can help reverse the epidemic of obesity in this country, while promoting physical activity and healthy eating. A variety of strategies are available to reduce TV viewing among youth. Parents should monitor and limit children's TV viewing to no more than 2 hours/day, and encourage alternative entertainment such as reading, hobbies, and athletics. Health care professionals should include questions about media use in their assessments of youth, and reinforce efforts of parents to monitor and limit TV viewing.

(Lowry *et al.* 2002: 420)

The authors make no mention of the high levels (relative to Whites) of over-weight and obesity in the US among Black and Hispanic Americans. Given the complexity of their results and the socio-demographic distribution of overweight and obesity, it is not at all clear *how* encouraging parents in general to limit tele-vision viewing (or, in fact, any of the other strategies they recommend) will help to 'reverse the epidemic of obesity'. We would argue that this is a conclusion that is simply not supported by the reported findings. It appears that confidence in this strategy derives solely from the weak and inconsistent correlation in the litera-ture between television viewing and overweight. Indeed, most researchers appear to concede their inability to comment on causation but, nonetheless, make recom-mendations on the need to reduce television watching in order to reduce obesity and improve public health (also see Salmon *et al.* 2000).

It is interesting to note that some researchers are prepared to declare proven the case for causation (e.g. Brownell and Horgen 2004; Dennison *et al.* 2004; Dietz 2001; Gortmaker *et al.* 1996, Hu *et al.* 2003) and, indeed, that some arrived at this conclusion nearly twenty years ago (Dietz and Gortmaker 1985). However, other researchers, such as some of those cited earlier, still see the matter as unresolved. This is not a matter of splitting hairs; it is *not* the case that these researchers appear to have basically accepted the case for causation and have moved on to fleshing out the details. Take the following example in which the researchers concede that the role television plays in childhood overweight and obesity is unclear but, at the same time, never question the assumption that a causative relationship actually exists.

The summary abstract for Hernández *et al.*'s (1999: 845) study of 712 Mexican children, published in the *International Journal of Obesity and Related Metabolic Disorders*, concludes with the sentence 'Physical activity and television viewing, but not VCR/videogames use, were related to obesity prevalence in Mexican children 9–16 y old'. While it is open about the lack of association between obesity and videos and computer games, the summary does not say that there is a 'correlation' or 'statistical association' between television and obesity, but rather a 'relationship'. In our view, this choice of a slightly ambiguous non-technical term appears to leave open the question of causation when, in fact, further reading of the full paper might suggest a different conclusion.

The researchers found a statistically positive association between television viewing and physical activity levels. They also found that children from higher income families watched more television, did more physical activity and were more likely to be obese, a set of findings very difficult to square with $T_1 = T_2 \quad T_3$. In this context we might wonder why the study's abstract did not include a statement to the effect that children who watch more television are more physically active. After all, this would seem a significant and interesting finding, not to mention one that enjoys some empirical support. Instead, it appears the only aspect of the study's findings that conforms to conventional wisdom about technology – the statistical correlation between body weight and television viewing – is the one the authors chose to highlight in the paper's abstract, rather than the other findings which are not. We need to read through to the study's last page to find that the authors concede that they are not able to comment on causation. That is, there is nothing in the paper on which to base a conclusion about the *nature* of the 'relationship' announced in the paper's abstract.

The researchers point out that three *causative* theories exist to account for the association between obesity and television watching. They describe these theories as 'plausible, although unproven' (Hernández et al. 1999: 851). The first theory they mention, that sedentary activity displaces physical activity is clearly not supported by this study and they say nothing more about it. The second theory is that television viewing causes children to snack on high-fat junk food more often, perhaps because of the advertising for these products, which children are exposed to. However, in this study there was no correlation between reported snacking and obesity levels and correlations between television viewing and food intake – particularly high-fat foods – in other studies have tended to be weak or non-existent (Robinson 1999). Moreover, while a number of researchers have proposed this theory, to our knowledge none have done so *and*, at the same time, addressed the problem of a lack of empirical support for childhood overeating as a cause for overweight and obesity.

Hernández et al. (1999) also mention a third theory of causation, in which television is said to displace not physical activity, but other sedentary pursuits which, while still classified as 'sedentary', consume more calories than watching the television. The theory that television viewing is *more* sedentary than other sedentary activities, whatever these may be, is supported by one study and not-supported by others (Dietz et al. 1994; Grund et al. 2001).

Whether these are 'plausible' theories or not would at least seem open to debate. Certainly, with respect to these last two theories we might wonder whether they have been proposed because a 'plausible' case exists, or simply because the assumed connection – that television detracts from the amount of physical activity children do – seems less and less tenable. Hernández et al. (1999) speculate about a number of theories of causation (as is their right), but do not canvass the possibility that no such causative relationship exists. This possibility is simply not considered even though it would seem just as valid an interpretation of the data they present. With respect to the television viewing/overweight and obesity association in general, it would also seem at least as defensible to argue that overweight and obese children are more likely to choose television as a form of recreation than other forms, such as sports. The physical education profession, for example, has long been concerned about the ways in which overweight and obese children avoid, and are stigmatized within activities, that involve physical exertion. It is perhaps not surprising that many overweight people, young and old, arrive at the conclusion that sports and other forms of physical activity are not for them. There is data to suggest that overweight and obese people, including children (Strauss and Pollack 2003), may also be more socially isolated and that this occurs for reasons connected to their feelings about themselves and the way others treat them. Yet another interpretation is that the association between television viewing and overweight and obesity among particular groups could at least be partially explained by the prohibitive costs of many other forms of leisure and recreation.

As we saw in the previous chapter, the idea that televisions, VCRs and computers play a causative role in childhood overweight and obesity is widespread and often held to be a straightforward truth. However, in addition to those we have already made, there are a number of other points worth bearing in mind before accepting this idea. Researchers in this area seem comfortable with making generalized claims about the causative relationship between technology and overweight and obesity. However, most of the existing data have been collected in the US. In addition, very little data exist concerning computers and video games even though computers seem to figure prominently when people blame the 'obesity epidemic' on technology. Perhaps more importantly, the conclusions about causation that some researchers have come to are based almost entirely on self-report data, and a wide variety of different methods have been used to calculate television watching time, physical activity levels and even body weight.

Finally, it may be objected by some readers that some data exist which appear to offer empirical support for the case for causation in a more direct way. A study by Robinson (1999), in particular, is often cited in this respect. This is an interesting study because the author begins by describing research findings about the relationship between fatness and television watching as 'consistently weak':

> Cross-sectional epidemiological studies have consistently found relatively weak positive associations between television viewing and child and adolescent adiposity. Prospective studies are less common and have produced mixed results. The consistently weak associations found in epidemiological studies may be due to the measurement error in self-reports of television viewing ... a causal relationship can only be demonstrated in an experimental trial in which manipulation of the risk factor changes the outcome.
>
> (Robinson 1999: 1561–2)

In passing, it is worth noting the author's assertion that causation has yet to be established. Robinson then reports on a Californian school-based intervention that broke third- and fourth-grade students into two groups. One group acted as a control while the other received school-based tuition that encouraged students to cut down their use of televisions, VCRs and video games and to be more 'selective' television viewers. Students in the intervention group were also encouraged to participate in one ten-day period without television, VCRs and video games and, thereafter, to limit themselves to a total of seven hours a week. Televisions in the homes of participating families were fitted with electronic devices that limited the amount of time the television could be watched by particular household members, although families could request for their television 'budgets' to be increased without cost. Two-thirds of intervention group students completed the ten-day television 'turnoff', 55 per cent handed in at least one written parental confirmation that the student had stuck to their weekly television budget for the previous week, 42 per cent of participating parents reported installing the television limiting devices and a little over a quarter of all families in the study asked for increased television 'budgets'. Students' body compositions were measured at the beginning of the study and again seven months later.

At the end of the study the intervention group, students were comparatively leaner than the controls and, not surprisingly, reported watching less television and eating fewer meals in front of the television. However, there were no statistically significant reductions in VCR or video game usage or consumption of high-fat foods, and there was no effect on physical activity levels or physical fitness. The author concludes that based on this data 'a causal inference might be made' (Robinson 1999: 1565–6). The results of this study support none of the existing causative theories that have been proposed and, in fact, cast no light on the apparent intervention effect. The author makes no attempt to explain this result except to offer that the self-report nature of much of the data collected may have hidden important causative pathways.

This far from conclusive small study and the mixed results of another by Gortmaker *et al.* (1999) have carried a heavy weight in the obesity literature and are regularly cited by other researchers as evidence for causation. However, a recent third study, Dennison *et al.* (2004), used a similar research design to Robinson (1999) with pre-school children. While the intervention group students reported watching less television, there was no significant difference in fatness compared to the control group at the end of the study. Even at this early stage the pattern of inconclusive and contradictory results that dogs the obesity literature in general may have already set in. These studies do not settle the question of causation and as the founder of the television–childhood obesity literature himself, William H. Dietz, seems inadvertently to concede, twenty years of research has yielded precious few if any meaningful insights:

> Opportunities for spontaneous play may be the only requirement that young children need to increase their physical activity. Reducing the amount of time that children are allowed to watch television is one strategy that offers children opportunities for activity, and it is likely to alter requests for advertised foods as well. These are not novel approaches: a generation ago, because there were few alternatives, these practices were the norm. Although there is no data to show that these interventions prevent obesity, none of these interventions are likely to have adverse effects, and all of these interventions will improve the quality of family life.
>
> (Dietz 2001: 314)

In the face of such disarming honesty it might seem uncharitable to wonder on what basis Dietz concludes that his suggestions are 'logical' or likely to 'improve the quality of family life'. In fact, perhaps we are getting closer to the truth here. Perhaps in the absence of compelling data both to blame television viewing for overweight and obesity and to hope that limiting television might cure them, we are actually beginning to see what is at stake. In the previous chapter we saw how the Australian newspaper columnist Angela Shanahan blames childhood obesity on the decline of 'family values'. Dietz also seems to see television as an assault on 'traditional family life'. And in one of the world's most prestigious biomedical science journals, the *British Medical Journal*, Dietz follows the previous passage with what may have been the thing worrying obesity researchers about television all along: that televisions are symptomatic of modern life's departure from an earlier, 'better' of way of living:

> Strategies to change families' patterns of eating and activity must be adapted to the social and economic pressures of today's world. However, in view of the rapid increase in the prevalence of obesity and its implications for chronic disease, a return to basics seems to be essential.
>
> (Dietz 2001: 314)

Given that Dietz sees the solution to lie in a 'return to basics', we doubt whether he or others who blame technology for the 'obesity epidemic' will be much impressed by new generation video games that require players to be extremely physically active. For example, some games use small cameras to take the image and actions of the flesh-and-blood moving player and project these into the action on the screen. Reports concerning Australian research which suggests that televisions and computers actually encourage children to be more, not less, active (*Daily Telegraph* 2003) are likely to be less welcome still. However, our assessment of the case against televisions and computers is that it is not actually about food and physical activity at all. Instead, they seem only to rehearse age-old suspicions that technology will not only turn our bodies and minds to mush, but also lead to households where nobody talks to each other and, as we will see in later chapters, precipitate the disintegration of Western civilization itself.

What do we know?

It is surely telling that leading journals continue to publish claims by medical researchers about the fattening effects of *computers and video games* on children when supporting data is virtually non-existent (for two striking examples see Baur 2001 in the *Medical Journal of Australia* and Strauss and Pollack 2001 in the *Journal of the American Medical Association*). But even more troubling is the way televisions, computers and video games are regularly described as 'attractive' (Dubbert et al. 2002: 123; Hill and Peters 1998: 1373; Hill and Melanson 1999: S517) and 'seductive' (Strauss and Pollack 2001: 2848). In the obesity literature, technology often appears as a kind of evil temptress, 'turning the heads' of children away from more 'wholesome' pursuits. Even in the exalted pages of the journal *Science*, Hill and Peters (1998: 1372) can make the unreferenced claim that: 'The appeal of television, electronic games, and computers has increased the time spent in sedentary pursuits among children and adults alike.' In our view, no compelling data whatsoever exist to support this claim.

We would contend that a more compelling reading of the existing data is that children can be friends with both technology and physical activity. We are also puzzled by studies (e.g. Lowry et al. 2002) which find that poorer children watch much more television than children from wealthier backgrounds and, regardless of whether television viewing correlates with inactivity and obesity, implore *all* parents to restrict television usage. The fact that there is no evidence that this strategy will reduce childrens' body weight is almost beside the point. What is even more noticeable is that researchers who find that poverty or low education levels are often (though not always) associated with obesity, inactivity, television viewing and 'unhealthy diets' are prepared to advise poor parents about how they should manage their children, but rarely call for a reduction in poverty or more funds for school and university education. Blaming technology for the ills of society has a long history in Western culture. It is also easy to do. By investing evil powers in inanimate objects, the difficult and potentially political work of questioning the way our societies are organized can be neatly avoided.

The mechanistic thinking, which produced the theory of physical activity displacement, is also exemplified by the energy-in/energy-out law of body weight and the search for laws or patterns linking physical activity and health. We have not addressed the literature concerning food and health here because of space limitations, but there is ample literature to suggest that this field is equally driven by a mechanistic search for regularity and similarly characterized by inconclusive findings and ongoing controversies.

In our view, the empirical uncertainties discussed in this chapter cast doubt on the certainty with which scientists have described the 'obesity epidemic' as a health crisis. For example, researchers such as Colditz (1999) and Colditz and Mariani (2000) have attempted to calculate the economic costs of obesity and physical inactivity. These calculations are based on quite precise judgements about the contribution of body weight and inactivity to a number of different diseases *and* on being able to separate out the respective contribution of body weight and physical inactivity to these diseases. Our reading of the relevant literature suggests that the imprecision of existing research does not support the assumptions with which they begin, such as 22 per cent of colon cancers and 18 per cent (Colditz 1999) of osteoporotic fractures could be prevented if people were not 'inactive or obese'. Whether or not these estimates are conservative, as they claim, is at present a matter of conjecture. It is also noticeable that their projections do not allow for any of the reported (although we would hasten to add, not conclusively proved) health benefits of increased body weight (e.g. Edelstein and Barrett-Connor 1993; Kabat and Wynder 1992; Tverdal 1986; Vatten and Kvinnsland 1992), nor for the costs of what has been called the 'epidemic' of exercise-related orthopaedic injuries and over-exercising (Goldstein 1992: 89). There is also no acknowledgement that the weight loss industry keeps many people employed and, presumably, protects them from the negative health effects of unemployment and poverty, which, as it happens, includes increased risk of overweight and obesity. This kind of research appears to assume all costs and no benefits. At the very least, these authors do not address doubts raised about the efficacy of this style of health cost calculation (Hatziandreu *et al.* 1988; Russell 1986), which suggest that the case for net economic benefit is far from straightforward. It is not that any of these doubts are refuted, it is that they are ignored. We would concur with Flegal (1999: S511) who argues that: 'The net health implications of the increases [in overweight and obesity] are not completely clear.' She also points out that in many countries it appears that hypertension, elevated cholesterol, cardiovascular mortality and average blood pressure have dropped as overweight and obesity have gone up, while cardiovascular risk factors also remain high among the non-overweight and non-obese in the US.

But even if we accept that the current situation *is* a crisis, it is not at all clear that the science of overweight and obesity has helped us to respond in constructive ways. We are not completely alone in this view. From within obesity science itself Brodney *et al.* (2000) argue that the field's preoccupation with food (energy-in) and body weight (energy balance) has delivered overwhelmingly disappointing results for overweight and obese people. We would not share Brodney *et al.*'s confidence that shifting the focus to physical activity (rather than food and body weight) is necessarily a more justifiable or promising course of action. However, their arguments should at least remind us that the idea that science might sometimes lead nowhere is not an altogether foreign one.

It is curious that obesity science appears to have unquestioning faith in the energy-in/energy-out law while, at the same time, it seems to generate so few answers. Our contention is that the problem with the model is not so much that it produces untrue knowledge. In the end, the question of what is 'true' about the causes and consequences of overweight and obesity will probably prove to be immaterial. The important questions, as we will go on to argue, will probably be political, cultural and social. But while there may be those who would argue that the science of obesity *is* concerned with cultural and social questions, we would simply point to the example of children and television. Scientific study of this phenomenon has produced blanket calls for parents to limit children's access to television and the naive assumption that the effect of television on childhood overweight and obesity can be measured and manipulated in reasonably straightforward ways. This assumption derives from the mistaken belief that human societies themselves work like machines, an idea known as functionalism and long since dispensed with by the social sciences as a way of conceptualizing people and their lives.

Note

1   Text references in quotes here and elsewhere are cited in the originals and have not been altered. They are not given in the references section at the end of this book.

4 'Modernity's scourge'

A brief history of obesity science

In his foreword to the edited volume *Child and Adolescent Obesity*, William H. Dietz writes:

> Rarely have we had the opportunity to observe an epidemic of chronic disease occur before our eyes. The questions and challenges that the epidemic provokes provide us with an exciting and unique opportunity to shape a new field. As Winston Churchill once said: 'Now this is not the end. It is not even the beginning of the end. But it is, perhaps, the end of the beginning.'
>
> (Dietz 2002: xvii)

Although Dietz does not explicitly say when the epidemic – which has occurred 'before our eyes' – actually began, he does claim that the year 1980 is significant (2002: xv) and marks the beginning of a rapid acceleration in obesity rates. Our reading of the literature suggests that scientific opinion concurs roughly with this view, although points five or ten years before and after 1980 are mentioned. For example, Booth *et al.* (2003) surveyed existing childhood overweight and obesity data in Australia and found that between 1985 and 1997:

> the prevalence of overweight increased by 60–70%, the prevalence of obesity trebled, and the prevalence of overweight and obesity combined doubled. Although we cannot be quite so confident about the findings for the period 1969–1985, the results do indicate that changes in the prevalence of over-weight and obesity were far smaller during this 16-y period than they were for the ensuing 12 y. Our findings are generally consistent with studies conducted in the United States, Spain, and Britain.
>
> (Booth *et al.* 2003: 33)

As with most of his peers, Dietz blames this new epidemic of chronic disease on people's food intake and exercise habits, thus repeating the core scientific premises on which the entire field of obesity studies rests: the idea that over-weight and obesity are bad for your health and that excess food intake and insufficient physical activity are the root causes of this disease.

This sense of newness is absolutely central to the construction of a crisis. If it was the case that obesity has been a problem for, say, one hundred years, it would be much more difficult to talk of a crisis or, we suspect, an 'epidemic'. This is important because, to reiterate, this book does not dispute that severe obesity is experienced negatively by many (although not all) people who are so classified. What is at stake is the idea that we are witnessing a 'crisis': a new situation, which, if Dietz's choice of Churchillian inspiration is any indication, requires a 'war on obesity'.

In the previous chapter we questioned the usefulness of the intellectual tools obesity scientists use to understand human body weight. In particular, we argued that the 'body as machine' model appears to fail on two fronts. First, it has not produced a robust and empirically verifiable account of why people become overweight or obese. Second, and perhaps more importantly, it has generated precious few insights for solving the problem it claims to study. Instead, the first decade of the twenty-first century is as awash with fad diets, weight loss powders and gimmicky exercise machines as any that preceded it, as well as experts repeating the same, familiar advice to eat a balanced diet and exercise regularly.

Our assessment of obesity science may seem unduly harsh to some readers. However, the full extent of obesity science's failure comes more sharply into view when we consider what experts have said about overweight and obesity during earlier historical periods. While many areas of science and medicine have made astonishing advances, in this chapter we show how obesity science is caught in a perpetual loop. Its enduring faith that the human body really is a machine has condemned it to asking the same questions and producing slight variations on the same answers. Space does not allow a comprehensive history of obesity science here, but in what follows we offer a glimpse of the closed circle in which scientific ideas about overweight and obesity exist. In particular, we look at obesity science during the pre-'obesity epidemic' period between the late 1880s and the late 1950s and find a field wresting with the same dilemmas and thinking about human body weight in the same way as we saw in Chapter 3.

Outside and inside

There has been no shortage of writers, both academic and popular, who have expressed misgivings about the modern age's demonization of fatness (e.g. Atrens 2000; Campos 2003; Chrisler 1996; Fitzgerald 1981; Gaesser 1998, 2002; Germov and Williams 1996; Hall and Stewart 1989; Jarrett 1986; Wooley and Wooley 1984). Some of these writers suggest that anti-fat sentiment is a quite recent and peculiarly Western phenomena and that, in times past, fatness was celebrated as a marker of high status. This is a simplistic and naive argument. The attitudes of different cultures towards fatness during different periods of history have varied widely. This argument also tends to homogenize non-Western cultures as uniformly fat-accepting, often by pointing to an artistic artefact of some kind. But as West (1974) points out, an image depicting an extremely overweight man or woman may simply indicate a culture's expectation that their monarchs or gods should be a particular shape rather than evidence that the wider population coveted fatness for themselves. Some writers also forget that, just as with contemporary Western culture, celebration and stigmatization of fatness could have existed simultaneously both within and across the different social strata of different cultures. The study of history does not deliver a consistent and unified attitude towards fatness against which contemporary Western attitudes can be easily contrasted. For example, while West (1974) tends to argue that a suspicion of fatness and a celebration of leanness (particularly for men) has been fairly constant through history, Brown and Konner (1987), on the other hand, claim that anthropological data suggest that a substantial majority of 'traditional' cultures have seen plumpness as desirable.

A more compelling way to think about people's contrasting feelings and attitudes towards body weight is to see them as different threads of thought stretching back into the past. At particular points in history these threads have intermingled to produce new 'patterns' of thinking so that certain ideas about fatness – for example, as a sign of high status, sickness or strength or weakness of character – have been more or less widespread at different times and among different groups of people.

Taken together, the work of historians such as Schwartz (1986), Goldstein (1992) and Stearns (1997) suggests that Western anxiety about overweight has ebbed and flowed throughout history as far back as we care to look (for a brief assessment of medieval attitudes see Stunkard et al. 1998). Bray (1990), for example, tracks the pathologization of fatness from Hippocrates and Galen during ancient times through to the sixteenth century and then onwards. Writing in the 1950s, Ayers (1958) also surveys the works of ancient, medieval and Renaissance intellectuals, noting their regular concern with the medical (not just moral) risks of fatness, physical inactivity and overeating. She dates the beginning of modern medical interest in fatness from around the time of Thomas Bedoes' 1793 work *Observations on the Nature and Cure of Calculus*.

Thus, despite the vast amount of late twentieth century research devoted to settling the issue (much of it inconclusive), belief in the idea that excess fatness is bad for human health appears to be very old indeed. This is not to say that the case against fatness (particularly overweight and moderate obesity) has ever, in any period of history, been conclusively made, either via empirical science or any other means. In fact, at *both* the beginning and the end of the twentieth century, the precise nature and severity of health risk related to excess fatness (however it is measured) remained poorly understood. Indeed, part of our motivation for this book was to question the labelling of people, who happen to carry a level of fatness above some arbitrary level, as 'sick' or 'diseased'. Therefore, in noticing the long history of belief in the idea that fatness is unhealthy, we are certainly not suggesting that longevity indicates the soundness of the idea. In the following chapter Bruce Ross tackles the health implications of overweight and obesity more directly. For the moment, though, we are simply flagging the fact that the strength of existing scientific evidence has rarely, if ever, had any bearing on people's desire to see fatness as unhealthy. Obesity writers themselves, such as Shell (2002), often provide potted histories of fatness, reminding us that Hippocrates, the ancient Greek physician, and Galen, the first-century anatomist, both saw fatness as a sickness and prescribed dietary restraint and physical exercise. Shell also writes that:

> Ibn Sina, the tenth-century Arabic physician and tireless author of more than one hundred volumes of prose, lists obesity as a disease in his magnum opus

Kitab al-Qanum, and suggests treating it with a regimen of hard exercise, lean food, and – contrary to Hippocrates' teaching – judiciously timed baths.

(Shell 2002: 25–6)

Shell also describes two periods in particular, the mid-1700s and the early 1900s, when sections of the Western medical establishment became especially interested in fatness. Stearns' (1997) description of the period between about 1890 and 1920 paints a picture of an initially reluctant medical profession gradually and then enthusiastically joining the anti-fat movement in the US. By 1927, obesity was firmly established as a medical condition in the widely used *Cecil Textbook of Medicine* (Chang and Christakis 2002). According to Sobal (1995), a new phase in the relationship between the medical profession and body weight began in the early 1950s, with the proliferation of medical procedures, journals, conferences and professional bodies, all devoted to the treatment of excess body weight. However, as far back as the 1880s, medical journals had been publishing papers about excessive fatness.

Jacab Gutman, writing in a 1916 edition of the *New York Medical Journal* lists a long list of chronic ailments caused by fatness (or 'excess adiposity' as he puts it), particularly of the cardiovascular system, and concludes that: 'From the foregoing it may easily be concluded that the harm accomplished by excessive adiposity is varied and of serious consequence. Hence the imperative advisability of its reduction is evident' (Gutman 1916: 162).

J. B. Hurry (1917: 164), in *The Practitioner*, describes 'obesity and its vicious circles', which include cardio-vascular, respiratory, digestive and nervous disorders. Hurry reminds readers that not only did Hippocrates write that: 'Persons who are naturally very stout are more liable to sudden death than are thin persons', but that Aristotle also observed: 'Fat persons age early and therefore die early' (Hurry 1917: 178). Hurry warns that: 'The numerous vicious circles associated with polysarcia convert it into an obstinate, a pernicious and often a lethal disorder' (Hurry 1917: 177). And in a pre-echo of the contemporary writers we discussed at the beginning of the previous chapter, he uses the idea of energy imbalance to explain why people become obese:

A careful investigation of the mode of life must first be made, so that the precise aetiological factors may be elucidated. There may be excessive or injudicious food, with or without an abnormal appetite, too little exercise, or too much sleep. The deviation from the normal standard may appear unimportant, if estimated by daily measurements. But small items multiplied by 365 days in the year, especially when the excess extends over several years, may involve a total accumulation of fat that spells disaster.

(Hurry 1917: 179)

Both parts of Ibn Sina's prescription of 'hard exercise' and 'lean food' have had their respective proponents throughout the history of obesity science and, as we have seen, they remain the primary weapons in the 'war on obesity' to this day. In an 1893 edition of *The Lancet*, T. D. Savill informed readers that he cured a patient's obesity 'by an exclusively nitrogenous diet and copious libations of warm water' (Savill 1893: 133). Savill reports:

I still see him occasionally, and though he takes ordinary diet, *avoiding beer* only, he keeps at about 16 1/2 st. and in good health ... It was certainly very successful in this case, for the man was not only thinner, but was in much better health in every way and able to resume work. The permanence of the improvement after resuming ordinary diet is a fact worthy of special attention.

(Savill 1893: 133–4, emphasis in original)

In sharp contrast and at around the same time, a correspondent to the *Journal of the American Medical Association* reported attending a meeting of the Basle Medical Society conference at which:

Professor Massini, the President, made a short address and introduced Professor Bunge, who read a paper on 'The Formation of Fat in the Body, and the Causes of Obesity,' the subject being treated from a strictly scientific and chemical standpoint. He showed clearly that fat is produced from fat, other hydro-carbonaceous food and albuminous substances. The causes of fat accumulation were attributed to want of muscular exercise and consumption of alcohol. He said that dieting in the treatment of obesity was useless and often dangerous, and advised as the safest, most rational and most efficient treatment, active muscular exercise and abstinence from alcoholic drinks. As no one responded to the invitation to open discussion on the paper it must be taken for granted that the views advanced represented those of the members present.

(Senn 1887: 348)

Readers of contemporary obesity science will be aware that strong doubts about the value of diets and the suggestion that people should eat normally and do more exercise are among the stated positions of many of today's experts (Anonymous 1993; Atrens 1988; Gaesser 2002; Germov and Williams 1996; Katz 2003; Williams and Roughan 1986). On the other hand, perhaps a more widely held view is that a *combination* of dietary restraint and exercise is the best way to attack overweight and obesity. Such advice would have been entirely familiar to I. N. Love who described his own approach in a 1900 edition of the *Journal of the American Medical Association* as follows:

I prescribed proper purgation and a course of medication and diet which would antagonize the constipation and favor a general activity of the secretions, regulating the diet by proscribing fats and sweets, and instructing him to eat freely of fruits and vegetables, such as tomatoes, cabbage, spinach, sauerkraut, etc. I also ordered him to pay especial attention to all hygienic rules, such as bathing and massage, and in particular to take plenty of exercise, walking, running, jumping, horseback riding, croquet, and all out-door athletic games.

(Love 1900: 975)

As we noted in the previous chapter, the study of genetics currently plays an important 'black box' role in salvaging the 'body as machine' model. However, the science of genetics is just the latest of a number of other black boxes that have preserved the idea that a science of body weight is possible. For example, Love was one of the many scientists of his day who felt that obesity was caused by thyroid gland dysfunction:

> In this department of work the already established value of the thyroid gland in myxedema, obesity, idiocy, some forms of insanity and other conditions due to interrupted or misdirected metabolism is familiar to all, and favorable clinical evidence is accumulating constantly.
>
> (Love 1900: 975)

On the other hand, W. J. Hoyten (1906) writing in the British Medical Journal, is more cautious about the efficacy of thyroid treatments:

> Young persons of both sexes, as a rule, show no falling off in weight even when the gland substance is taken for some months. On the other, females between the ages of 25 and 45 years come under its influence speedily, and weight decreases rapidly, whilst in males of a corresponding age the results are uncertain, the fat in only a certain proportion being permanently reduced.
>
> (Hoyten 1906: 197)

During the first half of the twentieth century, perhaps one of the best-known proponents of the idea that obesity is caused primarily by too much food was Hilde Bruch, the controversial and influential German psychiatrist. Bruch published widely on childhood and general obesity and argued that dietary restraint was the fundamental mode of obesity treatment. In particular, she saw the energy-in/energy-out law as the basis for understanding obesity and was highly critical of those who argued that obese people generally suffered from metabolic (including thyroid-related) dysfunction. In a 1944 article she writes:

> You will find in textbooks and journals detailed enumeration of all possible 'causes' such as heredity, endocrine disorder, metabolic and neurogenic disturbances, and so on. Overeating, if mentioned at all, is considered only in connection with those uninteresting cases of 'simple' or obscure obesity to which no long scientific label can be attached. It is my opinion that this type of approach, in which complex disorders are 'explained' in terms of one specific cause, is in need of revision. The line of inquiry and method of investigation determine to a large extent the result of any scientific enquiry. It is therefore not surprising that workers so often find evidence for what they had set out to prove. This type of scientific investigation may lead to complicated theories which overlook the obvious, such as the relationship of overeating to obesity.
>
> (Bruch 1944: 361)

She goes on:

> For a long time, the trend in obesity research had been to look for errors in energy expenditure, and countless thousands of basal metabolism tests were

done in an effort to demonstrate that the energy requirements of an obese person were particularly low and that the metabolism functioned with a saving which was then stored as excess fat. All kinds of glandular dysfunction were postulated to explain these metabolic peculiarities which could not be validated by less enthusiastic examiners.

(Bruch 1944: 361)

In the context of this book, Bruch's work is extremely interesting because she clearly saw her research as rigorously empirical and was highly critical of work she saw as insufficiently scientific. But Bruch also lived in the immediate post-Freudian era in which all manner of human illnesses and abnormalities were being attributed to psychological abnormality. Even though she saw herself as a scientist, her work is littered with extremely dubious moral judgements about obese people and their families. In fact, Bruch was one of the first modern commentators to explicitly blame mothers for childhood obesity, something she did repeatedly and, as we will see later in this book, this is a practice that unfortunately endures to this day. In short, just like contemporary obesity science, Bruch's work was a cocktail of science, morality and (in Bruch's case, Freudian) ideology.

Bruch felt that childhood obesity often emerged within families run by nervous, 'bossy' and neurotic mothers and weak, 'energy' deficient fathers. She argued that the mothers of obese children consistently lied about the amount of food that they fed their children. Moreover, she believed that mothers overfed because of deep-seated anxieties and disappointments in their own lives, and children overate because of a lack of 'true' parental love. She writes:

We have accumulated information on more than 200 children who had grown obese before the age of puberty. These children showed striking similarities, not only in their physical appearance, their slow and awkward movements, their great interest in food, but in their total personality development and the way in which they handled their interpersonal relationships. It became clear in the course of these studies that excessive eating played an important role in the emotional life of these children. The giving and receiving of food was a tie of great significance in the relationship between a mother and her fat child, one which had retained, in a way, the same significance which food normally plays in early infancy. The expression of satisfaction which the warm and well-fed infant displays seems to express the acme of contentment and is the mother's reward for her work and trouble on his behalf. Normally, as a child grows older the relationship to the mother becomes less materialistic and parasitic ... This normal course of development presupposes that the mother, herself, is a secure and stable person who can permit her child to develop these new sources of satisfaction and thus to become an independent and self-reliant entity, and that she can find her reward in the growing maturity of his personality. Mothers of fat children are singularly unable to permit their children a normal unfolding of their personalities. These children are overstuffed not only with food; all other aspects of their physical care are greatly and anxiously exaggerated. The mothers continue to dress them, or to lead them by the hand and accompany them to school at an age when other children are well able to take care of themselves. As one gets acquainted with them one learns that many mothers live out their own problems and frustrations in these children. They cannot give them the respect nor permit them the dignity to which they are entitled as individuals; instead they try to realize in their children their own dreams of a life of luxury and idleness of which they themselves may have felt deprived.

(Bruch 1944: 363)

A number of recent popular books (Fumento 1997a; Pool 2001; Shell 2002; Vogel 1999) have attempted to chart sections of the history of obesity science, often by interviewing some of the important surviving scientists. Almost without exception, the psychoanalytically-driven period in which Bruch worked is described as a kind of embarrassing adolescent phase. Albert J. Stunkard, for example, is quoted as saying that during obesity science's psychoanalytic period 'the respect for data in this field was absolutely lacking' (Shell 2002: 45). This is an extremely debatable point of view. We would direct readers to Bruch's many papers, some of them voluminous published reports of painstakingly recorded data about the families of obese children (in particular, see Bruch 1941; Bruch and Touraine 1940). Similarly, Meloan's (1941) work on the 'excessive' appetites of 'maladjusted' children presents detailed case studies and family histories, often finding that 'weak', 'nervous', morally questionable or economically 'unsuccessful' parents (usually mothers) were to blame.

P. E. Craig's (1955) article, 'Obesity: a practical guide to its treatment based on a controlled study of 821 consecutive cases', for the *Medical Times* is another striking example where adherence to the energy-in/energy-out law and the importance of collecting empirical data went hand in hand with what many people would now see as highly dubious moral judgements. Craig exemplifies the dictum of energy balance, with which we are now familiar, as follows:

Obesity can be corrected only by creating a negative energy balance, expressed by a daily caloric deficit. In other words, eat less than the body requires and the stores of fat will be quickly drawn upon to supply that caloric deficiency.

(Craig 1955: 160)

He then goes on describe the treatment protocol used with his patients. This description includes the following comments:

It was further pointed out [to patients] that obesity not only is physically crippling but socially and psychologically disabling as well. No one loves a fat girl except possibly a fat boy, and together they waddle through life with a roly poly family ... Those who refuse to admit the existence of unsolved conflicts ... will do nothing to attack the problem directly or employ the positive substitute approach.

(Craig 1955: 160)

Earlier in the paper these 'unsolved conflicts' are described as 'unsatisfied social and sexual desires' (Craig 1955: 158). Craig concludes by informing the reader that: 'The patient is told bluntly that no one can reduce unless there are fewer calories consumed than are daily expended' (Craig 1955: 162). Craig reports that this controlled study led to very pleasing weight loss among patients.

Not only does the work of psychoanalytically inspired obesity researchers appear *not* to have been marked by an absence of or 'disrespect' for data, it drew on a thoroughly empirical line of research which asserted that theories about metabolic or endocrinal disturbance among the obese were erroneous. For example, Newburgh and Johnston's (1930) research, published in the *Journal of Clinical Investigation*, found that any discrepancy between a person's body weight and how much they ate could be explained by water retention. They claim:

> These considerations lead to the conclusion that the fundamental cause of endogenous obesity is not to be found in some type of metabolic aberration; but rather that these individuals, in common with all obese persons, are the victims of a perverted appetite. In normal people there is a mechanism that maintains an accurate balance between the outgo and the income of energy. All obese persons are, alike in one respect, – they literally overeat.
>
> (Newburgh and Johnston 1930: 199)

And later: 'Our evidence leads to the generalisation that obesity is always caused by an inflow of energy that is greater than the outflow' (Newburgh and Johnston 1930: 211). Bruch (1940) cites a number of other experimental papers by Newburgh and Johnston which, she argued, proved the centrality of overeating in the development of obesity. In fact, she wrote somewhat sarcastically of those who overlooked overeating and clearly saw them as lacking scientific rigour:

> Some writers even stated that their patients were poor eaters who grew stout and remained so on exceedingly low diets. Such publications give the impression that their authors considered obesity a condition in which the law of conservation of energy does not hold true.
>
> (Bruch 1940: 740)

As we saw in Chapter 3 and will see again in Chapter 6, much of what is *currently* said about the causes and consequences of the 'obesity epidemic' is said in a largely 'data free' environment, a situation some obesity scientists readily concede. Bruch's alarming and, at times, frankly silly conclusions about the psychological bases of obesity were not produced because of an absence of data or because she did not consider data important. She clearly did. Rather, the work of Bruch and others was guided by moral assumptions about what made a 'good' family and what qualities 'good' mothers and fathers should have, as well as an ideological commitment to psychological explanations of human behaviour. By calling this work 'data free', contemporary obesity scientists try to distance themselves from their field's patently moralistic and ideological past, and ask us to believe that it is now an exercise in 'objective' science. But as our discussion of television viewing and childhood overweight/obesity suggested, obesity science has not transformed itself into a morally and ideologically neutral enterprise. The moral and ideological commitments that obesity scientists bring to their research have simply changed.

In the previous chapter we saw that some contemporary researchers are not convinced that a simple excess of dietary intake causes many or even most cases of overweight and obesity. These doubts are not new. As the eighteenth-century physician Malcolm Flemyng noted (quoted in Frank 1993 in Chapter 3, p. 46), the relationship between a person's body weight, on the one hand, and their food and exercise habits, on the other, is not always a simple matter. This observation has led scientists to speculate about different forms of obesity, often called 'exogenous' and 'endogenous' forms; those forms that derive from the way the obese person interacts with the environment (exogenous) and those forms that are brought about by some malfunction or peculiarity concerning the internal workings of the body (endogenous). These two explanations have often been in conflict and this conflict survives today in debates between those who would emphasize 'modern Western lifestyles' and those who emphasize genetics when discussing the 'obesity epidemic' and the causes of overweight and obesity more generally.

Although (like Bruch) a proponent of dietary intervention and restraint in cases of obesity, E. E. Cornwall's (1916) article for the *Boston Medical and Surgical Journal* is uncanny in the way it also pre-echoes the discussions of overweight and obesity we encountered in the previous chapter, particularly Sobal and Stunkard (1989):

> It would be an easy matter to calculate the formula for reducing the fuel value of the food intake, if oxidation in the body were always regular and uniform. In such case the amount of reduction would have a caloric value, equal to that of the quantity of body fat which it is desired to burn up. For example, if the reduction in weight desired is at the rate of two pounds a week, which means the combustion daily of about four and a half ounces of body fat, the fuel value of the daily ration would have to be reduced about 1000 calories below the normal for size, age and activity. But the oxidation of fat in the body is not always regular and uniform, and does not always respond promptly and fully to the demands made on it by partial starvation. Extensive variation of this oxidation in different individuals is a matter of common observation: frequently small eaters are seen to remain persistently stout, while large eaters as persistently remain thin. Nevertheless, the formula suggested serves as a basis on which to work out the best formula for the individual case.
>
> (Cornwall 1916: 601)

It is important to stress that the significance of the similarity between this quote and those from Chapter 3 is not tied up with questions about the truth or otherwise of what these authors claim. What is significant is that these researchers appear to be thinking in the same way and offering similar advice. Following these introductory words about energy-in and energy-out, Cornwall goes on to provide dietary advice which would be familiar to twenty-first century readers:

> Include plenty of fresh fruits and vegetables in the diet in order to supply full rations of the body salts and vitamins; but use careful selection so as to include only fruits and vegetables which are comparatively free from objectionable

qualities, such as indigestibility, possession of purin or oxalic acid content, and offensiveness to the patient's idiosyncrasies.

(Cornwall 1916: 601)

Writing at about the same time, Gutman (1916, quoted previously) held that endogenous, rather than exogenous, forms of obesity were by far the most common:

> While it is true that systematic underfeeding will accomplish satisfactory results in cases of obesity, classed by von Noorden as exogenous, it will not suffice to accomplish similar results in the other class of cases, the endogenous. To the latter class belong cases resulting from the disturbances of the functions of the various endocrine glands. It seems to me, that the great majority of obesity cases belong to this class, and only a very few cases constitute the other, the exogenous class. To the latter [sic] category belong the cases of obesity caused either by overfeeding or by underexercising, or both. Repeated excessive intake of food, or diminished expenditure of energy disproportionate to the intake must leave a balance for accumulation within the organism. In the endogenous variety, on the other hand, this disproportion need not necessarily be an accompanying etiological factor. Such persons often take a moderate amount of food, and yet continue to add weight constantly.
>
> (Gutman 1916: 162)

Examples of researchers wrestling with the particulars of the energy-in/energy-out relationship can be found even earlier. Here, W. H. Allchin (1906), writing for *The Practitioner*, sets the scene for his later remarks on the dietary treatment of obesity:

> Inasmuch, then, as the body fat is derived from the food which represents the potential energy of the organism, which should normally be converted into actual energy chiefly by oxidation in the tissues, an accumulation of fat usually expresses a disturbance in the relation of the ingesta to the work done . . .
> Now, although it is quite true that large eaters may and frequently do become unduly fat, it by no means follows that they will of necessity do so; and indeed many persons, especially women who are excessively corpulent, are, on the contrary, very moderate or even small feeders, not consuming nearly the amount above set down as the normal. With this may be mentioned that some persons, who habitually exceed, even to a large extent, the normal intake, or may even be rather below than above the average weight, or may even be distinctly thin, and no amount of food will make such people fat; and such differences, which are constantly being met with among perfectly healthy people are not to be explained by their habits of life, the most important influencing circumstances in the writer's experience being heredity.
>
> (Allchin 1906: 517–18)

Thus, writing in the first decade of the twentieth century, Allchin rehearses the routine within obesity science of, first, stating that human body weight is governed by the difference between energy-in and energy-out, second, noting that this relationship is far from universal and, third, going on to provide advice about one or both parts of the energy balance equation. In this case Allchin is concerned with energy-in and offers, once again, rather familiar dietary advice:

> Each case must be treated in view of age, sex, heredity predisposition, habits of life, and previous amount of food and kind thereof, and not with a blind adherence to any one hard-and-fast dietary as applicable to all. It is well to commence gradually, and not suddenly, to feed a patient on a very restricted scale; the weekly loss in weight should not exceed three pounds.
>
> (Allchin 1906: 526)

In a 1954 edition of the *American Journal of Digestive Diseases*, A. W. Pennington's article 'Treatment of obesity: developments of the past 150 years' prosecutes the case that simple overeating *is not* the cause of most cases of obesity. Here, Pennington laments that a preoccupation with the orthodoxy of caloric restriction, driven by a faith in what we have called the energy-in/energy-out law, has retarded the development of effective obesity treatments. In particular, he argues that the high-protein diet championed by the nineteenth-century ear surgeon, William Harvey, and his later-to-be famous patient, William Banting, was, in fact, a major breakthrough. Pennington claims that the medical establishment greeted the Harvey/Banting diet with hostility simply because scientific knowledge could not yet supply a reason for why the diet worked. After an initial period of excitement over the Banting diet, Pennington argues, treatment reverted to adherence to the idea of energy balance: 'Thus, omniscience remained inviolate and an opportunity for scientific advance was lost' (Pennington 1954: 66). He goes on:

> As the 20th century advances, the view became ever more widely accepted that the cause of obesity was an inflow of energy greater than the outflow, the disproportion between the two being attributed to careless or perverted eating habits. These, in turn, were explained on a psychiatric or moral basis to which, later, a disorder of the 'appestat' was joined . . . On all sides, concepts of obesity were being dismissed with laconic references to the law of conservation of energy, accompanied by knowing nods.
>
> (Pennington 1954: 67)

Pennington's alternative conclusion, based on the 'classic' work of Claude Bernard and, later, H. R. Rony, was that:

> *Obesity, in most cases, is a compensatory hypertrophy of the adipose tissues, providing for a greater utilization of fat by an organism that suffers a defect in its ability to oxidize carbohydrate.* This concept of obesity will, doubtless, strike many as strange in view of its complete departure from the usually prevailing one. Part of its strangeness, however, will be due to the newness of some of the physiological facts on which it is based. As these come to be more widely known and the matter is explored in a penetrating manner, its strangeness, I feel sure, will disappear.
>
> (Pennington 1954: 68, emphasis in original)

No doubt Pennington would have been both gratified and disappointed with the progress of obesity science in the remainder of the twentieth century: gratified because the idea of a high-protein cure for obesity made a number of high-profile comebacks over the next fifty years and disappointed with the enduring energy-in/energy-out orthodoxy.

The sense that the scientific study of overweight and obesity has been asking the same questions and deriving small variations on the same small set of answers for at least 120 years is, to us, overwhelming. Interestingly enough, this is precisely the same, if considerably earlier, conclusion reached by F. M. Bell in his 1914 article, 'The "why" of obesity', for the *New York Medical Journal*. Noting the apparently intractable nature of debates about whether obesity was caused by exogenous or endogenous factors, he writes: 'Bound by the chain of tradition, occasionally forging a new link, we are still marching round and round the same treadmill' (Bell 1914: 731). Were Bell alive today, he might wonder why the science of obesity is *still* concerned with working out if, why and to what extent human body weight conforms to the law of conservation of energy.

Breaking the loop

Despite the mass-media's recent and sudden interest in the subject, the idea that modern Western living produces entire populations of people who are overweight and averse to exercise is also not new. Indeed, it is an idea that a variety of experts and writers of various kinds have consistently found hard to resist. This is interesting, not least because those who write about the 'obesity epidemic' often hark back to a quite recent pre-epidemic period. According to these experts, this was a time without televisions and computers when people ate less fattening home cooked meals and did more exercise more often.

For example, we have seen how print-media reporting has romanticized the 1950s as an era before society 'let itself go'. This idea is echoed in the scientific literature. According to Boreham and Riddoch:

> Today's 50–60-year-old adult is likely to have walked or cycled to school, played for hours outside the house, was not distracted too much by television, and eventually walked to work – which was probably a manual job. So, any baseline measurements of physical activity or fitness may be misleading, as we know there has been an inexorable decrease in activity levels in all sectors of society over the past 50 years.
>
> (Boreham and Riddoch 2003: 22)

Chakravarthy and Booth are equally certain:

> Given that children were less sedentary 50 years ago, we believe that by instituting similar lifestyle modifications (watching less TV, eating fewer higher-calorie fast foods, and being more physically active), the current rising physical inactivity and obesity epidemics can be thwarted.
>
> (Chakravarthy and Booth 2003: 731)

However, Sobal (1995) claims that the American Society of Bariatric Physicians, devoted to the treatment of excess body weight, was founded as early as 1949 and that the 1950s was, in fact, a period in which a new wave of medical and scientific anxiety about overweight and obesity began. In 1952, the *Science News Letter* (1952: 408) reported that 'Obesity is now no. 1 U.S. nutritional problem'. Mayer (1953: 472) claimed that: 'The increase in mortality accompanying obesity justifies, it seems, calling obesity the "Number One Nutrition Problem" and perhaps even the "Number One Public Health Problem" in Western countries at the present time.' Referring to Mayer's article, Ayers (1958: 23) announced that 'practically everyone will agree that obesity is the "number one health problem today"', and 1956 saw the formation of the President's Council on Physical Fitness amid widespread and growing concern about the physical activity levels and fitness of Americans. According to Shell (2002: 188), a study published in 1956 'concluded that American children, though among the best fed and healthiest in the world, were woefully underexercised', and in a 1960 *Sports Illustrated* magazine article titled 'The Soft American', John F. Kennedy committed his administration to improving fitness and sports participation levels among the nation's youth. Of course, Kennedy's interest in fitness must be seen in the context of cold war politics. This, in turn, is a reminder to us today that calls for improved population fitness may not spring from a purely scientific concern with body weight or health.

Western culture has a long tradition of suspicious ambivalence towards the process of modernization, with its urban lifestyles and labour-saving technologies, and it is clear the idea that modernization produces 'soft' and under-utilized bodies stretches back much further than the 1950s. In concert with what appears to be the almost universal tendency for adults from any period of Western history to see their children as insufficiently physically active, the story of physical decline is, it seems, one we all know. Socrates' often quoted words capture the joining together of these two ideas, such that each generation's allegedly lazy children are seen as a sign that society itself is going downhill:

> Children today love luxury. They have bad manners, a contempt for authority, a disrespect for their elders, and they like to talk instead of work. They contradict their parents, chatter before company, gobble up the best at the table, and tyrannize over their teachers.
>
> (O'Connor 1980: 265)

Erasmus Darwin (1731–1802), grandfather of Charles Darwin, maintained in his 1797 *A Plan for the Conduct of Female Education in Boarding Schools* (Darwin 1968) that the children of his day had become far too sedentary and were in need of vigorous daily exercising. Concern about the declining physical capacities of children, particularly ruling-class boys, played a vital role in the development of organized sports during the second half of the 1800s (Chandler 1996; Crosset 1990) as well as the rise of 'muscular Christianity'. And as a number of social historians have shown (e.g. Burt 1995; Schwartz 1986; Smith 1974), social reformers had been articulating variations of these concerns since at least the early 1800s. In fact, a case could easily be made that the fear of bodily deterioration, brought about by rapid urbanization, was one of the defining ideas of the Victorian age. For example, McLaren (1997) shows how the proliferation of office work in Europe and North America generated middle-class anxiety about both physical and moral 'vigour'. Similar concerns about the corrupting potential of civilisation where central to Pierre de Coubertin's inspiration for the modern Olympic Games and, in an extreme form, shaped both the language and iconography of European fascism (Hoberman 1995; Mangan 2000).

By the early twentieth century, the idea that modern living was unhealthy and lead to mass indolence had begun to find an important ally in the emerging field of scientifically grounded medicine (Stearns 1997). Elsewhere, in his ominously titled *The Word, the Flesh and the Devil* (1929), the distinguished scientist J. D. Bernal predicted that, unless new functions were found for the human body, which he saw as trapped in a rapidly technologically changing world, it would be dispensed with altogether through sheer lack of use.

In this context, physical education is also an interesting case in point. Generally a low-status school subject, physical education has been the subject of occasional government and general public interest during times of crisis, such as wars and social unrest. Howell and Ingham (2001) suggest that this was particularly true in the US around the time of the Korean War when authorities were dismayed by the number of young men who failed the physical tests. But as others have pointed, it is difficult to find an historical example in which Western governmental and/or medical authorities have been anything other than shocked by what tests have 'revealed' about the physical state of its citizenry (Gould 1981; Kirk 1998). As we saw in Chapter 2, recent university studies of the physical skill levels of Australian children were interpreted as evidence of a general physical deterioration, even though no data exist against which these tests could be compared. The release of these results was accompanied by calls for more time for physical education (Raethel 1998).

In the 1965–6 *Physical Education Yearbook*, the prominent education scholar, P. J. Arnold wrote:

> 'The Affluent Society,' as Galbraith has dubbed ours, has many features about it which can be associated with physical enfeeblement. The ease and softness of life no longer make demands on the human organism that test and strengthen. The numerous labour-saving devices may be rewarded almost as commensurate with body-weakening. The promise of a still further extension of the use of automation in the produce of goods is likely to reduce the necessity for physical powers still more. The growing obsolescence in the necessity for physical fitness and hardiness in our day-to-day living, which has accelerated considerably in the past twenty years, is in the long run debilitating to man's constitution.
>
> (Arnold 1965–6: 17)

In 1969, the *Physical Educator* reproduced an address to an 'Obesity Seminar' by Dr F. B. Roby of the University of Arizona. Roby (1969: 158) opened his address as follows:

Of all the ways in which twentieth century man has dis-avowed his biological inheritances, the diminished usage of his large muscles is proving to be one of the most serious. For as man sits more and exercises less, he tends to violate his body's own wisdom. This very neglect leads us to hold seminars on obesity – and sooner or later someone appears to speak on physical activity and its relationship to this national health problem. And while this seminar is directed toward the obese individual we must remember that most of us are potential candidates for this not-too-select club and, therefore, my remarks are designed to have personal meaning for all.

(Roby 1969: 158)

It is important to point out that in this chapter we have purposely put to one side the health consequences of increasing overweight and obesity rates in the last twenty to thirty years. We questioned the certainty with which these health consequences are discussed in the previous chapter and will return to them in the next. Instead, what we have tried to do here is to make explicit the intellectual tools which appear to be the mainstay of obesity science; the energy-in/energy-out law and the 'Western lifestyles' explanation. Taken together, the pre-'obesity epidemic' literature cited in this chapter suggests that these two ideas are, at best, habits of mind. In the case of the energy-in/energy-out law, we have suggested that it has successfully trapped obesity science in a kind of loop, where the only question of empirical interest seems to be the precise biological aetiology of individual people's body weight.

In somewhat broader terms, we have also noted the ubiquitous story of Western decline and, in particular, the idea that 'Western lifestyles' are making us fat. Here the problem is not so much one of a closed research loop, but rather that of a story that is so familiar to us that we find it hard to think past it. How does the 'Western lifestyles' explanation help us to make sense of the fact that different groups of people appear to have markedly different sets of priorities concerning health, physical exercise and food? How does it inform the way we engage with what appear to be the important socio-economic dimensions of the diseases that are most closely associated with overweight and obesity? Such questions might at least help us to acknowledge that people live in different ways and that the 'everyone everywhere' version of the 'obesity epidemic' has the potential to obscure this basic fact. Not coincidentally, this problem of obscuring social, cultural and economic differences between people is also a feature of the energy-in/energy-out law, and it is perhaps for this reason that it appears to co-exist so happily with the 'Western lifestyles' explanation.

The negative consequences of this co-existence of two flawed ideas can be easily seen in the obesity science literature. First, there are those who write about 'the ultimate triumph of obesity' and obesity as the 'unstoppable side-effect of modernisation' (Foreyt and Goodrick 1995: 134) and declare that childhood obesity is 'modernity's scourge' (Waters and Baur 2003: 422). 'Modernity' and 'modernization' are notoriously difficult concepts to pin down but they surely refer to a period of time far longer than an 'obesity epidemic' whose experts estimate it to be between fifteen and thirty years old. If 'modernity' and 'Western lifestyles' really are to blame for the 'obesity epidemic' then the explanation for why this is so has yet to be convincingly made. If nothing else, blaming 'modernity' would seem to pit all of us against the overwhelming weight of centuries of history and the massed forces (whatever they may be) of civilization itself. As Foreyt and Goodrick (1995: 135) put it: 'We seem to be helpless pawns under the influence of social influences beyond our control'. In the meantime, our conclusion is that this explanation is both intellectually unsound and probably counter-productive.

Second, having blamed 'modernity', obesity scientists then return to their energy-in/energy-out law almost as if their 'modernity' thesis no longer holds. After invoking the image of helpless pawns, in the very next paragraph Foreyt and Goodrick (1995: 135) write: 'The problem of obesity could be eliminated in a few generations if our children were raised to know and practice prudent eating and exercise habits'. Remarkably, the problem is now one of insufficient 'prudence'. And yet, in the same article they appear to concede that this approach has not been successful in the past: 'The immense research effort into obesity has not yet culminated in effective help for the overweight. 33 894 publications related to obesity have accumulated since 1966, with 4785 related to treatment' (Foreyt and Goodrick 1995: 135).

As we noted in the previous chapter, the conspicuous juxtaposition here of certainty ('the solution to the problem is simple') and uncertainty ('we really do not have any effective courses of action') is difficult to ignore. Taken together, the message that obesity science appears to deliver is that the pro-obesity forces are unimaginably powerful, our defences against them notoriously weak and unreliable and, worst of all, it is our own individual, imprudent inattention to energy-in and energy-out that has landed us in this situation.

In Chapter 6 we will show that the 'Western lifestyles' explanation for the 'obesity epidemic' enjoys virtually no empirical support whatsoever. In concluding this chapter, however, we want to make one final point. When people blame technology for a particular problem, as has happened in the television viewing/ childhood overweight and obesity literature, they often do so in a way that suggests there is more at stake than the problem itself. For example, the 'couch potato' child is not just overweight or obese, she or he may also be seen as being vulnerable to the 'corrupting' powers of television and computer games. In Chapter 2 we saw how Garry Egger connected technology usage with a fatal moral failing (presumably sloth) in human nature. In Chapter 3 William H. Dietz appeared to cast television as the enemy of harmonious family life, a point of view echoed here by the cultural commentator Allan Bloom:

> Parents can longer control the atmosphere of the home and have even lost the will to do so. With great subtlety and energy, television enters not only the room, but also the tastes of old and young alike, appealing to the immediately pleasant and subverting whatever does not conform to it.
>
> (Bloom cited in Green and Bigum 1993: 128)

These are, of course, all moral and ideological pronouncements of one form or another even though they pose as statements of fact and are often expressed in contexts (such as academic journals) that have all the trappings of science.

Whether or not readers of this book concur with this gloomy view of technology is, to some extent, unimportant. In terms of our discussion of obesity science, the crucial point is that it rests on two ideas: that the body is a machine and that modernity makes people physically soft and fat. These two ideas have not sprung from within obesity science itself, but rather have been imported from other areas of science, literature and culture. In addition, they both carry a particularly heavy moral and ideological weight, which, we have argued, renders them ill-suited to understanding human body weight. None of this means that the 'obesity epidemic' should suddenly disappear as an issue for public debate. However, and in keeping with the overall purpose of this book, destabilizing the assumptions upon which obesity epidemic' thinking rests may at least begin to open up spaces for new ways of thinking and, as it were, breaking the loop.

5 Fat or fiction

Weighing the 'obesity epidemic'

Bruce Ross

A caricature of a post 2000 AD male appeared in *Playboy* magazine sometime in the mid-1960s alongside an article by a prominent physical education academic. It depicted a pot-bellied, skinny-legged male primate with a large head, huge genitals and an overdeveloped index finger. He was called something like *homo inertis* and represented the writer's projection of what men would look like in the third millennium if they continued to sit around watching television, drinking beer and being preoccupied with sex (large genitals reflecting male belief that size matters and an overdeveloped index finger to change channels so must have been before the advent of remote controls). Presumably women would still look like the centrefolds.

The article was intended to shock young men into physical activity by arguing that twentieth-century male humans were degenerating physically because they were not as physically active as their pre-industrial counterparts. Consequently, they were getting fat bellies, their legs were atrophying from disuse but their sexual organs and dominant index fingers were growing, presumably from overuse. Apparently, future generations would inherit these acquired characteristics. Apart from misrepresenting the process of evolution, the article presumed that humans were naturally physically active so that before the advent of machines and sedentary entertainment men worked hard all day every day.

In 2004 we still take for granted the notion that early women and men were always physically active in order to survive and that our typical urban dweller is a slothful, mobile-phone toting, car driving, lift riding, TV watching greedy guts, surfing the knowledge wave to wealth, fatness and ill health. Belief in the fictional *homo inertis* is apparently still alive and well among physical education academics, work physiologists and health policy makers (Boreham and Riddoch 2003; Bouchard 2000; Ministry of Health 2003).

Recent evidence suggests that modern city folk are not much less active, if at all, than our distant ancestors or our recent ancestors as demonstrated by existing forager communities, or our foraging cousin primates (Panter-Brick 2003). So why do obesity scientists, physical educators, health educators, fitness gurus and many policy makers still believe this science fiction of indolent, physically degenerating Westerners? Are we really getting fatter and sicker?

This chapter discusses the evidence most commonly used to support notions of national populations getting fatter and that this weight gain is a major community health risk.

The evidence: how do we know about the 'obesity epidemic'?

Statistics about the number of fat people in our communities have been accumulated by a variety of surveys using the techniques developed by epidemiologists. Epidemiology is the study of the occurrence of diseases or health states in human populations along with aspects or factors that seem to be related to the development or transmission or status of these diseases. Epidemiologists record how widespread a disease is in a population, for example the number of people with HIV/AIDS in New Zealand. They also monitor the frequency of a disease over time and the varying intensity of a disease in a population over time, such as the increasing or decreasing numbers of SARS cases in Hong Kong in 2003. Epidemiologists also attempt to note environmental factors that may predispose people to a disease or have some bearing on the health status of a population, for instance the reuse of hypodermic needles in heroin addicts as it relates to the occurrence of HIV/AIDS. In addition, epidemiological studies monitor the effectiveness of intervention or treatment of diseases, for example by recording the demise of smallpox since the widespread use of vaccination (Beaglehole *et al.* 2002).

Epidemiology has made important contributions to the understanding of the origin and spread of infectious diseases. In 1854 John Snow recorded the address of every person who died of cholera in the 1848–9 and 1853–4 epidemics and showed that five times as many people died who drank water from the Southwark water company pumps as did those who drank water from the Lambeth water company demonstrating, for the first time, that cholera is transmitted in water (Cameron and Jones 1983). More recently, epidemiologists have linked environmental factors with disease, cigarette smoking and lung cancer (Doll and Hill 1964).

Epidemiology contributes essential information for public health policy and action but to make sense of the data accumulated about the extent of human fatness and its relevance to individual and community health some epidemiological terms need to be clarified. Readers are referred to the texts *Basic Epidemiology* (Beaglehole *et al.* 2002) and *A Dictionary of Epidemiology* (Last 1995) for detailed information on these terms.

Terms

Population and population at risk

A *population* for an epidemiological study can be all the children in one school, all the people in a country, all women aged forty-five to fifty-five years living in cities, even the entire human population. It defines the actual group of people studied to generate information about the frequency and occurrence of a disease or health state. What is important for epidemiological work is that the studied population is clearly defined so that conclusions are drawn for that population only. It is sometimes important to specify a *population at risk*, that is the population that is likely to be exposed to a disease. For example, a study of the occurrence of prostate cancer would include only men. Thus, the population at risk for an epidemiological study of prostate cancer could be all males in Wales aged between fifty-five and seventy-five years.

Often a population at risk is defined by a factor that is known or thought to contribute to a disease being studied in a population. Smoking is one such factor that has been shown to contribute to lung cancer (Doll and Hill 1964) so the population at risk is defined by the *exposure* of the participants to smoking.

Incidence and prevalence

Fundamental to epidemiology is the measurement of the occurrence or frequency of a disease in a given population. *Prevalence* and *incidence* are the terms that describe the occurrence or frequency of a particular disease. Prevalence defines the number of people who have a disease or health state at a particular time in a given population. Incidence describes the number of new cases of a disease that appear in a given population over a period of time.

It is easy to confuse these terms even though they are entirely different ways of measuring the occurrence of a disease or health state in a given population. Prevalence and incidence are measures that are most useful for tracking communicable diseases that occur with variable frequency in a population. For example, the cold virus infects only a small proportion of a city's population in one year: that is, the common cold has a low prevalence. During winter months, however, more people catch colds so the incidence of cold infection is high during the cold weather but low during the warmer months. So the prevalence can be low and the incidence can be high or low for communicable diseases that people tend to recover from. For other diseases that people do not recover from such as diabetes or sickle cell anaemia there can be high prevalence and low incidence in a given population – few new cases each year but most of the people in the population suffer from the disease.

When reading statistics on body weight it is important to remember that prevalence of fatness is a snapshot or index of the occurrence of fatness in a given population at a particular time. Few studies on fatness actually track the incidence or changing level of fatness over time in a given population. Most of the studies on human adiposity record the prevalence of fatness in a given population at a given time and compare this with prevalence of obesity in a comparable but not the same population at a different time. Thus, the difference in the prevalence of fatness of say middle-aged men in 1984 and middle-aged men in 2000 is, strictly speaking, not a measure of the incidence of fatness in middle-aged men as two different populations are compared for their fat prevalence. This difference between prevalence and incidence is crucial to interpreting statistics used to support the notion that obesity is a disease of epidemic proportions as we discuss the occurrence of fatness in terms of prevalence and the diseases that are linked to that fatness in terms of incidence.

For comparison between populations both incidence and prevalence are expressed as the number of cases or persons multiplied by the period of the data collection (usually in years) and standardized for 1,000, 10,000 or 100,000 persons or person-years (hence 10^n in formula). These calculations determine the *prevalence rate* and the incidence rate. Thus, the prevalence rate (P) for a disease is:

$$P = \frac{\text{number of people with disease at a specified time}}{\text{number of people in the population at a specified time}} \times 10^n$$

However, prevalence of a disease or condition is also expressed as a percentage of the population. The World Health Organization (WHO) mostly uses percentages to express the apparent prevalence of obesity (World Health Organization 2000).

A simple and easy to understand measure of disease occurrence or frequency is the *cumulative incidence rate* or risk (CI): the number of people who get a disease or change their health state in a particular time compared to the number of people free of the condition at the start of the study:

$$CI = \frac{\text{number of people who get a disease during a specified time}}{\text{number of people free of disease at start of study}} \times 10^n$$

Table 5.1 is adapted from Beaglehole *et al.* (2002) and reports the findings of a study of the incidence of cerebral stroke in a population of women. It illustrates the calculation of the cumulative incidence rate of stroke in an eight-year study of a population of 118,539 women. Two populations at risk were defined by their *exposure* to smoking: smokers and ex-smokers. The cumulative incidence rate or risk for the population of women smokers was 49.6 cases of cerebral stroke for every 100,000 person years of smokers compared to 17.7 cases of cerebral stroke for every 100,000 person years of non-smokers.

Risk is used here in the same sense that it is used by life insurance companies that list the cumulative incidence of male and female deaths for each age group of smokers and non-smokers in actuarial tables (Jarrett 1986; Keys 1980). The 'risk of death' referred to in actuarial tables is the actual risk to the insurance company, that is the likelihood of the number of payouts that a life insurance company will have to make for every 1,000 persons insured. It is not each individual's actual risk of death. Similarly, the risk of death in the stroke study is the probability that a comparable population of 100,000 women smokers, ex-smokers or non-smokers will have 17.7, 27.9 and 49.6 deaths respectively from cerebral stroke. It is not the likelihood or risk that each woman smoker, ex smoker or non-smoker has of dying even though this is how these data are commonly reported.

As Pearce (1996) points out there has been a recent shift in the orientation or philosophy of epidemiologists such that they now a focus on individual risk to personal health rather than the risk to a population containing individuals who succumb to a disease. Thus, although epidemiologists today study populations, they do so in order to study decontextualized individual risk factors, rather than

Table 5.1 Cigarette smoking and cumulative incidence rate of stroke in women

Smoking level	Stroke cases	Person-years	Cumulative Index /100,000 person-years	Prevalence at end of study % population at risk
Never smoked	70	395,594	17.7	0.14
Ex-smoker	65	232,712	27.9	0.22
Smoker	139	280,141	49.6	0.39
Total	274	908,447	30.2	0.30

Source: adapted from Beaglehole *et al.* 2002: 16.

to study population factors in their social and historical context (Pearce 1996). As a result much of the popular and 'obesity science for the people' writings (see Chapter 7) on the occurrence of obesity mistake the cumulative incidence rate or risk of obesity in a population for the actual chance that any member of that population has of becoming fat.

Table 5.1 also clearly shows that the prevalence of stroke is quite low (less than half of one per cent of the 118,539 women observed over the eight years suffered a stroke) but the incidence of stroke in women who smoked or were ex smokers was nearly two to three times that of the non-smoking women. See Table 5.4 and Figure 5.1 for prevalence of obesity.

Mortality and morbidity

Much of epidemiology depends on the collation of statistics on the number of deaths attributable to a disease or condition. The cumulative incidence rate of deaths is often referred to as the *mortality rate*[1] or 'risk of death' in insurance actuarial tables. *Morbidity rate* is the cumulative incidence of the detected or diagnosed cases of a particular illness or change of function. So records are kept of the number of people who die from HIV/AIDS – mortality figures – as well as those who are HIV positive – morbidity figures.

Mortality and morbidity rates are not always as straightforward as they seem. For example, it would appear that mortality rates for road accidents are a simple tally of deaths at or after vehicle crashes. But what if someone dies from a heart attack or stroke before the crash? Are they legitimately a car crash statistic? Similarly, if someone with HIV/AIDS contracts pneumonia and dies, what cause of death should appear in the official record?

Obviously the usefulness and meaning of mortality and morbidity rates depends on the clinical and contextual accuracy of the diagnosis. It is interesting to note that obesity is rarely listed as a cause of death even though it is considered to be a disease (Jeffcote 1998; World Health Organization 2000). This anomaly probably arises from the difficulty in diagnosing obesity – distinguishing between normal fatness, corpulence and obesity and the fact that most fat people die for the same reasons that most thin people die.

Comparing populations for disease occurrence

Epidemiology provides useful information about public health when populations that differ in one or more characteristics are compared. Just as John Snow drew attention to the link between water organisms and cholera by comparing the mortality rates from cholera in a population of those who drank from one water company with those from a population who drank water from another water company, epidemiologists have demonstrated other health hazards by comparing populations. For example, smoking was shown to be a health hazard by comparing the lung cancer mortality rates of cigarette smoking physicians with those of non-smoking physicians (Cameron and Jones 1983; Doll and Hill 1964). Table 5.1 also illustrates the apparent relationship between smoking and the occurrence of stroke in women.

Risk ratio

A common way of comparing the occurrence of a disease in a population is to compare the cumulative incidence rate of a disease in a defined population with the cumulative incidence rate of that same disease in a population that differs in some clear way. For example, we can compare the cumulative incidence rate of stroke in female smokers with the cumulative incidence rate of stroke in a similar population of female non-smokers by consulting Table 5.1. Usually these cumulative incidence rates are compared as a ratio of the population at risk compared with the population not at risk. Thus to calculate the *risk ratio* (RR) of stroke for non-smokers and smokers:

$$RR = \frac{\text{Cumulative incidence rate of stroke in women smokers}}{\text{Cumulative incidence rate in women non-smokers}}$$

Using data presented in Table 5.1:

$$RR = \frac{49.6 \text{ per } 100,000 \text{ person-years}}{17.6 \text{ per } 100,000 \text{ person-years}} = 2.8$$

Obviously this means that the occurrence of stroke in a population of women smokers is nearly three times that of a population of women non-smokers. But it does not necessarily mean that each and every woman smoker is three times more likely to suffer from a stroke than a non-smoker. However, if the risk ratio is large like the risk ratio of thirty observed for the occurrence of lung cancer in heavy smokers compared to non-smokers then there is very likely an increased risk of getting lung cancer for all smokers (Doll and Hill 1964).

Now, what is most striking about epidemiological studies of obesity is that the risk of obesity is reported in terms of obesity being a defining character of a population, that is, an exposure that may predispose individuals to develop a disease. So just like smoking exposes women to the risk of cerebral stroke, excess fatness is identified as a factor that exposes people to the risk of ischaemic heart disease and non-insulin dependent diabetes mellitus (Bray 2000; World Health Organization 2000). Consequently, evidence to support both the disease status of obesity and the risk to health report the risk ratio of the incidence of ischaemic heart disease or non-insulin dependent diabetes mellitus in a population at risk defined as over-fat or obese people compared to a population of 'normal' people.

The evidence

Two important questions need to be addressed when discussing the epidemiology of obesity. Firstly, what is obesity and how is it measured; secondly is obesity a disease?

What is obesity?

How do we define obesity? When does 'healthy weight' become 'overweight' and when does 'overweight' become obesity? In his classic text (Garrow 1978: 6) simply states: 'Obesity is a condition caused by an excessive amount of adipose tissue.' He deliberately avoids using 'excessive fat' in his definition as adipose tissue, the padding below the skin that seems to change as we gain or lose weight is not just fat; it is 80 per cent fat – glyceryl esters of fatty acids – 2 per cent protein and 18 per cent water (Garrow 1978).

However, in practical terms we think of overweight and obese people as being fat not just having a large body size (de Garine and Pollock 1995; Mayer 1983b; Pollock 1995). So the problem with defining obesity is deciding what is excessive. How much adipose tissue do we need? How fat is obese? What are the advantages and disadvantages of being fat? And how fat do we have to be to be personally disadvantaged or a burden on society? Or how fat do we have to be to be classified as ill?

The term obese comes from the Latin *obedere* 'to eat up, to devour', and so carries the implication that fat people overindulge, eat too much, are greedy. Consequently identifying someone as 'obese' is judging their behaviour as well as their apparent physical state.

The WHO defines obesity as: 'a condition of abnormal or excessive fat accumulation in adipose tissue, to the extent that health may be impaired' (World Health Organization 2000: 6).

Now, the extent to which obesity impairs health has been estimated by comparing various disease states with measures of excess fat. How is human fatness measured? Life insurance company actuarial tables compiled from about 1911 probably provided the first epidemiological evidence that large body weight for a given height was associated with early death. But these tables do not take into account variations in physique or 'frame size' so that large muscled individuals would be rated as fat and therefore charged a higher insurance premium (Garrow 1978; Jarrett 1986; Keys 1980). As height–weight tables alone are poor indicators of body composition, a variety of measures have been devised to measure fatness (Bray 2003; Cahnman 1968; Keys 1980). Consequently, the body mass index (BMI) devised by Quetelet over 150 years ago is now used as the main measure of fatness as it seems to be a better indicator of total body fat in adults than simple measures of height and weight (Bray 2003). BMI is body weight divided by height squared:

$$BMI = \frac{Weight\ (kg)}{Height\ (m)^2}$$

It is the most widely used measure of body size in English speaking countries and when first used, a BMI of between 20 and 30 kg/m^2 was considered a desirable height weight ratio for Western adults (de Garine and Pollock 1995). Prior to 1999 a BMI of 29 kg/m^2 was considered to be 'overweight' but this was reduced to 27 kg/m^2 and now many health advocates claim that a BMI above 25 kg/m^2 indicates 'overweight' presumably because BMI does not correlate with levels of fat in people with a BMI less than 25 kg/m^2 (see Table 5.2) and does not appear to be associated with various non-communicable diseases (Bray 2003; Meek 2003; Seidell 2000).

However, BMI is a highly problematic measure of fatness. At best it accounts for between 60 and 75 per cent of the variation in body fat content of adults. It does not account for the differences in percentages of body fat for the same

Table 5.2 Classification of adult obesity according to BMI

Classification	BMI kg/m²	Health risk
Underweight	<18.5	Low (but there are health risks associated with low BMI)
Normal Range	19.5–24.9	Average
Overweight:	≥ 25.0	
Pre-obese	25.0–29.9	Increased
Obese class I	30.0–34.9	Moderate
Obese class II	35.0–39.9	Severe
Obese class III	≥ 40.0	Very severe

Source: adapted from Table 2.1 *Obesity: Preventing and Managing the Global Epidemic* (World Health Organization 2000).

BMI in different ethnic groups, nor for variation in human physique (size and amount of fat, muscle and bone). It is not suitable for assessing body composition in children, does not account for what seems to be natural age-related changes in body composition and distorts the fat assessment of women who tend to be shorter and have higher levels of adipose tissue than men (Bray 2003; Burstyn 1990; Keys 1980; Rush *et al.* 1997; Swinburn *et al.* 1999; World Health Organization 2000). Consequently, BMI is not a 'gold standard' for measuring human fatness or obesity. Table 5.2 shows how obesity is classified using BMI.

In his contribution to an Australian Association for Exercise and Sports Science round-table discussion on the BMI, the sports scientist Bill Ross argues that 'the BMI is almost useless as an index fatness' (*Australian Association for Exercise and Sports Science Newsletter* 1999: 3). Drawing on data from a study of 12,282 male and 6,593 females, he notes that BMI correlated only moderately with the sum of five skinfolds ($r = 0.50$), a more direct measure of fatness, but also showed a similar level of correlation with the girths of muscular body parts ($r = 0.52$) and a standard set of bone breadth measurements. As Ross puts it: 'In other words in the combined sample there were roughly similar relationships between the muscle, bone and fat estimates with the BMI. BMI might just as well be used as a predictor of muscularity or bone mass!' (*Australian Association for Exercise and Sports Science Newsletter* 1999: 3).

Other attempts to measure fatness accurately have involved measuring the triceps and subscapular skinfold thickness, lean body mass and the ratio of waist to hip circumference.[2] All of these measures are problematic in terms of the accuracy and repeatability of the actual measures as well as their precision in assessing excess fat or adipose tissue (de Garine and Pollock 1995; Garrow 1978; Hardman and Stensel 2003; Jarrett 1986; Seidell 2000). However, it does seem as if measurement of waist and hip girth in association with BMI can provide a profile of fat distribution that seems to correlate with various diseases better than BMI alone (Bray 1979; World Health Organization 2000):

> However, obese individuals differ not only in the amount of excess fat that they store, but also in the regional distribution of that fat within the body. The distribution of fat induced by weight gain affects the risks associated with

Table 5.3 Girth measurements that reflect 'excess' fat

	Waist circum 'alert zone'	Waist circum 'action zone'	'Normal' waist–hip ratio
Women	≥ 80 cm	≥ 88 cm	≤ 0.80
Men	≥ 94 cm	≥ 102 cm	≤ 0.95

Source: adapted from Seidell (2000: 22).

obesity, and the kinds of disease that result. Indeed, excess abdominal fat is as great a risk factor for disease as is excess body fat *per se*. It is useful, therefore, to be able to distinguish between those at increased risk as a result of 'abdominal fat distribution', or 'android' fat distribution, in which fat is more evenly and peripherally distributed around the body.

(World Health Organization 2000: 6)

So the WHO acknowledges that variation in body composition can alter the association between measures of fatness and various diseases but the prevalence of obesity worldwide is still reported on the basis of BMI (World Health Organization 2000). And waist and hip measures are used to classify obesity based on averaged data that, again, do not take into account variations in physique apart from gender differences (see Table 5.3). Obesity classification using a tape measurements of hip and waist circumference also neglects the large measurement errors inherent in such an exercise (Boreham and Riddoch 2003; Bray 2003; Burstyn 1990; Cahnman 1968; Flegal *et al.* 2002; Garrow 1978; Hall and Stewart 1989; Hardman and Stensel 2003; Jarrett 1986; Kahn *et al.* 1997; Mayer 1983a; Rush *et al.* 1997; Seidell *et al.* 1989; Swinburn *et al.* 1999; Wooley and Wooley 1984; World Health Organization 2000).

To summarise: obesity is defined as excess fat that impairs health and is routinely measured using height and weight to calculate a BMI or by measuring hip and waist circumference. The classification of obesity depends on the BMI or waist circumference or the ratio of waist to hip circumference that appear to relate to increased occurrences of various non-communicable diseases. As both BMI and girth measures are problematic, all statistics on the levels of obesity in human population need to be interpreted with a great deal of caution to avoid science fiction being represented as science fact.

Is obesity a disease?

'Obesity is a chronic disease . . .', according to a WHO report (World Health Organization 2000: 2), a disease that has at its base an 'undesirable positive energy balance and weight gain' (World Health Organization 2000: 6). However, the disease status of this 'undesirable weight gain' seems to depend on its association with various illnesses not because fatness or weight gain itself is a disease.

as standards of living continue to rise, weight gain and obesity are posing a growing threat to health in countries all over the world. Obesity is *a chronic disease*, prevalent in both developed and developing countries, and affecting children as well as adults. Indeed, it is now so common that it is replacing the more traditional public health concerns, including undernutrition and infectious disease as one of the *most significant contributors to ill health*.

(World Health Organization 2000: 1–2, emphasis added).

Note how the WHO substantiates the status of obesity as a disease by its contribution to ill health, not by obesity being a specific state of ill health like lung cancer or heart disease. We would not classify car crashes as a disease yet they contribute significantly to ill health as does poverty and industrial pollution. In other words, obesity is not a diagnosable illness in its own right, meaning that if you are fat you are ill. Some fat people are well and some thin people are unwell. So classifying obesity as a disease seems to depend upon the association between obesity and particular non-communicable diseases such as ischaemic heart disease or non-insulin dependent diabetes mellitus (Ezzati *et al.* 2002; Ezzati *et al.* 2003; Garrow 1978; Gilman 2004; Keys 1980; Mayer 1983a; Meek 2003; Murray and Lopez 2000; Must 2003; Pi-Sunyer 2002; Seidell *et al.* 1989; World Health Organization 2000). It seems illogical and scientifically weak to call obesity a disease as the reasoning equates obesity with bad health by assuming obesity *causes* diseases such as non-insulin dependent diabetes mellitus rather than *being symptomatic* of particular diseases like non-insulin dependent diabetes mellitus (Cameron *et al.* 2003; Gilman 2004; Keys 1980; Pi-Sunyer 2002; Seidell *et al.* 1989; Stehbens 1992; World Health Organization 2000). However, as Sander Gilman has explained in his cultural history of fat boys, the identification of fat men as sick and dissolute has a long, complex history, embedding into our Western consciousness the notion that 'obesity is antithetical to long life thus standing for moral as well as medical failures' (Gilman 2004: xi). Thus, modern medical discussions of obesity are not entirely based on recent evidence as claimed by the WHO but are coloured by our collective cultural prejudice that personal sinfulness and irresponsibility are responsible for obesity.

This book questions the classification of obesity as a disease. Many fat people live healthy, active productive lives and live beyond the lifespan of many thin people so it seems a nonsense to say that fatness is a disease (Burstyn 1990). This is not to say that very, very fat people do not have problems in moving about, using public spaces, breathing when lying down or buying clothes that fit. That is, some very large people are disabled in our society. And some of them may be sick – suffering from high blood pressure, heart disease, cancer, non-insulin dependent diabetes mellitus, damaged joints or emphysema. Many thin people also suffer from these diseases, yet we do not call thinness a disease.[3] Calling obesity a disease because obesity is associated with various non-communicable diseases is like identifying short men as ill because of the established association between short stature and ischaemic heart disease (Parker *et al.* 1998).

Prevalence of obesity

With the development of modern techniques in epidemiology and the ability to crunch numbers in computers, epidemiologists have been able to demonstrate a relationship between the degree of obesity and the occurrence of various non-communicable diseases (Cameron et al. 2003; Ezzati *et al.* 2003; Krieger 1994; Murray and Lopez 2000; Seidell 2000; World Health Organization 2000). They have also attempted to track the apparent prevalence of obesity and overweight in many societies during the twentieth century (Ministry of Health 2003; World Health Organization 2000). Some of this recent data on the prevalence of obesity is represented in Table 5.4.

There is a remarkable similarity in the mean BMI for the countries represented in Table 5.4, despite the disparity in the fraction of obese people in each country, particularly men. The mean per cent obese for the women in the various countries, excluding the US, is 21.6 per cent (range = 19.2–23.5 per cent), while the mean for the same populations of men is 18.3 per cent (range = 14.7–21 per cent).

Even though mean BMI for each country does not reveal the variability in body composition within each country (a distribution that seems skewed towards higher BMIs for US citizens (Flegal *et al.* 2002) and is not adjusted for age), its similarity for these populations suggests that a BMI between 26 and 27 kg/m^2 is a 'normal' value. Identifying a BMI in excess of 25 kg/m^2 as being abnormal rests on two assumptions. First, the association between BMI and some non-communicable diseases, a relationship that seems to hold for all values of BMI above 19 kg/m^2 and, second, the assumption that the minimum healthy BMI is demonstrated in those countries that have low BMI. Thus the WHO have set a theoretical minimal BMI of 21 ± 1 kg/m^2 for all adults regardless of age and sex (Ezzati *et al.* 2002; Ministry of Health 2003; World Health Organization 2000).

A graphical representation of recent data on the prevalence of obesity in forty-one countries is presented in Figure 5.1 and shows the range of obesity levels in various countries where BMI has been measured. However, these data do not necessarily accurately represent the total populations of these countries as few of the surveys randomly sampled adults from all age groups and the numbers of people actually measured are rather small. So care must be taken when interpreting these figures.

Table 5.4 Mean BMI and prevalence of obesity for selected countries (most recent data)*

Country, year surveyed	Mean BMI kg/m^2		Obesity %**	
	Females	*Males*	*Females*	*Males*
Australia 1999/2000	26.4	26.9	22.2	19.3
England 2001	26.7	27.0	23.5	21.0
Europe*** 1990/1995	26.5	26.7	21.0	17.0
New Zealand 1997	26.1	26.2	19.2	14.7
Scotland 1998	26.5	26.5	22.1	19.6
US**** 1999/2000	26.1	26.3	33.4	27.5

Notes:
* Adapted from Table 80 (Ministry of Health 2003).
** BMI ≥ 32 kg/m^2 for Maori and Pacific Island people; 30 kg/m^2 for other ethnic groups.
*** Average of MONICA project data from (British Heart Foundation 2004).
**** BMI for US is 1988–94 data from British Heart Foundation (2004).

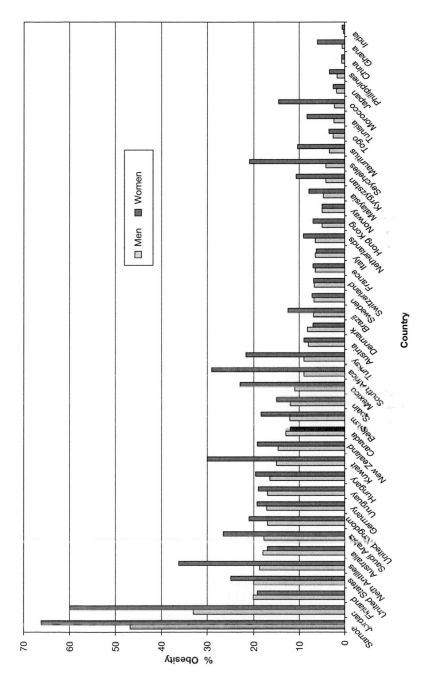

Figure 5.1 Worldwide prevalence of obesity based on BMI measures* (most recent data**).

Notes

* Data ranked from highest to lowest male % obesity with data from US, Australia, UK and NZ highlighted.
** Redrawn from data compiled by B. Swinburn for WHO (British Heart Foundation 2004).

The prevalence of obesity ranges from ≥ 1 per cent to 65 per cent of given populations, with women classified as having approximately twice the male obesity levels in fourteen countries. As they stand, it is difficult to know what these data mean. It is impossible to determine from Figure 5.1 what is a 'normal' healthy population level of obesity. The low levels of obesity in China and India do not represent healthy populations, as countries like Australia and New Zealand and Europe have a longer life expectancy and lower death rates for both men and women at all adult age groups than do Chinese and Indian populations (World Health Organization 2004). Clearly, the different obesity levels between women and men in countries as diverse as Ghana, Morocco, Kuwait and Samoa suggest that the roles women are expected to play in various societies affects their body size in ways that are not necessarily related to affluence or the adoption of Western food and exercise habits. However, these data contradict Table 5.5 (adapted from Seidell 2000) that indicates levels of obesity are higher in states with Western economies than in other countries.

It is not the intention of this chapter to discuss the social and economic factors that may be associated with different levels of body fat. Tables 5.4 and 5.5 and Figure 5.1, however, do illustrate that human obesity is a complex phenomenon and that the data on the prevalence of obesity lacks reliability and accuracy. Thus, statistics on the world prevalence of obesity need to be interpreted with healthy scepticism.

Apart from the apparent high prevalence of obesity in the world human population, much concern has been expressed about what seems like a dramatic *change* in the prevalence of obesity in the last decade; a change that the WHO has described as an epidemic (Ministry of Health 2003; World Health Organization 2000). In the US the prevalence of obesity has increased from 25.4 per cent in 1994 to 33.4 per cent in 2000 for females over twenty years and from 20.2 per cent to 27.5 per cent for males over twenty years (Flegal *et al.* 2002). Between 1993 and 2001 the prevalence of obesity in England rose from 16.4 per cent to 23.5 per cent in females over sixteen years and from 13.2 to 21.0 per cent for a comparable group of males (Ministry of Health 2003). In Australia the age-standardized prevalence of obesity has risen from 7.1 per cent in 1980 to 18.4 per cent (Cameron *et al.* 2003) in 2000, while in New Zealand the prevalence of

Table 5.5 Estimated obesity prevalence in states with different economic status

Region	Population 15 yrs+ (in millions)	Obesity (%)
Established market economies	640	15–20
Former socialist economies	330	20–25
India	535	0.5–1.0
China	825	0.5–1.0
Other Asia and islands	430	1–3
Sub-Sahara Africa	276	0.5–1.0
Latin America and Caribbean	280	5–10
Middle East	360	5–10

Source: adapted from Table 2.3 (Seidell, 2000) data obtained in 1996.

obesity has increased from 9.5 per cent to 14.7 per cent in males over fifteen years and from 12.6 to 19.2 per cent in females over fifteen years (Ministry of Health 2003).

Although these increases seem large, both the variability in the data for each country and the lack of precision in the measurement of obesity using BMI or waist circumference mean that most of these differences between the comparable but different populations are not statistically significant (Flegal *et al.* 2002). Consequently, we cannot be sure that the mean differences actually represent a large increase in the actual incidence of fatness, that is all individuals are actually accumulating more fat, or whether it is part of a long-term trend for an increase in overall body size in well nourished nations, or whether it is an artefact of measurement, population sampling and the resetting of arbitrary criteria for obesity (Flegal *et al.* 2002).

In summary, the prevalence of obesity and overweight seems high in many Western countries and it appears that the prevalence of obesity is increasing in most nations. However, because BMI or waist measures are crude measures of human adipose tissue and the populations sampled are not truly representative of each country, the actual prevalence of obesity is uncertain. It is also seems problematic that 50 per cent or more of many populations are classified as over-weight or obese and thereby labelled as being ill. It seems that the prevalence of obesity and its denigration as an 'epidemic' is a construct of highly suspect measure-ments and the setting of arbitrary universal criteria for overweight and obesity, criteria that inflate the levels of overweight and obesity in many populations to what seem like alarming levels. The extent of this inflation can be seen when we compare the average 14 per cent obesity of all New Zealand men with the mortality rate from ischaemic heart disease for each age group (Table 5.6). These data show that the incidence of a diagnosable cause of death – a real illness – ranges from 3.9 deaths per 100,000 men (0.004 deaths per 100 men) for 25–34 year olds to 845 deaths per 100,000 men (0.845 deaths per 100 men) for 65–74 year olds, while the average prevalence of obesity is 14 men in every 100. It seems odd that the prevalence of obesity is several orders of magnitude greater than deaths from an illness that is reported as a major cause of death when, in fact, the mean BMI *decreases* slightly for men aged 35–44 years even though the death rate from ischaemic heart disease for the same age group *increases*. Hence our suspicion that measures used to assess obesity paint a distorted picture of the prevalence of fat people in most communities.

Table 5.6 Ischaemic heart disease mortality and BMI for New Zealand males 1997

Age years	25–34	35–44	45–54	55–64	65–74	75+	Total
Deaths/100,000	3.9	28.3	106.5	312.8	845	2,626	291.4
Deaths/100	0.004	0.028	0.107	0.313	0.845	2.626	0.291
Mean BMI kg/m^2	25.8	26.9	27.5	27.4	26.7	25.3	26.2
BMI SD kg/m^2	4.1	4.3	4.4	4.4	3.4	2.8	4.4
Average obesity %							14

Source: adapted from Ministry of Health (2003).

Health risks of obesity

Obesity is considered to be a disease by the WHO because it is associated with an increased incidence of various diseases compared to the non-obese. Table 5.2 rates the 'risk' of diseases associated with increasing levels of BMI as 'average', increased and moderate. The impression is created that as individuals get fatter they increase their chances of becoming sick from a variety of diseases. However, as already mentioned, the 'risk' referred to in epidemiological studies of obesity is the prevalence of a given disease in populations of people with a BMI over 30 kg/m². It is not the actual personal risk that a person who has a BMI of more than 30 kg/m² has of getting that disease. As seen in Table 5.1, the relative risk of stroke in a population of women smokers compared to those women who have never smoked is 2.8. Similar comparisons of all cause mortality have been made between populations of people with a BMI ≤ 24.9 kg/m² and populations with BMI ≥ 25 kg/m² (Bray 2000, 2003; Jarrett 1986; Seidell *et al.* 1989; World Health Organization 2000). As can be seen from Figures 5.2 and 5.3, the relative risk of death plotted against BMI reveals a curvilinear relationship that is either a J-shaped curve (Figure 5.2) or a U-shaped curve (Figure 5.3) with the relative risk of dying being greatest for the very lean (BMI < 21 kg/m²) and the very fat (BMI ≥ 31 kg/m²). In both these figures it can be seen that the relative risk of people dying in a population of individuals with a BMI above 30 kg/m² is between 2–3 times greater than in a comparable population with a BMI below 30 kg/m². This means that in a group of people with a BMI ≥ 30 kg/m² it is probable that

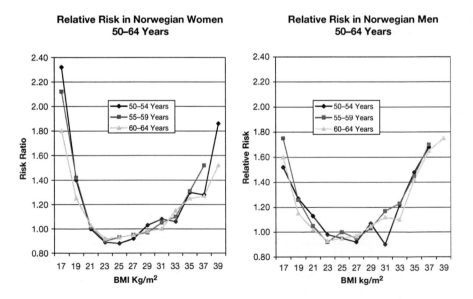

Figure 5.2 Relative mortality in Norwegian women and men*.

Source: Redrawn from Seidell *et al.* (1989).

Note: *Data compiled from the 200,000 deaths recorded by cause in a population of approximately 1.8 million Norwegian women and men followed for an average of ten years.

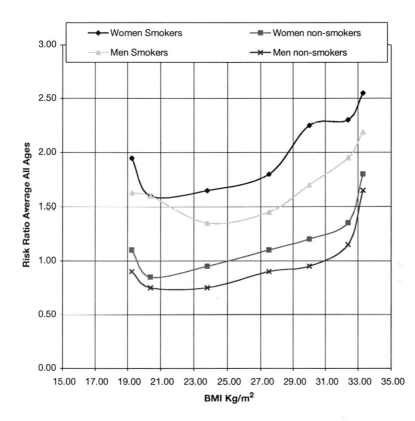

Figure 5.3 Average mortality risk for all age groups in relation to BMI in American smokers and non-smokers.

Source: Seidell *et al.* (1989).

2–3 people will die for every 1 person who dies in a comparable group of people who have a BMI ≤ 29.9 kg/m². It does not mean that any given person with a BMI ≥ 30 kg/m² is 2–3 times more likely to die than an individual with a BMI ≤ 29.9 kg/m².

It is also important to put into perspective the magnitude of the problem. If we use the ischaemic heart disease mortality rates for New Zealand males aged 45–54 listed in Table 5.6, we see that in 1997 312 men in every 100,000 died from ischaemic heart disease. Now, if we assume that 14 per cent of these 100,000 men were obese then that equates to 14,000 obese men. Assuming that the ischaemic heart disease mortality rate of these obese men is twice the average mortality rate of all the men aged 45–54 (Table 5.6), then in 1997 it is possible that 87 of the 312 ischaemic heart disease deaths were obese men. In other words, more than three times as many New Zealand non-obese men aged 45–54 years died of ischaemic heart disease in 1997 than obese men.

Unlike ischaemic heart disease, which seems to show a risk ratio between 1 and 2.5 with increasing body mass (Table 5.4), non-insulin dependent diabetes mellitus seems to be up to sixty times as prevalent in obese people than it is in non-obese (Bray 2000, 2003; Ezzati *et al.* 2003; Keys 1980; World Health Organization 2000). Consequently, non-insulin diabetes is considered to be a disease triggered or caused by obesity. However, it is not possible to graph the risk ratio of the incidence of non-insulin dependent diabetes mellitus and BMI because non-insulin dependent diabetes mellitus is not usually listed as a cause of death and the criteria for diagnosing it varies over time and locality (World Health Organization 2000).

Associations between levels of fatness and other diseases have been reported in several studies but as these diseases have a relatively low prevalence they are not discussed here (Bray 2000; Ministry of Health 2003; World Health Organization 2000).

Although the association between obesity and two common non-communicable diseases, ischaemic heart disease and non-insulin dependent diabetes mellitus seems clear, the WHO in its report on managing the global 'obesity epidemic' draws attention to the difficulties in evaluating the actual health consequences of obesity. It is difficult to design epidemiological studies that follow a cohort of people long enough and in enough detail to show a clear relationship between the incidence of a disease and the incidence of obesity. Most studies report the prevalence, not the incidence of obesity in a population, and relate that to the incidence of various diseases over relatively short periods of time. Alternatively, they compare the prevalence of obesity and the incidence of diseases in a population for a given cohort with a comparable cohort several years later. Thus, at best, the correlation between obesity prevalence and disease incidence provides an indication of a possible link between body size and health for a population. These population studies provide little or no information about the impact of fatness and changing levels of fat on the health of individuals. It is important to reiterate this point because, as Pearce (1996) has made clear, there is a tendency for epidemiological findings to be reported as risks to individuals rather than as population risks. Consequently, much of the rhetoric around the so-called 'obesity epidemic' is based on the spurious claim that obesity *causes* or is one of the important *multiple causes* of non-insulin dependent diabetes mellitus or ischaemic heart disease (Krieger 1994). In fact, if the evidence that associates obesity with disease is examined using the criteria laid down by Bradford Hill (1977) then we have no justification at all in saying that obesity causes ischaemic heart disease or non-insulin dependent diabetes mellitus (Bradford Hill 1977; Skrabanek 1992).

Bradford Hill's canons for inferring causality

THE STRENGTH OF THE ASSOCIATION

There must be a strong association between the disease and the observed variable. That is, the risk ratio must be large. For example, studies suggest that the death from lung cancer is 9–10 times higher (risk ratio = 9–10) in a population of middle-aged male smokers than in a population of middle-aged male non-smokers and 20–30 higher in a population of middle-aged male heavy smokers than in a population of middle-aged male non-smokers (Doll and Hill 1964).

On the other hand, the death rate from coronary thrombosis in the same population of male smokers compared to those middle-aged men who are non-smokers is no more than twice or less (risk ratio ≤ 2). Thus, it is difficult to separate smoking from other possible environmental factors as a primary cause of coronary thrombosis in middle-aged men (Bradford Hill 1977). The risk ratio for the incidence of ischaemic heart disease and a BMI greater than 27 is between 1.1 and 2 for all age groups of men and women (Bouchard 2000; Bray 2000; Ezzati *et al.* 2003; Garrow 1978; Keys 1980; Ministry of Health 2003; Pi-Sunyer 2002; Seidell *et al.* 1989; World Health Organization 2000). Thus, the association between high levels of body fat and ischaemic heart disease is rather weak, certainly not as strong as the association between cigarette smoking and lung cancer for all age groups (Doll and Hill 1964).

On the other hand, there is a strong association between over-fatness and non-insulin dependent diabetes mellitus that suggests a causal relationship. However, there is some concern about the accuracy of diagnosis of both the disease and obesity so these data remain problematic.

CONSISTENCY

The association is observed repeatedly with different studies that differ rather than being exact repetitions of the same study. For example, a variety of studies have shown a clear link between lung cancer and smoking (Bradford Hill 1977). As can be seen outlined earlier, there is a consistent finding of a weak relationship between ischaemic heart disease and excess body fat but the studies mostly rely on measuring prevalence of obesity and comparing that with the incidence of the disease so it is not clear that fat or changing levels of fat are what are implicated in the disease–obesity link. The same argument holds for the apparent consistent relationship between obesity and non-insulin dependent diabetes mellitus.

SPECIFICITY

The association is limited to a specific population or environment and particular types of diseases and there is no association with other causes of dying then there is a strong argument for causation (Bradford Hill 1977). This is not the case when examining data that associates obesity with ischaemic heart disease or non-insulin dependent diabetes mellitus. Ischaemic heart disease, non-insulin dependent diabetes mellitus and obesity have associations with age, sex, ethnicity, social standing and poverty, associations that are impossible to disentangle. (Boreham and Riddoch 2003; Bouchard 2000; Fogelholm *et al.* 1999; Garrow 1978, 1992; Hall and Stewart 1989; Hardman and Stensel 2003; Jarrett 1986; Jeffcote 1998; Keys 1980; Klein 1996; Knapp 1983; Mayer 1983a; Murray *et al.* 1999; Must 2003; Panter-Brick 2003; Pi-Sunyer 2002; Pollock 1995; Schoenfielder and Wieser 1983; West 1974)

CLEAR RELATIONSHIP IN TIME

The temporal relationship of the observed association must be considered carefully – which is the cart and which is the horse? This is most important for slow developing, so-called 'degenerative' diseases. Does a particular diet lead to obesity and ischaemic heart disease or do the early stages of ischaemic heart disease lead to particular dietary habits and obesity? Do people without a predisposition to ischaemic heart disease have a natural predisposition to physical activity or not gaining weight? Does the development of insulin resistance associated with non-insulin dependent diabetes mellitus cause people to gain weight or does weight gain trigger insulin resistance? Clearly, we do not know the temporal relationship between large weight gain and non-insulin dependent diabetes mellitus or ischaemic heart disease.

BIOLOGICAL GRADIENT

Some associations show a dose response curve as in the relationship between the number of cigarettes smoked per day and lung cancer (Doll and Hill 1964). The complex aetiology of obesity makes the slight increase in ischaemic heart disease and non-insulin dependent diabetes mellitus with increasing body fat a difficult biological gradient to interpret and the gradient between overweight and non-insulin dependent diabetes mellitus is certainly not a clear linear relationship as one would expect from a dose response curve (Boreham and Riddoch 2003; Bouchard 2000; Bray 2000; Ezzati et al. 2002; Garrow 1992; Hardman and Stensel 2003; Ministry of Health 2003; World Health Organization 2000).

BIOLOGICAL PLAUSIBILITY

A causal association is more likely if there is a clear biological mechanism, such as bacillus bacteria causing TB or the carcinogens in tobacco causing lung cancer. But we cannot always expect this as the biology may not be known to science, as in the case of malaria and mosquito before the discovery of the parasite carried by the anopheles mosquito, or cancer in chimney sweeps in the eighteenth century before the understanding of carcinogens in soot. The biology of obesity is complex and the physiological relationship between adipose tissue and ischaemic heart disease or non-insulin dependent diabetes mellitus is unclear even though it is tempting to accept the individual biological malfunction argument that weight gain is a simply either eating too much or not exercising enough (Brownell and Stunkard 1989; Critser 2003; Fitzgerald 1981; Garrow 1978; Hall and Stewart 1989; Hardman and Stensel 2003; Le Fanu 1987; McKenna and Riddoch 2003; Martînez-Gonzàlez et al. 1999; Schoenfielder and Wieser 1983; Shell 2002; Stacey 1994; Swinburn et al. 1999; Tremblay et al. 1983; West 1974; Westerterp 1999; Wooley and Wooley 1984).

COHERENCE OF THE EVIDENCE

The cause-and-effect interpretation of an association should not seriously conflict with the generally known facts of the natural history and biology of the disease. The incidence of ischaemic heart disease should show coherence with changes in activity patterns, diet and levels of excess fat over time – all overweight and obese people must over eat or not exercise. Clearly this is not the case with every obese person. It seems that the incidence of ischaemic heart disease is declining along with an apparent decrease in activity patterns and increasing body mass. Similarly, not all obese people are pre-diabetic. Some thin people also suffer from non-insulin dependent diabetes mellitus. So the data linking obesity with disease is too lumpy to assume a causal link.

EXPERIMENT

Experimental studies should agree with the epidemiological evidence. Although there are some metabolic studies that suggest exercise ameliorates the insulin resistance characteristic of non-insulin dependent diabetes mellitus by improving glucose transport into muscle cells, there is no direct evidence to show that the excess adipose tissue in fat people is directly responsible for the development of insulin resistance (Hardman and Stensel 2003; Viru and Harro 2003). It is just as likely that the resistance to insulin by muscle cells results in high levels of circulating insulin which in turn facilitates the storage of fat. Similarly, experimental studies that have attempted to reduce excess body fat by manipulating diet and deliberate exercise have failed in the long-term to significantly alter the body composition of most, if not all, obese people even though increased fitness may have improved their cardiovascular function and their susceptibility to ischaemic heart disease if they continue to exercise. Thus, the experimental evidence to support a causal link between obesity and ischaemic heart disease is highly problematic (Burstyn 1990; Garrow 1992; Hardman and Stensel 2003; Jeffcote 1998; Keys 1980; Pi-Sunyer 2002; Saltin *et al.* 1968; Shephard 1997; Tremblay *et al.* 1983; Viru and Harro 2003; Westerterp 1999).

In summary, there is insufficient evidence to support the common assumption that obesity causes non-insulin dependent diabetes mellitus or ischaemic heart disease. Bradford Hill's (1977) criteria for establishing cause using epidemiological data are not met by any of the epidemiological studies of obesity and it is obvious from the experimental studies on exercise and diet that the apparent increase in average body weights of people all over the world cannot be explained by the biological malfunction of individuals. Nancy Krieger (1994) argues that epidemiology can limit our understanding of the complex 'intertwining ensemble' of biological, environmental and social factors that make up human life and health if epidemiologists adhere to single or multiple causation theories to explain their observations. The same is true, I suspect for exercise physiologists and much of medical science. Consequently, the responsibility of scientists, physical educationists and other health professionals is to be aware that our understanding of the 'obesity epidemic' depends on how we perceive the 'facts' and 'fictions' that construct this apparent modern plague. This chapter challenges the science facts and fictions that underpin the arguments of those who advocate that we are in the midst of a modern-day pestilence, a pestilence called the 'obesity epidemic'.

Summary

Although the statistics suggest that the world population is getting fatter and that there appears to be an association between levels of fat and a variety of non-communicable diseases, there are several reasons why we must be sceptical about the claims of an 'obesity epidemic':

- BMI is not a sensitive or accurate measure of human adiposity. It does not take into account the diversity of male and female human physique so the classification of people with a BMI greater than 25 kg/m^2 as overweight and a BMI of 30 kg/m^2 as obese is, at best, an arbitrary index of fatness.
- Recent changes in the BMI classification of overweight from 27 kg/m^2 to 25 kg/m^2 highlight both the arbitrary nature of BMI as a measure of fatness and the tendency to conflate corpulence with extreme levels of fatness.
- Population measures of obesity using BMI do not accurately represent most of the populations studied.
- It does not make sense to classify large body size as a disease simply because it has a weak association with various non-communicable diseases.
- There is little or no evidence to support the assumption that obesity *causes* non-communicable diseases such non-insulin dependent diabetes mellitus and ischaemic heart disease rather than being a symptom of these diseases.
- When the prevalence of obesity is related to the incidence of non-communicable diseases some 20 per cent or more of a population is classified as obese and unwell and some 30 to 50 per cent classified as overweight and potentially ill, creating a science fiction spectre of hordes of large, ill people populating our planet.
- There is an assumption that the root cause of the prevalence of obesity in various populations can be explained by the malfunction of food intake and energy output of individuals, a malfunction that can be managed by every normal person.

Conclusion

The simplification and misreading of the evidence about human body size reinforces our cultural prejudices about the sinfulness of being fat rather than alerting us to the mysterious, dynamic and contingent processes of biological and cultural evolution that continue to shape individuals and societies.

Notes

1   Strictly speaking mortality and morbidity rates differ from cumulative incidence rate in that the number of deaths are reported with respect to the average population over a given time rather than the actual number of people in a defined population. Thus the mortality rate for HIV/AIDS for 1997 in NZ is calculated by cumulating the number of HIV/AIDS deaths in 1997 and expressing them in relation to the average population for NZ in 1997.
2   Fat levels in humans can be measured accurately using sophisticated methods from underwater weighing, isotope dilution, magnetic resonance imaging, bioelectrical impedance and dual-energy X-ray absorptiometry but these techniques are expensive and not suitable for population studies (Bray 2003).
3   It is interesting that anorexia nervosa is seen as an eating disorder rather than as a disease. Recent books on the perils of overweight not only accept that obesity is a disease but also claim that it is a behavioural and eating disorder (Critser 2003).

6   The search for a cause

It is not always the case that in order to solve a particular problem a precise understanding of its cause or causes is needed. A number of scholars have pointed out that the European health reformers of the nineteenth century had very little knowledge about the medical aetiology of the major health problems that afflicted the urban poor. Dubos (1971) argues that these reformist campaigns, which agitated for cleaner food, water and air, were motivated mostly by humanitarian rather than scientific impulses. It would be some years before the microbial origins of these diseases were discovered and there are those who seriously question whether these later scientific discoveries contributed significantly to improvements in public health (McKeown 1979).

So far in this book we have raised questions about the legitimacy of describing overweight and obesity as diseases and as a looming health disaster. But if we leave these issues to one side and engage with the 'obesity epidemic' on its own terms, what can we say about the most popular causal explanations, particularly the idea that 'Western lifestyles' are responsible? Our argument will be that, first, this claim is extremely difficult to justify given the available evidence and second, that it is, in reality, quite meaningless, misleading and decidedly unhelpful. Unlike many who claim expertise in this area, we think that the reasons for changes in the levels of overweight and obesity in Western countries remain largely mysterious and that scientific research has done little to clarify the current situation.

It is hardly an original insight on our part to point out that, faced with mystery, humans have historically resorted to telling stories as a way of making sense of their world. But we should never forget also that stories are rarely disinterested, neutral accounts of the way things are. Either wittingly or unwittingly, they present partial and partisan accounts of how the world works and how it should be. Therefore, our argument is not only that existing causational explanations of the 'obesity epidemic' rest on largely unsubstantiated claims, but that they also avoid and obscure other ways of interpreting obesity statistics and thinking about body weight.

Our purpose in all of this is not to suggest that these other ways of thinking are ideologically neutral or that we have offered the last word about the science of overweight and obesity. Despite our collective air of certainty and claims to 'expertise', all of us – epidemiologists, exercise scientists, sociologists, medical practitioners and physical educators – work in a context of profound uncertainty. What is interesting is not so much that people cling to a story in order to manage this uncertainty, but that so many cling to the same story.

The evolutionary explanation

The scientific literature generally claims that overweight and obesity have exploded over the last twenty or thirty years, usually pointing to what would appear to be quite low levels of Western overweight and obesity during the 1960s and even 1970s. And yet, when it comes to demonstrating how 'modern Western lifestyles' have changed (and, therefore, *caused* rapid rises in body weight) scientists rarely look closely at Western life during the 1950s or any other period from the relatively recent past when, at least according to the contemporary scientific literature, overweight and obesity were not the catastrophic problems they are today.

Quite apart from the unresolved nature of the biological processes that lead to overweight and obesity (see Chapters 3 and 4), research into how much people eat, how much recreational exercise they do and how many calories they use going about their average daily lives is beset with methodological problems (also see Chapter 3). These problems multiply when attention turns to large populations or when the time-frame of interest is a number of days or longer. Needless to say, precise comparisons between entire populations are difficult and extremely scarce in the literature.

In this context, it is perhaps not surprising that studies comparing the energy consumption and expenditure of large populations during different periods of history are also rare. One of the few areas of empirical study to attempt comparisons of this kind is what is known as 'comparative primate energetics' (Leonard and Robertson 1997). In this work, our contemporary lives are compared with those of our pre-*Homo sapiens* ancestors alive millions of years ago (Eaton *et al.* 1988; Park 1988).

Given the problems involved in measuring the energy intake and expenditure of populations alive today, it is difficult to see how comparisons with our prehistoric ancestors could be anything other than speculative and very imprecise. For those wishing to explain the 'obesity epidemic' it would also seem to be an extraordinarily indirect route to take, akin to going from London to Manchester via the South Pole. For those interested in comparisons, we surely know much more about day-to-day Western lives during the 1950s or, for that matter, the 1850s. But apart from vague references to 'technology' and the alleged disappearance of 'manual labour', *precisely* how *contemporary* Western lifestyles differ from those of fifty or 150 years ago is a question few appear prepared to tackle.

The explanation that the 'obesity epidemic' has come about because our current lifestyles are out of step with our prehistorically formed genetic make-up is now widespread in the scientific literature (e.g. Friedman 2003; Peters *et al.* 2002). Klein writes:

> Until recently in our evolutionary history, we kept obesity at bay by maintaining a reasonable balance between our genes, which are geared to consume and store energy, and a harsh environment, which kept energy intake down and energy expenditure up. Nations that have become technologically evolved with labour-saving devices, sedentary jobs, and abundant food supplies have found that these technological successes have dealt a serious blow to the precarious energy balance equation. The United States and other industrialized

countries are getting fatter and obesity is a major and growing public health problem throughout the world.

(Klein 1999: 1061)

Blair *et al.* provide slightly more detail:

> Remains of our early, human-like ancestors, *Australopithecus afarensis*, have been dated as 3.5–3.8 million years old. Nearly 4 million years of evolution of the human family, *Hominidae*, produced modern humans, *H. sapiens*, by approximately 35,000 years ago. The earliest hominids were scavengers; but, by about 1 million years ago, hunting and gathering was firmly established as a way of life for human beings. A hunting and gathering lifestyle involves high energy expenditure for several days a week, with peak bouts of strenuous physical activity. The next major change in human sociocultural development was the domestification of plants and animals and the rise of agriculture, which occurred only 10,000 years ago. Industrialization advances over the past 200 years led to further urbanization and the rise of the middle-class. But, even during this period, most individuals had relatively high energy expenditures compared with those of society at the end of the twentieth century.

(Blair *et al.* 1992: 99)

One of the most striking aspects of this form of explanation is the enormous leaps in time. In fact, most writers in this area are content to jump from a few million years BC or so to today in a single bound. In this respect, Blair *et al.*'s mention of the intervening industrial revolution makes theirs a comparatively detailed account.

It is important to notice the way our prehistoric past is woven into discussions about the 'obesity epidemic' while, at the same time, keeping in mind the scientific literature's contention that the 'obesity epidemic' is a new phenomenon. If, as Damcott *et al.* (2003) claim, our genes have not changed in the last thirty years, what then is the value of talking about evolution at all? Of course, we are currently living through a period in which evolutionary explanations for almost every aspect of human life are being proposed. We might then wonder whether the inclusion of evolution and genetics in discussion about recent changes in human body weight owes more to intellectual fashion than scientific parsimony.

One of the problems with using evolutionary theory to explain the current state of human affairs centres on the use of what are often called 'just-so' stories (Fuller 1997). A 'just-so' story is a story about the past that is invented in order to explain the present. Rather than being a story based on evidence, it is a story wheeled in 'after the fact' to support an existing hypothesis; a hypothesis about a hypothesis as it were.

It is important not to misinterpret our point here. Many brilliant natural historians have devoted their careers to developing quite detailed accounts of the lives of our primate ancestors. However, this is a very different matter from calculating their average daily caloric consumption and expenditure against which other populations can be compared. As we have pointed out, comparisons of this kind between populations of people separated by much less time or geography are rare.

Panter-Brick's review of the small existing literature concerning the average physical activity levels of populations has warned against simplistic assumptions about our ancestors:

> descriptions of hunter-gatherer life – whether ancestral or modern – all too often promote over-simplified portrayals of levels of physical activity. There are few studies that do not lump together men and women, that portray the activities of children as well as adults, or that appraise variability in daily activity patterns. The net result is a stereotypical view of levels of activity to characterise the activity of humans.
>
> (Panter-Brick 2003: 264)

Her review arrives at conclusions some may find surprising. For example, studies of university students and urban residents found 'moderately high' physical activity levels. In other research, some present-day hunter–gatherer societies (often used in research as a proxy for ancient hunter–gatherers) recorded higher physical activity levels while others had levels lower than existing estimates for Western urban populations. Chimpanzees, with 98 per cent genetic similarity to humans, had very low levels and few cases of obesity. In some groups of hunter-gatherers, men did most of the strenuous physical work while women did it in others. In general, the hunter-gatherer data exhibited a great deal of variation between studies and some researchers postulate similar variability across seasons. In short, some comparisons suggest Western populations are more active than current hunter-gather/forager populations and others suggest the opposite.

Elsewhere, Panter-Brick (2002: 627) also describes assumptions that physical activity decreased when humans moved from hunting to agriculture or that men were more active than women in either context as 'facile'. Both of these literature reviews lead to an important, if not all that surprising conclusion: while it may tempting to romanticize about our ancestors living simple, television-less and fast food-less lives, in balance with their surroundings, eating only what they need to survive and never far away from their next health-enhancing bout of exercise, the truth is almost certainly more complex. Stereotypes are rarely a credible substitute for the messiness of reality. And as Panter-Brick points out, there is probably very little about the biomedical health of hunter–gatherers (contemporary or ancient) that we would wish for ourselves.

There are probably a number of explanations as to why obesity researchers talk about a period in the history of life so distant and yet with such confidence. But perhaps the most obvious reason is the fact that very little scientific data exist to support the conclusion that Western populations have become more sedentary in recent decades (discussed later). Therefore, it is probably much safer to speculate about the behaviour of populations – 'they consumed x thousand calories per day and expended y thousand' – that are millions of years dead because there are few, if any, solid arguments for rejecting one estimate over another.

It will be objected that the reason why pre-*Homo sapiens* energy consumption and expenditure is of interest is because it was during the approximately three to four million year period prior to the emergence of *Homo sapiens* that our current genetic make-up was established. Further, it will be argued, it is this genetic make-up, the so-called 'thrifty gene' theory, which *now* predisposes our society to overweight and obesity in times of relative plenty. In response, we would make four points as rejoinder.

First, no amount of talk about 'thrifty genes' alters the fact that our knowledge about the energy consumption of these distant civilizations is only ever likely to be extremely imprecise. We would remind readers how hard it is to arrive at firm estimates regarding populations (not to mention individuals) alive today. Recall too our earlier point about contemporary populations: not only do we have only crude techniques for estimating pre-*Homo sapiens* energy consumption and expenditure at our disposal, we have no way of knowing how accurate any given estimate is since there is nothing to compare it to. The 'thrifty gene' theory is, in this sense, quite unfalsifiable.

Second, in the context of trying to explain the 'obesity epidemic', recourse to prehistory is a 'high-risk' strategy. For the 'thrifty gene' theory to hold true it is necessary to argue that following the millions of years in which the 'thrifty gene' was established, human societies existed in relative energy balance, or at least never got to a point where energy *imbalance* was particularly widespread. Thus, the 'obesity epidemic' must represent a tipping point when Western societies, *en masse*, suddenly crossed over a threshold, which had remained uncrossed for millennia. If *this* is true, then the vague argument that 'Western lifestyles' are to blame begins to look even more unhelpful. What is needed here are clear and specific arguments about concrete events that have caused increasing overweight and obesity in some, but not all, communities, not vague allusions to society in general.

Third, as with many 'just-so' evolutionary stories, the 'thrifty gene' theory appears to imagine our prehistoric ancestors to be of one kind and to have lived in particular ways. How else do scientists arrive at estimates of the daily caloric estimates for these creatures? But what if, as seems likely, the millions of years at stake in this theory were marked by different ways of life, in different places, changing over centuries? Which would we choose to be the 'gold standard' 'thrifty gene' moment? Of course, the artefacts that scientists study are given to us by luck; they do not have the luxury of being able to choose which period to study. From whence comes the confidence that the partial snapshots of life derived from these artefacts are representative of the period in which the 'thrifty gene' was established?

Fourth, even if the 'thrifty gene' idea is true, it is not at all clear how this helps us understand the present. Does anyone actually doubt that we live rather different kinds of lives to our pre-*Homo sapiens* ancestors? What exactly are we to do with this knowledge? Adopt prehistoric lifestyles? The hypothesis that pre-*Homo sapiens* developed 'thrifty genes' is actually quite independent of questions about their average daily caloric expenditure. The 'thrifty gene' hypothesis is more concerned with unstable food supplies – 'feast or famine' – and it is difficult to see how any energy expenditure estimates – very high or very low – would have any bearing on this hypothesis. In terms of the 'obesity epidemic', talk of evolution and 'thrifty genes' is almost certainly a rather large red herring. Contrary to what McMichael (2002) has claimed, evolution and 'thrifty genes' are not the key to understanding what makes us 'tick' or 'sick'.

As we have seen, there are scientists who are convinced that human energy expenditure has dropped significantly over the last *fifty* years. We will see in the remainder of this chapter that this claim is not supported by data. However, we have far more artefacts to study from the 1950s than three million BC and so anyone curious enough could at least try to assess whether we were more physically active in the 1950s. But at present it remains the case that most obesity scientists who express an opinion on the matter speak more confidently about energy expenditure during our distant prehistory than during periods we know much more about.

'Environments' and human nature

There is precious little evidence that the positions scientists hold differ greatly from the generalized notion of the 'environment', which we saw articulated in print-media coverage of the 'obesity epidemic' in Chapter 2. Readers will recall that the idea of a generalized environment that is 'obesity conducive' is central to the construction of the current situation as an 'epidemic'. In other words, if it is true that we are all at risk of falling victim to the same disease then we must all be exposed to the same risk factors. This is the 'everyone everywhere' version of the 'obesity epidemic' and it is a version that appears to shape the thinking of contributors to magazines, newspapers and scientific journals alike.

As with the print-media, people writing for scientific journals use words such as 'Western', 'population', 'our', 'society' and 'environment' apparently without hesitation. In the midst of their scholarly analysis of the allegedly catastrophic economic costs of obesity to the US and what they call 'sedentarism', Colditz and Mariani conclude:

> With this added understanding of the magnitude of the burden of inactivity, we might then better motivate the political will to support the social changes necessary to increase energy expenditure in our society and avoid the excess weight gain that is associated with our Western ways of living.
>
> (Colditz and Mariani 2000: 62)

In *Medicine and Science in Sports and Exercise*, Hill and Melanson write:

> As the environment becomes more obesity-conducive (as has the environment in the United States), the average body weight and fatness of the population will increase. Genes may protect some individuals from becoming obese and contribute to differences in the extent to which obesity occurs, but environmental factors may be overwhelming our genetic defenses against obesity.
>
> (Hill and Melanson 1999: S515)

It is interesting to note here that one's genetic make-up is seen as the main mediating factor between people and the obesity inducing 'environment' rather than, say, one's financial income. In the same edition of this journal, Claude Bouchard and Steven Blair go even further, generalizing this already generalized view of the 'environment' to the entire world:

> The increase in the prevalence of overweight and obesity cases worldwide is occurring against a background of a progressive reduction in the energy

expended for work and occupational activities as well as for the accomplishment of personal chores and daily necessities. The reduction in energy expenditure associated with physical activity brought about by automation and changing job and professional environmental circumstances has been nothing but dramatic in the second half of this century. In contrast, the energy expenditure of leisure time physical activity may have increased slightly but not enough to keep pace with the changes brought about by urbanization and automation.

(Bouchard and Blair 1999: S498)

In Chapter 2 we also saw that, hand in hand with the idea that we live in a generally obesity conducive environment, goes the idea we are all weak of will and prone to gluttony. It is worth noting that these two generalizations are not necessarily compatible. For example, if our objective were to explain why the 'obesity epidemic' was happening we could argue that the great majority of humans find themselves in an environment that they did not explicitly choose. Therefore, it is not moral failing that makes us fat but rather the world in which we are forced to live. A contrary argument might suggest that nobody is being forced to drive cars or eat junk food. The more alarmist claims about the potential spread of overweight and obesity notwithstanding, it is still the case that many Westerners manage to maintain a 'healthy weight'. Thus, according to this line of thinking, overweight and obesity are simply a matter of people choosing to live a certain way, and for this they have only themselves to blame. Putting to one side the veracity of either of these arguments, notice how generalizations about people or the 'environment' are absolutely indispensable if one's purpose is to account for an 'epidemic' – a sickness which is affecting 'everyone everywhere'. Without these generalizations it is distinctly possible that the thing you are trying to explain will look less and less like an 'epidemic'. Furthermore, without these generalizations a more detailed look at who is and who is not affected might be called for.

In 'obesity epidemic' thinking, these two line lines of argument are usually brought together to form a worst of all possible worlds scenario: we live in an obesity conducive environment *and* we are morally weak. In fact, as the epidemiologist Garry Egger argued in Chapter 2, the 'fact' that we live in an obesity conducive environment can actually be seen as *an expression* of our slothful nature – we eat fatty foods, avoid exercise and build physical and social environments that reduce physical activity all because human nature is geared towards finding the easiest and most comfortable way of living. It scarcely needs to be pointed out that this is not a point of view that has been arrived at by weighing up scientific evidence. Above all, it is a moral judgement.

Eating ourselves sick?

In the previous section we argued that generalized notions of 'Western society' and the 'environment' do not offer sophisticated intellectual tools for understanding the current situation. It is perhaps not surprising, therefore, that many obesity scientists lament the lack of success of existing anti-overweight and obesity strategies given that they begin with the assumption that we are all getting fat for roughly the same reasons.

The relative simplicity of the 'everyone everywhere' story is an extension of the simplicity of the energy-in/energy-out law discussed earlier. In other words, if we begin with the assumption that an individual's body weight is a simple consequence of how much they eat and the physical activity they do, then it is difficult to see how population-level increases in body weight could be addressed in a more nuanced fashion. Thus, many obesity researchers claim that the 'obesity epidemic' has been caused, at least in part, because people eat too much. For example, according to Bouchard and Blair: 'The availability of relatively inexpensive and highly palatable foods in almost unlimited abundance is undoubtedly contributing to the epidemic as some of the affected individuals eat many times a day and consume large portions' (Bouchard and Blair 1999: S499).

The lack of supporting references for this statement, usually a standard academic practice, is also apparent in Dionne and Tremblay (2000) who, in the following passage, appear to compensate for this lack of evidence by invoking the scientific authority of evolutionary theory (discussed previously):

> During the first stages of humanity, man had to hunt and fish for foods. More recently, man became able to cultivate and breed his foods. Nowadays, new technology has enhanced the availability of food and facilitated its preparation. Foods are now much more palatable and plentiful. In the meantime, the fast pace and variety of social events in the modern lifestyle have directed the population to select fast meals, often rich in fat and simple sugars, frequently accompanied by alcohol consumption. Taken together, these changes are very likely to have contributed to an overconsumption of energy-dense foods.
>
> (Dionne and Tremblay 2000: 151)

In another example, Peters *et al.* invoke the vague notion of 'the environment' to make their case:

> The environment promotes low energy expenditure, largely because little or no physical activity is required for daily living. (1) Simultaneously, the environment encourages overeating through an abundant food supply that is high in fat and energy density, easily available, relatively inexpensive, good tasting and served in large portions (1).
>
> (Peters *et al.* 2002: 70)

This passage is interesting because the digit '1' in parentheses, indicating a supporting reference, refers to an article written by two of the four authors (Hill and Peters 1998), published in the journal *Science*, which, rather than providing supporting evidence for both claims, simply restates them. The impression created, at least for us, is that these claims are held by the authors to be self-evident. A number of other researchers appear to claim that increased food intake has self-evidently helped to bring about the 'obesity epidemic' (e.g. Chakravarthy and Booth 2003; Magarey *et al.* 2001; Nestle and Jacobson 2000).

However, supporting evidence for the idea of a food-led 'obesity epidemic' is quite difficult to find. Rolland-Cachera and Bellisle's (2002) review of the literature concerning the nutritional determinants of childhood overweight and obesity is a case in point. They begin by referring back to a similar literature review by Whitehead *et al.* (1982) that found a consistent decline in average energy intake among Western children between 1935 and 1978. Rolland-Cachera and Bellisle's review of studies published since Whitehead *et al.*'s paper strongly suggests that this trend has continued: that is, a consistent reduction in the average energy intake of boys and girls (but especially girls) from a number of Western coun-tries. In fact, almost all the studies included reported a reduction in energy intake (one study reported no change) and all reported a reduction in fat intake. They conclude:

> today's children, in both developing and industrialized countries, are taller and heavier than in the past, in spite of relatively stable or falling energy intakes among children from industrialized countries. Their fat intakes are falling and the percentage of total energy derived from protein is rising. Lower energy intakes are apparent even among young children and seem to be more pronounced in girls than in boys.
>
> (Rolland-Cachera and Bellisle 2002: 74)

They also consider studies of adult dietary intake from Britain, Japan, the Netherlands and the United States, all bar one of which reported reductions in average energy intake (one found no change). In addition, only the Japanese study found an increase in fat intake; the others all reported decreases. Rolland-Cachera and Bellisle conclude that evidence pointing to a widespread increase in the proportion of protein in the diet is a more compelling causal explanation for increased overweight and obesity:

> In summary, it is often suggested that high energy or high fat intakes pre-dispose to obesity. No clear evidence for this emerges from epidemiological studies conducted in children – although similar inconsistencies are reported in adults. Thus, contrary to the usual views, protein excess, rather than fat excess, may well account for the various characteristics associated with obesity during growth.
>
> (Rolland-Cachera and Bellisle 2002: 79)

The obvious criticism of this conclusion, and one that is made by many researchers, is that under-reporting of dietary intake may play a significant role in these results. Rolland-Cachera and Bellisle concede the point. However, they point out that 'consistent tendencies do emerge from diverse studies' (Rolland-Cachera and Bellisle 2002: 74). We would add that in order to undermine Rolland-Cachera and Bellisle's findings, it would have to be argued that, not only is under-reporting a consistent problem in this research, the level of under-reporting must have *accelerated* since the 1930s. For example, a reasonably consistent level of under-reporting by people in nutritional research would consistently under-estimate people's total energy intake, but it would have no bearing on longitudinal comparisons *between* these totals. We might even speculate that in recent times, with food labelling and greater general nutritional knowledge, the average lay person is much better able to estimate their energy intake than was the case in the 1930s. Whether or not this speculation is reasonable, we are not aware of any evidence that the level of under-reporting in nutritional research has changed over time. And while some have speculated that overweight and obese children and adults are more likely to under-report what they eat than other people, supporting evidence is scarce (Fisher *et al.* 2000) and some studies suggest that under-reporting does not vary according weight status (Klesges *et al.* 1988; Myers 1988).

The sense that emerges from the 'obesity epidemic' literature on food intake is of a kind of split personality. On one side we have those who make unsupported generalizations about the role of food and, on the other, researchers who seem prepared to accept that population-level increases in dietary intake are not major, or even minor, contributors to the 'obesity epidemic'. Having claimed that overweight and obesity accelerated rapidly in the previous ten years, the Australian epidemiologist Wendy Brown writes:

> But during this period, the contribution of saturated fat to total energy expenditure is thought to have decreased (from about 16% in 1983 to 13% in 1995). So it would seem that, in the absence of an overall increase in energy intake, the main factor contributing to the overweight/obesity epidemic must be the increasing levels of sedentariness in our population.
>
> (Brown 2001: 9)

The declining-food-intake thesis appears to be accepted by many other researchers (Durnin *et al.* 1974; Grundy *et al.* 1999; Jebb and Moore 1999; Prentice and Jebb 1995; Salbe and Ravussin 2000; Seidell 2000; Sunnegardh *et al.* 1986; Weinsier *et al.* 1998; Willett and Leibel 2002), most of whom turn to alternative explanations for the 'obesity epidemic', although Bouchard (2000) appears to both concede that food intake is going down *and* blame the 'obesity epidemic' on food. Hanley *et al.* (2000) and Dubbert *et al.* (2002) suggest that, while total energy intake is not rising, the amount of dietary fat people eat is.

However, Heini and Weinsier's article 'Divergent trends in obesity and fat intake patterns: the American paradox' for the *American Journal of Medicine* examines existing longitudinal US data and concludes that:

> average fat intake, adjusted for total calories, dropped from 41.0% to 36.6%, an 11% decrease. Average total daily calorie intake also tended to decrease, from 1,854 kcal to 1,785 kcal (-4%). Men and women had similar trends. Concurrently, there was a dramatic rise in the percentage of the US population consuming low-calorie products, from 19% of the population in 1978 to 76% in 1991.
>
> (Heini and Weinsier 1997: 259)

It is worth recalling that the idea that it is not so much the total number of calories we consume that is important, but whether they come in the form of fats, carbohydrates or proteins, represents a departure from the energy-in/energy-out law of body weight. Scientific opinion appears to be quite divided on the validity of this idea. Willett (1998) and Willett and Leibel (2002) argue that dietary fat has not played an important part in the 'obesity epidemic' and that fat intake has been falling (see Bray and Popkin 1998 for a generally opposing point of view and reply to Willett 1998). As we have just seen, Rolland-Cachera and Bellisle (2002) are inclined to blame protein, not fat, while, as some readers will be aware, there has been no shortage of popular writers willing to implicate carbohydrates in recent years (e.g. Atkins 2000). Meanwhile, reviews of the effectiveness of low-fat (Pirozzo *et al.* 2003) and low-carbohydrate (Bravata *et al.* 2003) diets consistently find that these diets are no better than simple caloric restriction.

Two points emerge from this literature. First, whether total calories or the source of calories is the more important aetiological factor in the development of over-weight and obesity appears to be, at best, unresolved despite a long history of empirical interest in the subject (see Chapter 4). Second, the consensus among a significant group of researchers that average energy intake has been declining and continues to do so is simply impossible to reconcile with much of the existing popular and scientific literature, which takes widespread gluttony among Western populations to be a given.

The literature we have cited in this section refers to a number of different countries and some readers may be uncomfortable with the way we have glossed over this potentially important point. For example, could it be that food intake is going up in some countries and going down in others, or that different sections of particular Western populations are eating more while others are eating less? We have not considered these potential differences here precisely because the scientific literature rarely addresses them. After all, were the dietary intake situation markedly different in different Western countries, this would severely complicate the idea of a generalized 'obesity epidemic'. Is it possible that the same phenomenon – rapidly increasing body weights – has emerged in many different countries for different reasons? Perhaps these potential complications are not addressed in the obesity science literature because to do so would make the rela-tively straightforward idea of an 'everyone everywhere' 'obesity epidemic' much more difficult to sustain.

Finally, it needs to be acknowledged that apart from those researchers who seem to simply assume that dietary intake is rising, there are others who mount an empirical case for this point of view. These researchers rely on what is known as 'food disappearance' data, which purports to show how much food is being produced and, having adjusted for a certain amount of wastage and spoiling, estimates how much is eaten (e.g. French *et al.* 2001; Nestle 2002). At present, existing data for this approach is largely limited to the US and suggests very significant rises in the consumption of some high-fat and high-sugar foods.

It is difficult to see how acceptance of the 'food disappearance' case would not completely invalidate the epidemiological data discussed previously. In other words (and putting to one side the possibility that both are wrong), either the epidemi-ological data, based largely on surveys, or the 'food disappearance' data have produced a severely inaccurate picture of average dietary intake. We can simply see no way of reconciling these two positions. This is not a trivial matter. Epidemiological data (the vast majority of it self-report and survey data) have been the bedrock upon which scientific claims about the links between body weight, health, food and physical activity have been built. Indeed, it is this epidemiological data that is used to make the case for why we should be concerned about increasing overweight and obesity levels. We are not aware of any attempt in the literature to explore the potential consequences of this sharp divergence of opinion.

An epidemic of inactivity?

Scientific journals that deal with overweight and obesity appear not to be the least bit hostile to the proposition that Western human beings are basically lazy. For example, Lee and Paffenbarger begin an article for *Research Quarterly for Exercise and Sport* with:

> Almost 60% of all U.S. adults today engage in no physical activity or only irregular physical activity despite ample evidence that higher levels of physical activity and fitness are associated with decreased risk of chronic diseases, as well as increased longevity. Thus, while the relevant question should be 'How much physical is optimal for health?' most, sadly, will ask, 'How little physical activity must I carry out in order to still remain healthy?' Blair and Connelly's (1996) thoughtful article arguing for the merits of moderate amounts and intensities of physical activity with respect to improved health and enhanced longevity should, therefore, come as welcome news for this nation of physical activity sluggards.
>
> (Lee and Paffenbarger 1996: 206)

Writing in the *Journal of the American Dietetic Association*, Rippe and Hess (1998: S31) claim that: 'The United States is facing 2 major lifestyle-related epidemics that are intricately linked: an epidemic of obesity and an epidemic of inactivity'. As we saw in Chapter 3, Chakravarthy and Booth (2003) characterized Western life as a 'sedentary death syndrome'. Recently, a group of thirteen leading obesity researchers attended a conference to produce a 'consensus statement' regarding the amount of physical activity people needed to do to avoid 'unhealthy weight gain'. The outcomes of this meeting were published in 2003. The article claimed that: 'A decline in daily physical activity levels (PALs) is clearly a major factor contributing to the current obesity epidemic affecting both developed and developing countries in the world' (Saris *et al.* 2003: 101).

At the risk of stating the obvious, statements of this kind are not simply suggesting that lots of people do not do enough exercise. An 'epidemic of inactivity' means that 'inactivity' is spreading – rapidly – and that no one is immune. Let us now consider the argument that people are generally less active than in previous times.

A number of the authors cited in the previous section argue that, since a strong case for gluttony cannot be found, the cause of the 'obesity epidemic' must be sloth. Heini and Weinsier propose that:

> Reduced fat and calorie intake and frequent use of low-calorie food products have been associated with a paradoxical increase in the prevalence of obesity. These diverging trends suggest that there has been a dramatic decrease in

total physical activity related energy expenditure. Efforts to increase the average American's total exercise- and nonexercise-related physical activities may be essential for the prevention of obesity.

(Heini and Weinsier 1997: 259)

This appears to be a position shared by a number of others (Astrup 2001; Blair *et al.* 1992; Bray *et al.* 2002; Brown 2001; Fogelholm *et al.* 1999; Jebb and Moore 1999; Prentice and Jebb 1995; Salbe and Ravussin 2000; Swinburn and Egger 2002). Noting the apparent decline in food intake, Jebb and Moore conclude:

This implies that there have been even greater decreases in physical activity. Unfortunately, there are no direct measurements of secular trends in physical activity, but good data exist to show significant increases in the time spent watching TV (a proxy measure of leisure-time sedentary activities) and increased car ownership (a proxy measure for the decline in the personal energy cost of transport).

(Jebb and Moore 1999: S535)

Jebb and Moore's tentative comments about physical activity are in stark contrast to Astrup's confident diagnosis:

The American Paradox, the observation that obesity prevalence is increasing despite a slight decrease in population dietary fat consumption, *is easily explained* by the concomitantly decreasing physical activity, which reduces fat requirements and counteracts the beneficial effect of a slight reduction in dietary fat.

(Astrup 2001: S46, emphasis added)

However, the case for increasing sedentariness among Western populations may not be quite as open and shut as this quote suggests. Grundy *et al.* (1999) are somewhat non-committal about general physical activity levels: 'In spite of long-term societal trends in activity patterns, these have not been assessed quantitatively; moreover, leisure-time activity apparently has not changed much over recent decades' (Grundy *et al.* 1999: S503). Pointing to the methodological difficulties associated with measuring average population physical activity levels, particularly for children, Sleap *et al.* (2000) argue that we have very little evidence on which to base conclusions about physical activity trends. In another example, French *et al.* assert that: 'It is an accepted fact . . . that the changes in eating and exercise behaviours that are driving the obesity epidemic are largely due to an environment that encourages the former and discourages the latter' (French *et al.* 2001: 309). And yet later they claim that the number of Americans who report no leisure time physical activity is falling. They go on to say:

Overall, government-sponsored, population-based survey data suggest little, if any, change in physical activity levels during the past few decades, although the most recent data are 6 years old. There seems to have been a small decrease in the percentage of the population who report being completely inactive, a small decrease in the percentage reporting regular physical activity, and a small increase in the percentage reporting regular vigorous physical activity. Data from other population-based surveys and trend data on sports and recreational participation between 1961 and 1985 suggest a more dramatic increase in leisure-time physical activity.

(French *et al.* 2001: 319)

French *et al.* argue that this apparent paradox can be attributed to car, television, computer and labour-saving device usage. As well as the misgivings about blaming television and computers articulated in Chapter 3, we would point out here that it is by no means universally accepted that levels of television viewing are increasing. For example, Biddle *et al.*'s review of the childhood obesity literature finds that:

although more children and youth have greater access to TVs than in previous generations, the amount of TV watched per head has not changed for 40 years. Preliminary findings from Project STIL suggest that inactivity is more complex than we sometimes think. Indeed, measures of 'couch potato-ism', such as TV viewing, may be inappropriate markers of inactivity.

(Biddle *et al.* 2004: 29)

Writing in the *British Medical Journal*, Morris claims that 'present evidence suggests that increasing sloth is not an important factor in the current steep increase in obesity' (Morris 1995: 1569). Morris cites British evidence that television viewing has been falling while walking has been increasing among some sections of the population, and sports participation has been increasing across all age and social groupings.

In their literature review concerning the physical activity levels of American children and adults, Pratt *et al.* write:

It is widely believed that participation in physical activity is declining among adults in the United States. However, national survey data are not able to support this contention. Levels of physical activity and inactivity as measured by the BRFSS and NIS have been remarkably stable during the past decade. Data sources consistent enough to adequately assess trends before 1985 do not exist. A synthesis of noncomparable surveys suggests that leisure-time physical activity probably increased between the 1960s and 1980s. The stability of leisure time over the past decade or more may mask an overall decline in physical activity. Several authors have postulated that there have been substantial decreases in overall energy expenditure driven by large decreases in the amount of physical activity required for work, transportation, and routine daily tasks.

(Pratt *et al.* 1999: S530)

Pratt *et al.* also point to a number of studies that suggest participation in recreational physical activity has gone up significantly among girls and women. They go on to argue that:

The public perception of an increasingly sedentary way of life among children is even more widespread than for adults. However, there is even less good information available on national trends in youth physical activity or fitness than for adults. No fitness data exist since the completion of NCYFS II in 1986. The YRBS physical activity questions have been standardized only since 1993 and provide information only on young people attending school in grades 9–12. There has been no significant change in reported vigorous physical activity between 1993 and 1997: 1993, 65.8%; 1995, 63.7%; and 1997, 63.8%.

(Pratt *et al.* 1999: S531)

With respect to Australia, Bauman and Owen (1999) come to basically identical conclusions: a mostly unchanged picture over the last twenty years with small increases in some types of physical activity. In passing, it is worth keeping in mind that although a number of studies suggest that people become less physically active as they age, particularly from childhood to late adolescence (e.g. Anderssen *et al.* 1996; Telama and Yang 2000), this cross-sectional finding has no bearing on the question of whether people of all ages are less active than they were in the past.

The apparently fragmented state of scientific opinion about physical activity levels must also be seen in relation to other scientific debates we discussed in Chapter 3. For example, we saw that considerable uncertainty exists concerning whether inactivity causes overweight and obesity or whether, conversely, (for whatever reason) overweight and obesity lead to lower levels of activity (also see Petersen *et al.* 2004 for evidence for this latter proposition). Perhaps even more importantly, because the precise relationship between physical activity and health remains poorly understood, conclusions about the health effects of long-term physical activity trends (whether they are going up or down) would seem even more speculative. As Livingstone *et al.* put it:

Evidence suggests a high prevalence of inactivity in adults, but whether or not inactivity is increasing cannot be assessed currently. Similarly, no definite conclusions are justified about either the levels of physical activity of children, or whether these are sufficient to maintain and promote health. Data to support the belief that activity levels in childhood track into adulthood are weak. Inactivity is associated with an increased risk of weight gain and obesity, but causality remains to be established.

(Livingstone *et al.* 2003: 681)

In this context it is interesting to note the way some obesity scientists have both blamed alleged decreases in physical education for the 'obesity epidemic' as well as seeing physical education as a potential cure (e.g. Booth *et al.* 2002; Hill and Melanson 1999). There is also now a small literature consisting of studies, which have tried to measure the amount of physical activity children do in physical education classes. Leaving to one side those studies that have been part of intervention programmes explicitly designed to increase physical activity, the findings of these studies have been reasonably consistent (e.g. McKenzie *et al.* 1995, 2000; Simons-Mortons *et al.* 1993, 1994; Yelling *et al.* 2000). In general, physical education lessons are found not to provide children with the amounts and kinds of physical activity that scientists deem sufficient to enhance health (bearing in mind that we have no data to determine what these amounts and kinds might be). On the other hand, these studies report a wide range in the frequency, duration and intensity of physical activity during physical education lessons. Some children, for example, apparently get large amounts of physical education, boys and children from more affluent families appear to derive more opportunities for physical activity than other children (e.g. Mallam *et al.* 2003)

We have no data from earlier periods of history, which would help us to make a comparison between physical education classes of different eras. Furthermore, some contemporary data suggests that children tend to derive the bulk of their recreational physical activity outside of school time (e.g. Booth *et al.* 2002). So despite reports that some (but by no means all) schools are devoting less time to physical education, it is not at all clear what the implications of this is. It is hard to see how the small amounts of physical activity that appear to happen during classes might affect average body weights one way or the other, a point that applies equally to individual students as it does to national populations. In addition, the preoccupation of scientific researchers with measuring the time children spend walking, running and sitting down during physical education may be counter-productive. If the purpose of physical education is to encourage lifelong partici-pation in physical activity, then it is not difficult to see how highly physically demanding classes, particularly those that focus on fitness, might have the oppo-site affect to the one desired. For example, there is evidence that when it focuses on physical fitness and activity for activity's sake, children are much less likely to enjoy physical education (e.g. Hopple and Graham 1995; Pangrazi *et al.* 1996). To put the point simply, it is possible that many children do not view the issue of childhood fitness with quite the same urgency as some adults and will resent these anxieties being visited upon them. This may be particularly true for those students whom scientific researchers see as needing to do more physical activity. What is telling about obesity science's sudden interest in physical education is that it seldom acknowledges that others have been researching the subject for some time and may have useful things to contribute about children and physical activity. Twenty years of sustained physical education scholarship (e.g. Ennis 1999; Evans and Clarke 1988; Kirk 1996; McKay *et al.* 1990; Siedentop 1996) has contributed to sophisticated curricula and programmes that aim to develop skills, knowledge and attitudes to help students enjoy a wide range of recreational and sporting activities during and beyond school. However, in the context of an 'obesity epidemic', where principals, teachers, parents, health promoters, doctors and scien-tists see children's body weight as the primary health concern, physical education is often reduced to the most efficient and rudimentary means of burning energy. For example, some obesity scientists (e.g. McKenzie *et al.* 2000; Simons-Morton *et al.* 1994) really do claim that good quality physical education experiences are ones in which children burn lots of calories, an idea that surely derives from the vision of the body as a machine, rather than a serious consideration with the social, cultural and emotional lives of children.

The end of hard work?

The last suspect in the search for the 'obesity epidemic's' *cause* is what obesity scientists often call 'incidental physical activity', which refers to the activity we do in order to live our lives minus recreational or leisure time physical activity. Bouchard and Blair put the case as follows:

> The increase in the prevalence of overweight and obesity cases worldwide is occurring against a background of a progressive reduction in the energy expended for work and occupational activities as well as for the accomplishment of personal chores and daily necessities. The reduction in energy expenditure associated with physical activity brought about by automation and changing job and professional environmental circumstances has been nothing but dramatic in the second half of this century. In contrast, the energy expenditure of leisure time physical activity may have increased slightly but not enough to keep pace with the changes brought about by urbanization and automation.
>
> (Bouchard and Blair 1999: S499)

But right from the very beginning, there is something odd about this. The case now appears to be that the 'obesity epidemic' has been caused by cars and remote controls. Is this plausible? Western civilization has been producing labour-saving devices for centuries but we are being asked to believe that the most recent crop has triggered a health crisis. We are inclined to wonder whether obesity science has ended up at incidental physical activity because there is simply nowhere else to go. If body weight *is* simply a matter of energy-in/energy-out then this law dictates that the reason for changes in body weight must lie on one side or the other. And as we have seen, epidemiological research into diet and leisure time physical activity has not produced the 'smoking gun'. But having arrived at this point, obesity science is left with the most difficult of all possible empirical problems: proving that recent changes in our normal daily lives have caused an explosion in overweight and obesity. Data to support this proposition is scarce. The problem with making claims about the decline of incidental physical activity is captured by Hill and Melanson:

> Although it is intuitively obvious that improvements in technology over the past few decades have substantially reduced the energy expenditure required for daily living, this has not been definitively documented. All indications are that work-related physical activity has declined.
>
> (Hill and Melanson 1999: S517)

Hill and Melanson offer no suggestions for what these 'indications' are. They go on:

> The amount of energy expenditure required for daily living also appears to be declining due to an increase in attractive sedentary activities such as television watching, video games, and computer interactions. Again, we do not

have good measures of sedentary activity that would allow us to examine changes over time.

(Hill and Melanson 1999: S517)

This lack of data brings us back to the point at which we began this chapter: researchers are driven to the prehistoric past to make the case that we are, indeed, more sedentary than in the past. In the meantime, few empirical attempts to quantify changes in incidental physical activity have been made, nor have there been attempts to compare these changes to apparent increases in recreational or leisure time physical activity.

Whither obesity science?

Over this and the previous three chapters we have argued that the scientific specifics of the energy-in/energy-out law has occupied obesity scientists for at least a century. To this point this scientific agenda has produced few certainties, little in the way of effective overweight and obesity population interventions and, as this chapter has shown, causational dead ends, that is, a series of grossly generalized explanations about why the 'obesity epidemic' has happened that enjoy frustratingly little empirical support. In Chapter 4 we described this as a research loop that prohibits other ways of thinking about human body weight which take into account social, cultural and political factors.

The socio-economic, racial and ethnic dimensions of body weight, food and physical activity in Western countries have been well documented (Bauman and Owen 1999; Bray 2000; Dubbert *et al.* 2002; Flegal 1999; Grundy *et al.* 1999; Seidell 2000; Siedentop 1996; Sobal and Stunkard 1989; Stunkard *et al.* 1972; Whitfield *et al.* 2002). Unfortunately, these differences have often been interpreted by scientists and health promoters as indicating insufficient knowledge and inappropriate attitudes towards diet and exercise among some groups of people. Obesity scientists such as Fentem (1994) and Bouchard and Blair (1999) often claim that the population as a whole has failed to act upon on the knowledge base generated by obesity science. However, millions of middle-class men and women around the world have enthusiastically taken up exercise and diet regimes, many of them in the form commercially available memberships, programmes and products. In some sections of society, behaviours really have changed in ways that should make the scientific community very pleased. However, this is rarely acknowledged in the universalizing propensities of 'obesity epidemic' proponents. At the same time, obesity science have given very little consideration to the reasons why people might organize their lives around priorities other than exercise and diet, much less monitor their energy-in/energy-out on a daily basis.

This point is neatly demonstrated by Barbara Ehrenreich's (2002) book, *Nickel and Dimed: Undercover in Low-Wage USA*, which records the author's experiences living for a year among the US's 'working poor'. Normally an upper middle-class journalist, Ehrenreich went 'undercover', taking low-paid work in diners, department stores and house cleaning. In the main, the book is a story about the dark side of the US's deregulated labour market and the grinding poverty, anxiety and sheer injustice that now appears to be the day-to-day lot for millions of American workers. However, Ehrenreich also describes a world in which 'junk food' and low-nutritional value food handouts play a vital sustaining role for people with not much money and even less time between part-time jobs. The gym clothes she brought with her go months unused, the idea of a 'workout' now a distant, self-indulgent memory. In any case, Ehrenreich reminds us that low-paid work is often extremely physically demanding and she spends most of the small amount of non-working, non-sleeping time she has watching television, partly because it is one of the few forms of entertainment she can afford, and partly out of complete exhaustion. To paraphrase Mark Twain, reports of the death of manual labour appear to have been greatly exaggerated.

7 Obesity science for the people

In a space somewhere between the hyperbole of the print-media and the generally (although not always) more considered tone of scientific journals, another kind of literature about the 'obesity epidemic' has appeared in the last decade or so. Contributors to this category of commentary usually claim to draw on the very latest science but with what is often called an 'educated lay audience' in mind. We might refer to this category as 'obesity science for the people'. Books such as Michael Fumento's (1997a) *The Fat of the Land*, Ellen Ruppel Shell's (2002) *The Hungry Gene* and Greg Critser's (2003) *Fat Land* are typical of this phenomenon. Although usually written in a deliberately non-academic style, they leave the reader in absolutely no doubt that they are intended as serious, scientifically informed contributions. As one dust cover testimonial says: '"*The Fat of The Land*" has the research of a doctoral dissertation yet reads like a compelling novel.'

Like Shawna Vogel's *The Skinny on Fat* (see Chapter 1), almost all of these authors represent themselves as being the true voice of science. However, as this chapter's selection of 'obesity science for the people' shows, they also present sharply contrasting views delivered with an air of unshakable certainty, often with withering contempt for different opinions. It is almost as if certainty in one camp forces others to take up equally rigid positions, creating a context in which uncertainty is simply not an option. And like Vogel, these authors not only claim to be faithfully presenting the current state of scientific knowledge, they also implore their readers to think in more 'scientific' ways.

The fact that a group of people all claim to be offering a rigorously 'scientific' perspective while arriving at very different conclusions should give us cause to reflect: are we looking at 'objective' assessments of the science or, instead, at different moral and ideological views dressed in the cloak of science? It is important to stress that, if the later turns out to be the case, this is not necessarily a bad or unusual state of affairs. All intellectual positions, including our own, rest primarily on moral and ideological assumptions, although these are not always made clear when people write or speak. The point to make is that the authors we consider in this chapter claim that science will lead us to the truth and, more specifically, that scientific ways of thinking are our best hope for solving the 'obesity epidemic'. Our purpose in considering these texts, therefore, is to suggest that thinking 'scientifically' is unlikely to deliver the definitive 'truth' about overweight and obesity. Nor is it likely to produce the 'obesity epidemic's' solution.

Our approach in this chapter attempts to tread a fine line between a detailed analysis of some of the claims made by these authors, on the one hand, and what might be seen as mean-spirited nit-picking, on the other. We would simply remind readers that all but one of the authors discussed in this chapter claim to be speaking the 'scientific truth' and they therefore invite close scrutiny. It is also worth remembering that, with the possible exception of Mary Eberstadt's (2003) article, 'The child-fat problem', 'obesity science for the people' is likely to reach a much wider readership than most academic journals and may actually be a more significant contributor to the flow of ideas in the public sphere.

We want also to draw readers' attention to the ways in which the arguments of these authors often turn on unsubstantiated appeals to 'common sense' in much the same way as we have seen in writing for scientific journals. This means that, at times, we will dwell on apparently insignificant remarks because we think they are anything but insignificant. These appeals to 'common sense' act as bridges between unrelated pieces of scientific data and the wider stories the authors want to tell, often about the moral decline of Western civilization. They are, in effect, forms of camouflage so that primarily moral and ideological agendas can be made to look like health and medical agendas supported by objective science. To return to the title of this book, it is not the state of science that these texts present, but rather the parcelling up of science, morality and ideology into a good story.

The heretics

First, let us consider two books which challenge the 'obesity epidemic's' conventional wisdom: Glenn Gaesser's (2002) *Big Fat Lies: The Truth About Your Weight and Your Health* and Dale Atrens' (2000) *The Power of Pleasure: Why Indulgence is Good For You and Other Palatable Truths*. Immediately we are struck by the use of the word 'truth' in both titles. The cover of Gaesser's book includes other text: 'Learn the astonishing facts' and 'Takes on the fat phobia that permeates so much of the research about obesity and health'. 'Truth' and 'facts' are clearly important to both authors.

Gaesser argues that a careful reading of the scientific literature reveals that overweight and obesity are not as bad for one's health as we have been led to believe and even presents data to suggest that both overweight and obesity might provide some health benefits. Rather than focusing on body weight, he suggests that we can achieve significant health benefits by looking elsewhere. For example, he claims that small increases in the amount of physical activity that people do and quite minor changes in their diets can lead to significant reductions in heart disease and diabetes.

On one level, this book might be seen as supportive of the concerns with 'obesity epidemic' thinking that we have discussed and it certainly does provide a useful summary of the biomedical arguments against what he calls 'fat phobia'. However, on another level, *Big Fat Lies* is simply another example of 'obesity epidemic' thinking. Gaesser, like most of the authors cited in this chapter, appears to believe that science *does* give us the answer to the question 'how should we live?' Gaesser's scientific answer is that we need to do just a little bit more exercise than we are currently doing, eat just a little less fat and eat just a little more complex carbohydrates – every little bit will help. This seems an extremely ambitious argument if, as we have argued, the precise effect of food and exercise on the human body is unclear. How is it possible to be so confident about such small variations in physical activity – Gaesser suggests a few extra flights of stairs every day can be health promoting – when our knowledge of the health benefits of physical activity is currently so imprecise? Gaesser's argument implies that the relationships between body weight, health, food and physical activity are so finely calibrated and so well understood that just a tweak here and a tweak there can produce measurable health improvements. But, as we have argued elsewhere in this book, these relationships are not well understood. Gaesser's book totally rejects the option of arguing that we do not know enough about body weight, health, exercise and food to be certain. For Gaesser, the truth is out there even though our 'fat phobia' prevents many of us from seeing it.

While Gaesser claims to offer a radical point of view, his final prescription for health could not be more familiar. His solution of a little more exercise and slightly better eating is anything but radical and differs from most other experts only in terms of the *extent* to which he thinks we are currently straying from health's 'straight and narrow'.

Dale Atrens' *The Power of Pleasure* also maintains that the dangers of overweight and obesity have been exaggerated. However, he appears to contradict Gaesser by arguing that *worrying* about exercise and food is bad for one's health. Atrens says that the idea of an 'ideal diet' is hopelessly misguided and that health benefits of exercise have been over-stated. He writes:

> The stress and loss of control associated with obsessional attitudes about food and exercise are very likely to compromise immunity and promote ill health. What is commonly portrayed as a healthy lifestyle is, in fact, a concerted assault on immunity. This goes a long way toward explaining why a theoretically healthy lifestyle is not healthy in practice.
>
> (Atrens 2000: 151)

We find Atrens' assessment of the science of nutrition compelling, in that it shows that research produces contradictory, complex and contingent results. In other words, the idea that we might feed a human body a certain selection of foods in certain quantities and that this will lead to predictable outcomes – the 'body as machine' model once again – is untenable. Atrens has similar things to say about exercise. However, in the world of 'obesity science for the people' authors must have a positive story to tell and Atrens' story is that the field of psychobiology tells us that happy people are healthy people. Thus, argues Atrens, part of the reason why wealthy people are healthier than the poor is because they have less to worry about.

At this point, it is difficult not to be reminded here of the literally hundreds of experts and scientists who have appeared over the centuries claiming that he or she has found the secret to health and happiness. Atrens' argument rests on a branch of scientific inquiry that remains speculative, controversial and open to multiple critiques. On a straightforward level we might ask how is it possible to tease out the contribution of 'stress' to various forms of cancer from other contributing factors? Atrens really does argue that worrying less about food and exercise will lead to less cancer because worry lowers the immune system. He appears not to have considered the possibility that exercise leads to less stress, which, although not an argument without its own serious problems, is at least as scientifically mainstream as the idea that worrying about food causes cancer. Indeed, there seems a simple stereotype operating in *The Power of Pleasure* that people who watch what they eat and try to fit some exercise into their lives are nervous wrecks. We might also ask *how* worried about food and exercise does one have to be to get sick? Atrens' argument never achieves this level of specificity and, as such, looks like yet another unsubstantiated variation on the 'body as machine' model that claims to reveal health's secret laws.

Atrens' take-home message is as old as it is startling and unsatisfactory: it is that we should cultivate our taste for the 'exquisite'. Just like well-to-do ancient Greeks, his formula is that we should savour, in moderation and in balance, the best things in life, particularly food:

> Weight loss and indulgence go hand in hand. You may have noticed how few food enthusiasts are fat. The secret is in cultivating a sense of the exquisite. If you can do this you will have made an enormous step toward being thinner and healthier as well as broadening your smile.
>
> (Atrens 2000: 182–3)

Presumably the 'food enthusiasts' he is talking about include the celebrity chefs whose images have proliferated on our television screens. Have they avoided over-weight because of the 'exquisite' food they eat or is it just that plump 'food enthusiasts' are less likely to be asked to host their own television shows? Either way, this seems a remarkably unhelpful, not to say elitist, piece of advice if, as it appears, overweight and obesity disproportionately affect the poor.

'Big Food'

How to be Alone (2002), a collection of non-fiction works by the American novelist Jonathan Franzen, includes a meditation on the recent wave of litigation against cigarette manufacturers. There has been, he argues, a disturbing self-righteousness about the way people have condemned these companies: could anyone really claim that they did not know that cigarettes are harmful? Recalling the very public denials of health risk by tobacco executives, Franzen points out that if our gut reaction is to demonize these people, we might pause to think about the other players in this conspiracy, if conspiracy is what it is: what about the institutions and individuals who have owned and profited from stock in these companies and the businesses and stores that sell cigarettes? In short, Franzen's discomfort is with the way a line is conveniently drawn around a small group of people so that they can be portrayed as the villains in this story, while the rest of us can look on with self-justified moral outrage.

Moral outrage is an important ingredient in Marion Nestle's (2002) *Food Politics: How the Food Industry Influences Nutrition and Health* and Eric Schlosser's (2001) *Fast Food Nation: What the All-American Meal is Doing to the World*. Schlosser's book is a journalistic exposé of the history and present-day workings of the massive American fast food industry. He wants his readers to know about the extraordinary things this industry does to animals, farmers and poor migrant, young and disabled unskilled workers in order to keep the price of fast food low. He wants us to think about the way it is marketed to children, the artificial means by which the food's taste is produced and kept uniform, and the industry's culpability for lethal food-borne pathogens. He urges us simply not to buy the products this industry sells and sees more government regulation as the only way to ensure a more ethical fast food industry.

The 'obesity epidemic' is mentioned in *Fast Food Nation* but is not the focus of the book. Schlosser's arguments are primarily moral and political; his position is that the conduct of 'Big Food' is self-evidently immoral and that unconstrained free-market forces and weak government bureaucracies do not lead to safe working environments, safe food, fair wages or the humane treatment of animals. Unencumbered with claims about scientific cause-and-effect, Schlosser focuses on the lives of real humans and animals, not theoretical machines, and is all the more compelling for it.

Food Politics is also a critique of 'Big Food'. Marion Nestle, an academic nutritionist, is particularly concerned with 'Big Food's' relentless lobbying of government officials and their sponsorship of academic journals, research, conferences and, it would appear, academics themselves. Unlike Schlosser, Nestle is *very* interested in the 'obesity epidemic' and includes working mothers and increased meals taken outside the home among her list of causative factors. More central to her argument, though, is the contention that the behaviour of 'Big Food' and, to a lesser extent, unethical academics has had the effect of confusing people about what and how much they should eat. In the book's second chapter 'Politics vs Science', Nestle seems to argue that the crystal clear waters of scientific nutrition have been muddied by the forces of naked corporate self-interest. Free of the unethical behaviour of 'Big Food', so her argument goes, the science of nutrition would wipe people's confusion away and better health would be the result. This seems a vulnerable argument because it ignores the extremely long history of dubious advice, both scientific and more populist, to which Western populations have been subjected (in particular, see Schwartz 1986). Exactly when was this 'golden age', when scientific nutrition spoke with a unified and coherent voice about healthy eating? How is the public supposed to know when the 'true' voice of nutritional science, and not some impostor, is talking?

For an author who sees science as the opposite of politics, Nestle strikes a surprising and consistently moral tone throughout *Food Politics*. She castigates 'Big Food' for advocating a 'permissive' attitude towards food and for refusing to call some foods 'good' and some foods 'bad'. Nestle gives every indication that she sees the idea that there is no such thing as a 'bad' food as a kind of nutritional blasphemy:

> Surveys indicate that people are interested in nutrition and health but are confused by conflicting information, suffer from 'nutritional schizophrenia,' and cannot figure out how to achieve 'nutritional utopia.' Surely, ambiguous guidelines must contribute to the confusion. This chapter explained how food

industries insist that guidelines be expressed positively and focus on nutrients rather than foods. Instead, food companies prefer thoroughly permissive principles that encourage consumption of all foods regardless of nutritional value: 'balance, variety, and moderation are the keys to healthful diets; there is no such thing as a good or a bad food; all foods can be part of healthful diets; it's the total diet that counts.'

(Nestle 2002: 91)

According to Nestle, this final sentence, which sounds to us like reasonably sensible and (perhaps more to the point) familiar nutritional advice, is actually an example of malicious and morally irresponsible 'Big Food' propaganda. For Nestle, science really does tell us that some foods are 'bad', an idea Dale Atrens would no doubt reject.

At the same time, scientists often say that 'sound nutrition' is really quite a straightforward matter. For example, Harvard University's Graham Colditz is quoted as saying that good health is reducible to the simple formula of 'eat fruit and exercise' and that experts have been giving this unchanged message for decades (Needham 2002: 5). If this true, then we might wonder about Nestle's argument that people are confused about 'good' and 'bad' food. Certainly the recent lawsuits brought against fast food companies alleging deceitful behaviour have not fared well, something Jonathan Franzen might have predicted. In our experience, people still seem to recognize chocolate cake and ice cream as 'sinful' 'indulgences' and understand that fizzy drinks contain a lot of sugar. In fact, advertising for what Nestle calls 'bad' foods generally rests on the assumption that people will recognize them as 'bad' – as an indulgence – hence their appeal.

The moral and ideological critique of 'Big Food' has been an important contribution to our understanding of the relationships between government officials, public policy, big business and the food we eat. However, the idea that the saving power of nutritional science, enacted through nutrition guidelines, has been violated by 'Big Food' would seem an unnecessary and difficult to sustain part of this critique.

Fat and 'family values'

What distinguishes thinking that is naively 'ideological'? This is never a simple question not least because it depends so heavily on one's point of view. Most of us find it much easier to accuse those with whom we disagree of being 'biased' or 'ideological', while we are more likely to see those whose views we share as 'unbiased' or 'objective'. This important qualification aside, perhaps the clearest examples occur when people arrive at the same conclusion regardless of the issue at hand. We might call this the intellectual equivalent of the 'one trick pony': although the issue or problem up for discussion may change, the answer never does.

We saw examples of this in Chapter 2, particularly the Australian 'family values' commentator Angela Shanahan for whom all of society's ills, including overweight and obesity, can be blamed on the dilution of Christian moral leadership. Interventions such as Shanahan's are interesting because, in a sense, they come from nowhere. Without any apparent formal expertise or history of interest in the subject, they make a kind of 'hit-and-run' contribution – barely bothering to consult research and then, by the time their next column appears, bringing their single analytical lens to bear on a completely different area of human affairs.

Another spectacular example of this is Mary Eberstadt's (2003) article 'The child-fat problem' for the magazine *Policy Review*. A research fellow at the conservative Hoover Institution, Eberstadt has argued for some time that America is in deep social decline and at the heart of the problem are absent mothers and what she calls 'latch-key children', children who return home to an empty house after school. In 'Home-alone America', Eberstadt (2001) argues that crime, schoolyard massacres, juvenile delinquency and general social breakdown are all the result of parents not spending enough time supervising their children. In particular, she singles out feminism, divorce and working mothers as the main culprits. For Eberstadt, the problem with society today is that nobody is telling children what they can and cannot do.

Turning her focus to rising childhood obesity, Eberstadt rejects the argument that the fast food industry is to blame, a not altogether surprising position for a member of the avowedly free-enterprise Hoover Institution. Instead, she argues:

> But it is at least as reasonable to suppose that the opposite is true – that fast-food franchises and the like are responding to demand rather than creating it. Maybe Americans are not in fact wallowing zombie-like to the trough because Colonel Sanders tells them to. Maybe fast-food and other companies unable to ignore our capacious appetites are just engaged in business as usual: trying to keep the customers – with apologies – fat and happy.
>
> (Eberstadt 2003: 5)

Notice the way Eberstadt's argument is framed around two extremes – people are either zombies with no free will (a position she rejects) or guilty of having 'capacious appetites', which they freely express (the position she endorses). And while Eric Schlosser and Marion Nestle have both written entire books about the marketing practices of fast food chains, the deregulation of food production and the behaviour of aggressively capitalist food corporations, Eberstadt dismisses these concerns with these brief sentences.

Surveying the existing 'whys', Eberstadt makes the dubious claim that heredity is the explanation of the 'obesity epidemic' that enjoys greatest support among other commentators. However, she rejects it, arguing that heredity could not possibly account for recent changes in obesity levels. This is in an interesting method for introducing the argument she is about to unveil since, far from being opposed to mainstream opinion, this is precisely the position articulated by most popular and scientific commentators – human genetic make-up changes far too slowly for it to be a significant factor in an 'obesity epidemic', which we are told is barely thirty years old. Having set up the (far from universally accepted) 'straw man' heredity argument, Eberstadt then casts her own explanation as a brave and original diagnosis that goes against current orthodoxies. Far from being unorthodox, however, her argument is merely a slight variation on the familiar story of Western decadence and decline. She writes:

Historically, either parents or extended family or both have controlled most of what and when children could eat. The fact that this control was typically born of necessity – i.e., of making sure there was enough to go around – does not refute its significance. After all, this parental or familial power has been exercised virtually everywhere in human history, from the savannah to the igloo to the Raj and back again ... Thus, the why underlying the child-fat problem can be formulated something like this: Given that parents and related adults across history and cultures have policed their children's eating habits, in what kind of social universe do adults cease to perform this task? The answer, which is as obvious as it is unwelcome, is that our universe has become one in which adults, particularly related adults in the form of parents, are not around to do the policing in the first place. In other words, there would appear to be an obvious relationship between absentee parents – meaning particularly, for reasons we will see, mothers – and overstuffed children.

(Eberstadt 2003: 9–10)

In the remainder of the article Eberstadt (2003: 10) sets about 'making the case for a connection between absent mothers and fat kids'. For reasons we will discuss below, our view is that Eberstadt fails to make this case. And yet the truth or otherwise of her position is less important in the context of this chapter than the way she builds it. After all, at some point in the future the Eberstadt thesis on childhood obesity may emerge as brilliantly prescient and the generally accepted analysis, our doubts about it notwithstanding. In the mundane present, however, her analysis flows seamlessly out of her well-known and often repeated moral and ideological commitments to free-market economics and 'family values'. These commitments are then blended with the air of scientific certainty to produce, as she sees it, her incontrovertible conclusion.

Perhaps the best example of this is her discussion of television watching. She begins:

Nothing, for example, is as firmly established in the fat literature as the fact that television watching and overweight children go hand in hand. This phenomenon, which has been studied many times over, is pretty easily grasped: The more television a child watches, the more likely he is to get fat. As to the mechanism at work here, this too appears clear. For one thing, people – including children – eat more in front of the television than they do sitting at a table. For another, the way in which metabolism slows to almost sleep-like levels after enough time in front of the tube means that the food taken is metabolized more slowly, hence in a more fat-friendly way, than would otherwise be the case.

(Eberstadt 2003: 11)

As we argued in Chapter 3, the link between television and obesity is anything but 'firmly established' in the literature, while the suggestion that eating while the metabolism is low rather than high is more likely to lead to fatness is, to our knowledge, without foundation. And while there are doubts about the robustness of the statistical correlation, the question of the causal 'mechanism' linking television and obesity is, as many scientists admit, a matter of speculation. For Eberstadt's readers, no trace of the underlying empirical uncertainty remains. Her move from an association between television viewing and obesity, for which some (although far from overwhelming) empirical support exists, to the speculative terrain of causal relationship is also accomplished without any sense of the empirical and scientific hurdles such a move implies. Instead, the phrases 'firmly established' and 'appears clear' smooth the way for the identical argument put forward in 'Home-alone America': working mothers are to blame.

To support her 'more working mothers = more childhood television viewing = more childhood obesity' position, Eberstadt cites a single study on the effects of Californian welfare reform. According to Eberstadt, although it had no interest in childhood obesity, the study 'incidentally uncovered' data that suggested that welfare reform had caused women to spend less time with their children and to increase children's average television watching. Remarkably, the author claims that this 'incidental' finding from one study 'puts to rest any notion that television-viewing is some class-based constant unaffected by other domestic variables' (Eberstadt 2003: 12).

This sentence concludes with a footnote that informs readers very little is known about whether computers and video games have the same (according to Eberstadt) fattening consequences as television and, therefore, she cautions that generalizations about technology in general are probably unwise. But in the very next paragraph of the article, the paragraph that concludes her discussion on television viewing, and with one solitary study and this cautionary footnote behind her, Eberstadt can restrain herself no longer – the dam now breaks and the story of the 'demon technology' is given full vent:

> Then again, how much social science do we need to tell us that when parents are away, kids will play? And they will particularly play at electronics. Again, to whose surprise? The screen in any color (and perhaps most especially the personal computer, that 'pool of electronic wonders,' in journalist Peter Hitchins's words) is a hypnotizing force. Of course children are more likely to turn it off if there is an adult around reminding them to do so. What could be more obvious, at a time when many adults need the same outside prodding in various forms – boss, co-workers, spouse, or children at home – to unplug from their own screens.
>
> (Eberstadt 2003: 12)

Despite her previous warning about conflating television and computers, by the end Eberstadt has forgotten about televisions, the only form of technology for which she presents research, and seems to be writing only about computers. It is interesting that having rejected the idea of people filing into fast food restaurants in a 'zombie' like state, she appears to have no difficulty in talking about the 'hypnotizing force' of computers. It is also telling that when people want to blame a particular element of society for a particular problem, be it fast food restaurants, televisions or computers, the element is often credited with the hypnotic power of making brain-washed zombies of us all. And at the risk of stating the obvious, when people begin to believe that things have malign hypnotic powers, it is apparent that we have moved out of the world of rational debate and into a world where evidence ceases to matter, and where no charge about the power of that thing to do harm is too fanciful.

Throughout this book we have encountered the anxieties that some adults have concerning the computerized world in which some – although, we hasten to add, not all – of today's children live. As with Eberstadt, these anxieties are usually expressed without recourse to evidence. It is the apparent strangeness of this computerized world that appears to be its only crime since, as Eberstadt herself admits, there is no scientific evidence which proves its guilt.

The article also includes sections that blame obesity on less breastfeeding and less adult supervized exercise for children with working parents. In both cases, propositions that are, in our view, speculative at best, are described as 'inarguable' and 'obvious'. Eberstadt claims that it is 'obvious' that absent parents lead to children doing less exercise: 'And though the evidence is anecdotal, it is surely highly suggestive. Ask yourself this question: Has any contemporary observer ever suggested that today's children get *more* exercise than their parents did?' (Eberstadt 2003: 15, emphasis in original).

For whatever reason, Eberstadt is unaware than some researchers have suggested exactly this (see Chapter 6), although whether these would fall into her category of 'observer' is impossible to know. More to the point, this is a clear example of how flawed assumptions tend to be treated as *evidence* for equally flawed lines of argument about causation.

Despite the apparent and consistent paucity of the research presented in this particular article, Eberstadt refers to her central argument as 'social dynamite' (2003: 10), 'undeniably ideologically explosive' (2003: 16), 'transgressive' (2003: 19) and 'incendiary' (2003: 19). And what is the argument? It is that a generation of feminism has torn women away from their natural place in the home with children and that *this has led to* rampant obesity among adults and children alike. As she puts it:

> perhaps part of the increase in overweight women, many more of whom are heavy or obese than men, reflects a similar yearning being answered by compulsive recourse to high-calorie food and plenty of it . . . Domestic life has its trials and traumas, without question, but it has its pleasures and consolations. Unable to enjoy these traditional comforts in anything like the doses which humanity has for better or worse been long accustomed, perhaps the Western child – and perhaps also the absent Western mother – uses food to try to compensate for other things being missed . . . So are American children fat and getting fatter because their mothers are? Or are both of them getting fatter in one another's absence, and for the same reason: because the worlds of home and work are out of joint? Maybe, just maybe, that is partly what the consolation of calories is about.
>
> (Eberstadt 2003: 19)

The article's 'explosive' and 'transgressive' argument is merely a twist on familiar conservative moral doctrine about the correct way to live and raise children, which Eberstadt and others have been making for many years. What *is* novel is the link she proposes between feminism, working mothers and obesity. Western anxiety about overweight and obesity is millennia old and the current panic has its roots in the late Victorian period (Schwartz 1986; Stearns 1997). Feminists have been blamed for many things since this time but never, to our knowledge, obesity. It is also worth remembering that Eberstadt's claim that 'many more' women than men are overweight in Western countries would come as a surprise to many obesity researchers, as would her implication that stay-at-home mothers are skinnier than working mothers. What is most revealing about Eberstadt's article is the kinds of things that become thinkable and sayable when the phenomenon being discussed is called an 'epidemic'. Without what we would contend is a kind of understated hysteria, which talk of an 'epidemic' has produced, the claim that feminism causes obesity would probably have seemed absurd. But as we have seen throughout this book, when the prevailing conditions are described as an 'epidemic', hyperbole no longer looks like hyperbole, ideology can look like common sense and moralizing can even look like science.

Class war?

At the beginning of this book we commented on the co-existence of the apparently opposing ideas of 'progress' and 'decline' in Western culture. Two opposite ideas can also be found in writing on the *nature* of the problem of the 'obesity epidemic'. The first is the idea that the 'obesity epidemic' is a *simple* problem. In this book's opening chapter, for example, we came across Claude Bouchard and Steven Blair's claim that the 'obesity epidemic' is a 'remarkably simple' problem. In Chapter 2, we also saw that journalistic comment is inclined to see the causes as 'obvious'. Running alongside this appeal to simplicity is the idea that the 'obesity epidemic' is actually a *complex* problem, one which has been brought about by a convergence of many and varied 'factors'. Unlike Eberstadt's article, which focuses on one factor, other 'obesity science for the people' writers have tended to adopt a more multifactorial approach to explaining the 'obesity epidemic's' causes. While this may seem like a more defensible approach than singling out one explanation, it has at least one serious weakness.

As a statistical concept, the term 'multifactorial' refers to a situation in which different factors are said to have a reasonably precise effect on a phenomenon being studied. To take a simple example, we might be interested in the reasons why particular students do well in mathematics compared to other students. In this case, we could collect information about a group of students, such as their sex, socio-economic class, ethnicity, educational history and any other factor we think might be important and then record their scores on a standard mathematics test. A multifactorial analysis could then be run on the results and it might reveal, for argument's sake, that 65 per cent of the variation between students' scores was statistically explained by socio-economic class, 25 per cent by ethnicity, 10 per cent by sex and the rest by other factors. And while we would need to be careful about generalizing too broadly from these results, they at least give us some sense of which factors might be most significant and perhaps how to provide help to those students who need it.

However, in the case of large-scale cultural and social trends such as an increase in population overweight and obesity, it is virtually impossible to design a study that could statistically explain the causes of this trend. The number of factors relating to how and why people form their food, exercise and general health behaviours is, at least in theory, endless. As with all epidemiological research, there is the dilemma of whether to study a small group of people and collect a great deal of extremely detailed information about their lives, or to study a large group of people, perhaps in the tens of thousands, and collect much less detailed information. Either way, the problem of demonstrating ultimate causation persists and a case can always be made to dismiss any individual study on the grounds that it has failed to take into consideration all the possible contributing factors. This intractable problem means that people who want to contribute to discussion about an issue like the 'obesity epidemic' are free to compile a virtual 'shopping list' of causative factors without feeling the need to offer precise scientific justifications for any or all of their choices. This is important because often these commentators will describe their contributions as 'scientific' when, in fact, little or no scientific justification for their selection of factors exists.

Among the considerable media attention that Greg Critser's *Fat Land: How Americans Became the Fattest People in the World* received, Critser's reported comments appear to match perfectly with the central argument of *this* book: that is, his primary interest is in what he sees as the *moral* dimension of the 'obesity epidemic'. In England's the *Observer* he is quoted as follows:

> 'Most of us are fat because we are slothful and gluttonous,' he says. 'People don't want to hear that. In the course of researching my book, I came to believe that, morally, over-eating is wrong. Look at Bosch's depiction of glut-tony: a man is eating; his child is tugging at his shirt; another man sits at the end of the table with nothing on his plate; his wife is waiting at the door for his next demand. Act the glutton, and you're not only worshipping your belly as a false god; you're involved in the dereliction of your secular duties as well. You're not taking care of your child; you're taking the food off some-body else's plate; you're neglecting your duties at work; you're not taking care of your body.'
>
> (Cooke 2003: 25)

In passing, it is interesting to note the way Critser moves seamlessly from talking about his research to the idea of people 'worshipping' their 'belly as a false god'. This neat linking of the author's 'research' with moral pronouncements is a consistent feature of 'obesity science for the people'.

Although an unequivocal statement of his general moral position, this passage alone does not account for Critser's explanation for what has changed, why we *now* have an 'obesity epidemic'. Critser's reported answer to *this* question comes next:

> That Critser is a liberal and a Democrat, rather than some toothy bible basher from the Mid-West, somehow serves to make his assertions all the more forceful. 'All this does have a spiritual, religious overtones,' he says. 'But I

think we can agree that, even in a secular sense, these things are morally wrong. I come from a generation that wants to avoid talking about moral absolutes, preferring instead to put the emphasis always on context. But now I think that there ARE moral absolutes, and the question is: what is a compassionate way to educate people about them? The people who accuse me of wanting to stigmatise fat people are just confused; I want to stigmatise gluttony, not the fat per se.'

(Cooke 2003: 25)

As *Fat Land* makes clear, Critser's culprits are the generation of baby boomers and their alleged attack on moral standards and boundaries that, he argues, had previously kept America thin. This is a daring argument because historians have argued that American history has, if anything, been marked by open hostility to frugality and dietary restraint (Schwartz 1986), notwithstanding the periodical proliferation of 'experts' – both religious and scientific – who have been convinced that gluttony was everywhere. But what of the specifics of this argument? What are 'these things' which Critser sees as 'morally wrong' and what are the 'moral absolutes' he wishes to defend and 'educate' people about?

The answer to these questions are not, at first, all that clear since he begins by suggesting that American obesity is partly the result of increased use of high-fructose corn syrup and palm oil in processed foods. We will not attempt to evaluate this claim here except to point out that critiques of his basic assumptions – that saturated fats and cholesterol cause obesity, atherosclerosis and heart disease – exist and are not addressed in the twelve short pages he devotes to this issue (see Garrety 1997, 1998 for critical discussions of this issue). While the truth or otherwise of this causational claim remains at least an open question, it is certainly not settled on the strength of the research presented here.

However, let us assume, for argument's sake, that Critser is correct to draw our attention to corn syrup and palm oil. Having accepted this point, we might then justifiably ask what more needs to be said? After all, Critser points out that increased usage of these products closely coincides with increases in American overweight and obesity. So is he suggesting that this is an important causative factor or an unimportant one? Could the corn syrup and palm oil factor be the 'obesity epidemic's' 'smoking gun'? If not, why not? What, exactly, is he claiming here?

While Eberstadt's 'The child-fat problem' is unambiguously and unapologetically conservative, there is a sense in *Fat Land* that the author wants to avoid criticisms of being overly partisan. So even though Critser's final moralistic 'take-home message' is scarcely different from Eberstadt's, he chooses not to let fast food corporations completely off the hook. Having dealt speedily with corn syrup and palm oil in chapter one, an even briefer chapter two (nine pages) considers the 'supersize' phenomenon – the aggressive marketing of oversize portions in order to boost the profits of fast and convenience food manufacturers and vendors. As with corn syrup and palm oil, Critser fails to address the significance of this phenomenon. Instead, the author makes brief mention of it and then has nothing more to say on the matter in the remainder of the book.

These are important omissions because research into the question of whether Western populations are actually eating more is equivocal – it is not at all clear that we are consuming more calories (see Chapter 6). Furthermore, as we have seen, many 'obesity epidemic' commentators see people's personal failings – gluttony and sloth – as the problem. So in terms of explaining why the 'obesity epidemic' has happened, how does the strategy of drawing attention to the behaviour of governments and multinational corporations, on the one hand, sit alongside the story of personal (and yet apparently population wide) moral decline, on the other? Certainly, in the absence of any further research or analysis, these two sets of factors could either be seen as perfectly compatible – working together to produce the same outcome – or incompatible – offering completely contradictory explanations – depending on your point of view. In Eberstadt's analysis, for example, the tactics of the fast food industry are dismissed as largely irrelevant and as simply satisfying the appetites that people already had. Critser takes a different path, suggesting that all these factors need to be considered, employing what we have called the 'shopping list' approach. However, Critser's 'shopping list' seems designed more to create the impression of ideological even-handedness rather than a serious empirical exercise. Rather than attempting to sort out the strong arguments from the weak, he simply lumps them all in together.

Critser's interpretation of the phenomena of supersizing is intriguing. While Schlosser's *Fast Food Nation* presents the marketing of fast food as a form of psychological trickery performed on a largely innocent and unsuspecting public, Critser sees it as a moral toxin that has broken down people's capacity to say 'enough!': 'The pioneers of supersize ... banished the shame of gluttony and opened the maw of the American eater wider than even they had ever imagined' (Critser 2003: 29). And yet this creates a similar problem to the one we have just discussed. In the remainder of *Fat Land* Critser blames people in general, and baby boomers in particular, for *choosing* to reject the moral constraints of the past. So who is to blame here: capitalism or ourselves? No doubt some readers will see this as a misleading, even meaningless question. We would completely agree, but add simply that this is the inevitable end point when commentators choose to analyse social issues through the lens of so-called 'moral absolutes'.

The next chapter, 'World without boundaries', signals the moment in *Fat Land* when Critser moves to the 'main game' of moral decline. The role of governments and corporations is now dwarfed by what he sees as the erosion of 'traditional boundaries' and 'old wisdom' (Critser 2003: 31). Critser's argument begins with the post-1960s movement of women into the workforce, moves to parents with less time and inclination to eat with children and to monitor the food they consume, then on to more meals consumed outside of the home and, finally, to increased obesity. The glue holding all the pieces of this puzzle together was and is, he says, the annihilation of 'self-control'. While he claims that an ethos of abundance has always been a powerful element of American culture and family life, the 'obesity epidemic' is the product of a baby boomer generation, which has purged itself of self-denial and is squeamish about saying 'no' to children.

As with Eberstadt's article, our inclination is to suspend judgement on Critser's overarching argument, partly through fear of descending into the same 'argument-by-generalization' that characterizes *Fat Land* and the 'obesity epidemic' literature in general. For the moment, we would at least point out that Critser's claim that Western moral boundaries, including but not only those relating to food, have dissolved is far from the self-evident truth he claims it is. For example, we might wonder whether the last thirty or forty years of advanced capitalism might not be more correctly characterized by *increased*, rather than decreased, moral injunction. Here we are thinking of moral concerns which would traditionally be associated with both the 'left' – such as human rights; racial discrimination; violence against children, women and other groups; the environment; and the unethical behaviour of institutions such as the church, police and government – and the 'right' – such as crime; juvenile delinquency; and what appears to be decreasing public sympathy and tolerance for welfare recipients, refugees, the unemployed and those exhibiting insufficient 'patriotism'. And on the matter of food, there are many who argue that food guilt has never been so widespread, nor have people ever felt more inhibited about food than is currently the case (e.g. Atrens 2000; Griffiths and Wallace 1998; Hesse-Biber 1996). Sociological health researchers such as Germov and Williams (1996) have used the word 'epidemic' to refer not to obesity, but to dieting among girls and women and even called for a moratorium on anti-overweight and obesity health campaigns.

As problematic as Critser's sweeping argument about the erosion of moral boundaries is, its ideological and moral dimensions come more sharply into view if we focus on the moments in *Fat Land* where he appeals to scientific certainty. For example, Critser is highly critical of the childcare and parenting books that proliferated during the 1980s and that, he claims, emphasized the 'important but ultimately squishy notions of "autonomy" and "empowerment"' (Critser 2003: 33). Critser's critique rests on the charge that the authors of these books mistakenly believed in 'the central dogma in the child-as-food-sage theology – that a child "knows" when he or she is full'. He paints the ideas of those with whom he disagrees as extremist 'theorizing', 'dogma' and 'theology' all of which fly in the face of 'overwhelming evidence' (Critser 2003: 38) to the contrary. He then summarizes a few studies he claims suggest that children need to be told what and when to eat and that parents should 'lovingly hassle' their children about food if they want to prevent or cure childhood obesity. Critser's verdict is unequivocal and certain: parents' increasing failure over the last twenty years to monitor and take active responsibility for what and when children eat has contributed significantly to the 'obesity epidemic'.

Is he correct? In their review of the literature concerning the influence of parents on childhood food intake and body weight outcomes for the journal *Obesity Reviews*, Schwartz and Puhl (2003) arrive at a very different conclusion. They argue that, far from being told to relinquish control, for decades parents have been bombarded with advice about how to manage what their children eat, much of it conflicting, and that parental intervention does not always have the desired effect. For example, some studies suggest that parental monitoring may *create* otherwise non-existent food anxiety among children, particularly when mothers restrict the food choices of daughters, and make 'bad' foods all the more desirable in children's eyes. This is particularly true, they argue, when 'bad' foods are incessantly promoted in shops and in the media, landing parents in the extremely unenviable role of 'food-police'. They point out that it is not at all clear whether children are by nature self-limiting eaters or not, but that there appear to be at least some circumstances in which children seem perfectly able to self-limit food intake without the verbal intervention of parents. They also suggest that it is unreasonable and unrealistic for parents to be held responsible for solving the obesity problem, particularly when they are struggling with the same cultural environment, the same mixed messages and the same pressures to both consume and resist 'bad' food themselves.

Critser then turns his attention to other factors, which he sees as having either created or perpetuated our 'world without boundaries'. For example, he provides a short history of the opening up of US government schools to the fast food industry, claiming that this was precipitated by the 'small-government' and economic rationalist policies of state legislatures during the 1980s. As Nestle's (2002) *Food Politics* also documents, many US schools have managed their straitened budgetary circumstances by negotiating business deals of various kinds with fast food and soft-drink vendors. On the whole, Critser appears to argue that this has been a self-evidently negative development, quoting statistics that suggest children's consumption of soft drinks increased during this period.

Once again, a reasonable question might be to ask who is to blame here? Although we might wonder about the role played by corporations who both supported legislation to restrict school funding and who profited handsomely from the resulting school funding situation, or the converging neo-liberal economic policies of both Republican and Democratic administrations – policies that were strikingly similar to those being enacted by conservative and social-democratic governments alike around the Western world – Critser blames what he calls 'Me Generation' citizens who voted for these policies. The picture he paints is of spoilt baby boomers putting their own hip pockets ahead of money for government services. As he puts it:

> In all of this ran a variant of the generational temper tantrum that Earl Butz [the person Critser 'credits' for increases in corn syrup and palm oil usage] had encountered only a few years earlier. The folk wanted what they wanted when they wanted it.
>
> (Critser 2003: 44)

Social commentators, particularly those of the 'left', are often criticized for offering an overly condescending assessment of the populace. But as we saw with the epidemiologist Garry Egger (Chapter 2) and here with Greg Critser, the idea of the 'obesity epidemic' appears to lock commentators into a view of people as childlike in their stupidity, short-sightedness and utter self-centredness. This is, as Egger claimed, our nature.

From here to the end of his book, no matter where Critser turns, he sees an American population addicted to soft options – ready to follow any fad diet in preference to simply eating less, abandoning traditional church teachings against gluttony, and even attracted to rap music's baggy clothing style which, he argues, has helped to erode the 'traditional' stigma attached to being fat. The manner in which Critser substantiates his baggy clothing thesis is yet another case of the way science is used to disguise or at least obscure moral and ideological agendas. In this case, Critser attempts to transform his argument about a slide in general moral standards into a scientific one by claiming that there is a 'small but important body of science upholding the theory' (Critser 2003: 61) that people who buy new loose fitting clothes are more likely to put on weight than those whose choose to stick with their tighter fitting old ones. By way of evidence, he offers one three-page clinical study concerned with patients who had undergone jaw wiring procedures which, published in 1981, actually pre-dates the popularization of rap music and its clothing by some time. The claim that rap's baggy clothing has played any role whatsoever in determining population obesity levels or general biomedical heath (which, after all, is Critser's ultimate stated focus in this book) has the ring of pure speculation and is not substantiated here. In fact, given that the one cited study predates the phenomena it is supposed to illuminate, no substantiation is really attempted.

Up to this point one of the more serious problems with *Fat Land* is the author's tendency first to take a moral position, second to find shreds of 'scientific' evidence that he sees as supporting his original position and third to claim scientific certainty on the basis of this evidence. This preparedness to put absolute faith in the find-ings of one or two studies evaporates in chapter four, 'Why the calories stayed on our bodies', in which Critser turns conspiracy theorist. He has two primary targets.

First, he blames the 'obesity epidemic' on the demise of 'traditional' physical education. Here Critser mentions government funding cuts, increasing educational emphasis on the 'basics', the fitness boom of the 1970s and the rise of private sports clubs for children. However, true to his agenda, Critser reserves his most serious criticism for physical educators (as opposed to government policies) who have turned their backs on 'traditional' physical education practices such as fitness testing children and callisthenics in physical education classes.

Second, Critser charts shifts over the last twenty years or so in scientific opinion concerning the amount and the kind of exercise people need to do in order to reduce their disease risk. As we have shown (see Chapter 3), during this period many experts have questioned the health (as opposed to fitness) benefits of vigorous exercise, while also suggesting that the value of 'accumulated' bouts of 'moderate' physical activity, such as walking and household chores, may have been seriously underestimated.

Critser's verdict on both of these issues is that physical educators and exercise scientists presented the populace, already on the look out for any excuse to take it easy, with an open invitation to take things even more easily, of 'lowering the bar' of exercise expectation. In addition, in both cases Critser argues that those in what he calls the 'exercise establishment' allowed themselves to be swayed by bad research into believing what they believe – if only they had been able to sort out the facts from the latest trendy fictions, his argument goes, then things would be different.

We have already discussed both the relevance of physical education and the exercise-for-health guidelines earlier in this book. At this point we would simply reiterate that the connection between physical education and lifelong exercise habits is not nearly as straightforward as Critser suggests. There is a consider-able amount of research that suggests many of physical education's practices of the past best suited those students who were already interested in sports and other athletic pursuits. For other students, the prospect of alienation from physical education, as Tinning and Fitzclarence (1992) put it, has been all too common. An approach to physical education that emphasises physical fitness and weight loss is unlikely to appeal to many students or to make lifelong exercisers out of less athletically inclined students. To put the point bluntly, the kind of physical education that Critser advocates has been criticized because many children do not (and probably never did) enjoy it and was, in this sense, potentially counter-productive, particularly for those students most alienated from physical activity already. At the same time, it is not at all clear, and Critser offers no evidence, that the fitness and fatness testing practices he advocates ever really went out of fashion with many teachers.

Critser's focus on physical education, although flawed, is not surprising since it rests on a misconception that plagues many *within* the physical education profession itself. This misconception is the idea that physical education can 'programme' children to be physically active throughout their adult life in the same way as we might program a computer to perform certain functions. In fact, this is actually another variation of the 'body as machine' model because it assumes that if we do something to a human body then something predictable will happen. However, it is an idea that fails to see that recreational physical activity is a dimension of, and is affected by, the day-to-day realities of people's lives. Commentators sometimes make the mistake of pointing to research that suggests that physically active children are more likely to become physically active adults as evidence to support the 'programming' argument. What this view overlooks is that a similar set of variables such as socio-economic class, gender, ethnicity, level of physical disability and geographical location influence both children's and adults' physical activity choices and opportunities. There is no magic here which physical education performs, transforming otherwise inactive people into regular lifelong exercisers.

This is not to say that Critser ignores socio-economic class as a factor in the 'obesity epidemic', although the manner in which he includes it highlights the central weakness in his overall argument about general moral decline. Critser acknowledges that wealthier people are less likely to be obese, more likely to do regular recreational physical activity and more likely to be able to articulate the health benefits of regular exercise and a balanced diet. But if, as Critser claims, obesity is primarily a moral issue, then these statistics push him close to the point of claiming either that wealthier people are also more virtuous or that the poor are simply more lazy and gluttonous. Critser gets himself out of this bind by claiming that the research into how much exercise we should do to maintain health is flawed because it has been conducted on largely affluent populations. As he puts it:

> These populations of lawyers and business executives may have looked much like average Americans; their body weights, rates of various diseases, and dietary patterns may have been not that different from those of a lineman for the telephone company or a data processor for an insurance company. But their total life experiences were very different. What made thirty minutes of accumulated activity a prophylactic against heart disease for the rich – with their already buffered existence – would likely, one might surmise, be much more dilute for the middle class, even more so for the poor. This is because

when the rich garden, even briskly, they are doing so with all the other health advantages that come with being rich. Their mini-dose of exercise is amplified by socioeconomics.

(Critser 2003: 92)

In short, while the wealthy might get away with small amounts of exercise, Critser's argument is that this is dangerous advice to give the less wealthy. Critser does not say it, but the end point of this line of argument appears to be that the poor should do more exercise than the rich. What he *does* say is that concern about excessive thinness, particularly anorexia, is primarily a middle- and upper-class anxiety and has been given too much attention. In fact, in an earlier article for *Harper's Magazine* (2000) Critser took this argument even further, suggesting that greater weight anxiety and anorexia among White middle-class girls was a relatively small price to pay if it kept them from becoming overweight and obese. And while much has been written and said about the possible harm caused by the women's fashion industry obsession with thinness, Critser is quoted elsewhere as claiming that thin fashion models represent moral virtue: 'there is something in a model's slimness that is good and that we recognise as good. Models tell us that it probably is better to be thinner' (Cooke 2003: 25).

Critser's class analysis boils down to a question of information. He interprets survey results, which show that Black and Hispanic children watch more television than White children and that people with a lower income are less likely to agree with the statement 'I would definitely exercise more if I had the time' (Critser 2003: 71), as proof that poorer people are simply ignorant. Not only might there be any number of other reasons besides ignorance why people might not agree with this statement, at no stage does Critser tackle perhaps the oldest and best documented of all health promotion problems: the disjunction between what people know and what they do (Hollis *et al.* 1986; Shepherd and Stockley 1987).

Critser also interprets research which suggests that African American girls are more likely to be happy with their body weight despite being more overweight than White girls as more evidence that they simply do not know what is good for them. The reason for their ignorance, his argument goes, is that the rich simply refuse to set a good enough example. Critser does not seem to consider the possibility that on some things, rather than being blind followers, poorer people may actively reject the behaviour and values of the rich. He goes on to blame exercise physiologists for lowering general population exercise guidelines (which Critser presumably believes the poor follow religiously) and postmodernists for daring to suggest that poor African Americans sometimes reject the pronouncements of middle-class medicine as a perfectly reasonable consequence of the failure of middle-class medicine to serve their needs in the past. Above all, Critser is un-relenting in his scorn for any suggestion that we should be happy with who we are. While some of us would empathize with people who might already have enough to worry about, such as the poor and ethnic minorities, Critser's argument is that these people should be *more* concerned about exercise and diet than more affluent groups.

This is a particularly confusing line of reasoning because he argues that the middle and upper classes are simultaneously much less obese, much more concerned about body weight, exercising more in private gyms, health clubs and sporting teams and *at the same time* sending the message to the rest of society that body weight and exercise are not important. And yet, this is precisely what Critser must argue given his focus on the socio-economics of overweight and obesity, on the one hand, and his utterly confused concern with 'moral decline', on the other. Because Critser is so committed to the idea that fat is first and foremost a moral issue, he fails to consider the well-documented association between general health and socio-economic class and the ways in which overweight and obesity might be similarly linked to disadvantage. What matters for Critser is only that the rich should instruct the poor about the 'moral absolutes' of life.

Fumento's fundamentalism

There could no clearer exemplification of our contention that the 'obesity epidemic' is primarily a moral and ideological phenomenon, rather than a scientific one, than Michael Fumento's (1997a) *The Fat of the Land: The Obesity Epidemic and How Overweight Americans Can Help Themselves*. At the time of its publication, Fumento was as a resident fellow of the American Enterprise Institute, one of the world's better-known right-wing think tanks. Fumento is the author a number of books on a remarkably wide range of topics, each adopting an impeccably conservative/pro-business/anti-liberal line. They include: *The Myth of Heterosexual AIDS* (1990) in which he blames a gay-lobby conspiracy for unnecessarily alarming heterosexual people and exaggerating their chance of catching AIDS; *Polluted Science* (1997b) which argues that environmental standards and regulations designed to reduce air pollution in the US are both unwarranted and unfairly restrictive on business; and *BioEvolution: How Biotechnology is Changing Our World* (2003) which, quoting the advertising blurb on Fumento's website, 'shows how biotech has already demonstrated the potential to cure almost any disease, extend human lifespans well past the 120-year range, and wipe out not only famine but malnutrition while using less land, less water, and fewer chemicals' (http://www. fumento.com/biotech/bioevolution.html).

In ideological terms, Fumento is what we might call a 'cultural warrior', very much a product of late twentieth-/early twenty-first-century US neo-conservatism. In his many newspaper columns and magazine articles he performs a kind of conservative 'gun for hire' role, ferociously attacking feminists, environmentalists, postmodernists and anyone else guilty of neo-conservatism's most deadly sin: liberalism. Why then, given his starkly partisan credentials, should we spend time discussing his contribution to the 'obesity epidemic'? The answer is that Fumento's writing is exquisitely emblematic (albeit in an extreme form) of the central problem that pervades 'obesity epidemic' thinking and its associated literature.

Fumento's writing is dominated by one rhetorical device – the purity of science. As the title of his other works – *Polluted Science* (1997b) and *Silicone Breast Implants: Why Has Science Been Ignored?* (an unpublished monograph in which he attacks those who have warned of the health risks of silicone breast implants) – suggests, he asks his readers to believe that science produces one, pure self-evident truth and that anyone who arrives at a different conclusion is guilty of an ideologically-driven misreading. In effect, he treats scientific literatures, whether they relate to SARS, AIDS or obesity, as if they were sacred texts, open only to one true interpretation: there is only 'good science' – which produces the 'truth' – and 'bad science' – which produces lies. And while other 'obesity epidemic' writers may come to different conclusions on some issues, they share Fumento's belief that only science will give us the answers we need and, just as importantly, that the only questions worth asking are the questions that science chooses to ask.

In the course of *The Fat of the Land*, Fumento presents body weight as a purely mathematical exercise – the difference between calories-in and calories-out – an idea which, as we have seen, is repeated regularly in the scientific literature. To do this, he takes a long list of scientific questions and controversies and irons them flat, claiming in effect that any suggestion that body weight is a complex matter, or that excess body weight may not always be a bad thing, is sheer myth making. For example, Fumento proposes that there is no such thing as benign fat, regardless of where you find it on your body, despite the existence of quite main-stream scientific opinion that people (more often men) who carry more body fat around the chest and abdomen are at greater health risk than those (more often women) who carry more of it on the buttocks and thighs. He claims that the percentage of total calories that we derive from dietary fat is completely unim-portant – the only thing that matters is the number of calories we consume, and whether they come from protein, carbohydrate or fat is immaterial. He dismisses concerns about the safety of the various weight loss drugs available or the possible injurious effects of 'yo-yo dieting'. And he ridicules the idea that human body weight is partly controlled by a person's individual metabolic rate and therefore resistant to change – the so-called 'setpoint' theory. In all of these cases Fumento does not merely suggest that, on balance, the evidence is on his side. Instead, those who arrive at different conclusions are either dishonest, stupid or both: 'The setpoint theory has its place, but its place is alongside goblins, fairies, dragons, honest high-ranking politicians, and other creatures of mythology' (Fumento 1997a: 107).

Regardless of which scientific controversy he buys into, the answer is always the same: body fat is bad for you, body weight can and must be controlled by individual force of will and any attempt to argue that losing weight is anything other than a matter of personal choice is simply an exercise in making excuses:

> But as with Scrooge, everything is ultimately up to you. I'm no spirit and regrettably possess no magical powers. But I've got one thing going for me that the spirits didn't have: empathy. I've been there. I've been fat. And though that's no longer the case, I still share the American culture, with its weaknesses and temptations. I just happen to have learned a few things others haven't.
>
> (Fumento 1997a: 26)

Or, more succinctly, Fumento refers to his own apparently victorious battle with overweight: 'As soon as I started losing my excuses I started losing weight' (Fumento 1997a: 115).

The point to draw attention to here is the way a moral position generates a particular way of reading and interpreting science. Because Fumento has a moral message to deliver – 'pathological slothfulness exists everywhere in this country' (Fumento 1997a: 49) and fat people are simply gluttonous, self-deceiving sinners – empirical complexity and uncertainty cannot be tolerated. If, as we would contend, the 'truth' of all of the scientific matters he writes about is neither resolved nor simple, then the moral force of his argument fades. It is not impossible to accept that, on the one hand, our knowledge about overweight and obesity is partial, contradictory and complex while, on the other hand, maintaining a moralistic and individualistic position on body weight. But, clearly, moral positions are simpler to defend when the 'truth' is said to be 'self-evident'.

It is also interesting to note the way Fumento's moral position, combined with scientific certainty, also forces him to recommend obesity 'cures', which became popular during the Victorian period of the nineteenth century. For example, he recommends slow chewing of food, wearing tight fitting clothes and, in perhaps the most disturbing section of the book, advocates the use of commercially available weight loss 'potions' (or 'drugs' in today's language) despite their well-documented, serious and sometimes fatal side effects. Once again, it is apparent that more scientific knowledge does not necessarily propel us into the future.

Fumento reserves his sharpest criticism for the members of what has become known as the fat acceptance movement (see Chapter 8), along with what Fumento calls their 'Aiders and Abettors' (Fumento 1997a: 120) within the scientific community. These writers have raised doubts about the health risks of fatness, particularly Glenn Gaesser, Steven Blair and Dale Atrens. Atrens, the author of *Don't Diet* (1988) and (well after the publication of *The Fat of the Land*) *The Power of Pleasure* (2000) (discussed previously), is guilty of pointing to the substantial literature that questions the value of caloric restriction. For Fumento, to cast doubt on dieting is to promote self-defeatism. Gaesser and Blair's sins are, if anything, more serious. Throughout *The Fat of the Land*, Fumento accuses these authors of foolishly putting lives at risk by suggesting that the amount of physical activity a person does is a more important health factor than their body weight:

> By great coincidence, both Gaesser and Blair work in the exercise field . . . Likewise, it's common to see those in the nutrition area (such as weight-loss clinics) downplay or dismiss exercise, while those who tout weight-loss drugs will sometimes downplay both diet and exercise. Parochialism is a common vice among people. But when you're dealing with other people's health and lives, you do have a responsibility to try to rise above it. Gaesser and Blair have not.
>
> (Fumento 1997a: 24)

Nothing appears to irritate Fumento more than the idea that we might accept ourselves the way we are. Self-esteem, he argues, only comes from achievement and it is our *responsibility*, a word he uses repeatedly, to be better, thinner people. He contends that there is no reason why people should accept gaining weight as they age and that his own success in returning to the weight of his twenties is proof.

Although Greg Critser is described as a Democrat (see p. 137), his argument is virtually identical to Fumento's 'neo-conservative-meets-obesity' agenda. According to both authors, the problem is that too many people, particularly 'bad' scientists, have been involved in creating a culture in which it is OK to be fat. Like Critser, Fumento blames the fashion for baggy clothing and sees the problem of what children eat as simply a matter of parents being firm and modelling the right behaviour. For Fumento, what children eat 'comes down to child-see, child-do' (Fumento 1997a: 18). Like Critser, Fumento wishes we could go back to 'real' physical education: 'When I was a kid in the 1960s, physical education was required and it was real. It was wind-sprints, circuit training, long-distance running, push-ups, pull-ups' (Fumento 1997a: 268–9). And for both authors, the 'obesity epidemic' could be solved if, first, scientists would only speak the truth rather than lies and, second, if American culture had not gone into deep moral decline and become only too willing to accept the 'OK to be fat' message.

And yet this is the most puzzling aspect of Fumento's book. While a number of researchers in both the medical and social sciences have described and lamented what they see as widespread and increasing stigmatization of obese people, for Fumento it is absolutely clear that we do not stigmatize enough. He argues that there are too many happy overweight people in television advertisements and thinks Hollywood films should not present overweight people in a positive light, an argument that runs counter to research suggesting that television tends not to present overweight and obese people in a favourable light at all (such as Greenberg *et al.* 2003). Indeed, he argues that we need to step up our stigmatization of obese people while, at the same time, claiming that obese people bring stigma upon themselves because their 'lower self-esteem' means they are 'less likable, less physically attractive' and have 'inferior social skills' (Fumento 1997a: 126). Lost in the late twentieth-century fads of 'self-esteem' and 'personal freedom', Fumento says that we live in societies (and here he is no longer talking only about the US) that stigmatize *thin* people and tolerate, even venerate, the fat. What we need is to make obesity 'gauche' (Fumento 1997a: 264).

One of Fumento's other arguments is that the media, the medical profession and governments have been virtually silent about the crisis of obesity while making far too much of illnesses like HIV/AIDS. This also seems a slightly surprising claim, although published in 1997, it is true that *The Fat of the Land* pre-dated by some years the crescendo of comment in 2003. In this sense at least, the book could be seen as prescient.

Machines within machines

Finally, we turn to Ellen Ruppel Shell's (2002) *The Hungry Gene: The Science of Fat and the Future of Thin*. As the title suggests, Shell's intention in this book is to tell a 'scientific' story about the 'obesity epidemic', one in which genetics plays a central role. This is interesting because obesity researchers, particularly those working in epidemiology, exercise science and what we might call 'traditional' medicine, tend to minimize the significance of genetics.

This is apparently not a view Shell shares. In fact, she appears to see the genetics of obesity as something of a saviour for the previously moribund field of obesity studies. She writes:

'Obesity science' has, in the last half-decade, been transformed from a lack-luster backwater into a vibrant field of inquiry attracting some of the most brilliant minds in science, and liberating overweight from the murky ghetto of 'character flaw' to the more potent status of 'disease.' Startling new insights into the genetic, parental, and environmental factors directing body weight have opened deeper questions and bigger challenges. They also point temptingly to concrete and viable approaches to prevention and treatment.

(Shell 2002: 4–5)

Throughout *The Hungry Gene*, either Shell herself, or others from the brave new scientific worlds she describes, lament the enduring focus on individual behaviour that has dominated obesity studies. In a similar vein to the critique we have offered in this book, Shell sees the individualism of pre-genetics obesity science as conservative and obscuring other more important lines of analysis. On this point, if not others, she articulates a similar point of view to the one offered in this book.

In many respects *The Hungry Gene* might also be seen as a rebuttal of Fumento's *The Fat of the Land*. Shell argues that human body weight is not really a matter of pure choice and, in fact, is largely determined by factors beyond individual control. She does this by pursuing two general lines of argument. First, Shell looks at three areas of medical and/or scientific activity. The first of these is gastric bypass surgery in which the capacity of the patient's stomach is reduced. Why this is included is not clear unless it is simply to provide an example of a developing non-behavioural form of obesity treatment. Next comes a series of chapters devoted to the genetics of human body weight. Shell provides a lively account of the major players in this research, their personalities and the intrigue that accompanied the worldwide race to be first to publish. Third, we are introduced to researchers who are convinced that the secret to overweight and obesity lies in evolution and understanding the prenatal embryonic environment. The theory here is that foetuses, which are deprived of sufficient nutrition early in pregnancy, develop into adults with a significantly higher risk of becoming overweight or obese. As Shell points out, these last two areas of science can be seen as contradicting the dominant behavioural approaches to overweight and obesity which see people's personal choices about food and exercise as the main problem. These surgeons, geneticists and prenatal theory researchers are the 'brilliant minds' alluded to in the beginning of the book. Indeed, they represent 'the science of fat and the future of thin', which the book's title announces.

And yet, having spent so much time talking about biomedical science, the book then takes an unexpected turn into her second line of argument, which deals with two decidedly social and cultural issues. The first focuses on the rapid influx of new consumer goods and high-fat and high-sugar foods into various South Pacific nations with disastrous health consequences. The second of these sees Shell covering (although in far less detail) much the same territory as Marion Nestle's *Food Politics* and Eric Schlosser's *Fast Food Nation*. She decries the manufacturers and marketers of fast and convenience food for their sophisticated and unapologetic exploitation of children, their infiltration of US schools and their ferocious resistance to government regulation.

This sidestep into the economics and politics of food raises two important questions which, although not exactly criticisms of *The Hungry Gene*, recall two serious problems with 'obesity epidemic' thinking discussed earlier in this book. First, Shell blames the obesity-related health problems faced by South Pacific nations as problems of 'Westernization'. However, this is an impossibly vague term, which seems to obscure, if not avoid, a careful analysis of the situation at hand. For example, there would seem a perfectly reasonable argument to be made here to the effect that the South Pacific situation is one of simple exploitation, where capitalist forces are being unleashed in a largely unregulated environment and, in fact, in a way which is *unlike* that in any Western country. Are these countries being 'Westernized' or are they simply being used as dumping grounds for a relatively small but profitable range of products? Might the conditions in which the trade of these products happens – between large economically powerful states on the one hand, and small impoverished ones on the other – perhaps better explain what is happening in the South Pacific? Certainly, when Shell turns her focus to the behaviour of fast and convenience food companies in the US she no longer talks about 'Westernization'. But why not?

Part of the answer is perhaps that she, like others, has become accustomed to discussing the cause of *Western* overweight and obesity in different – although no less vague – terms such as 'modern lifestyles'. If the forces of capitalism *are* playing a significant part in the rise of obesity in different parts of the world – and if people, in the end, decide that this is a bad thing – then it is hard to see how this problem will be solved without naming it. Shell, Greg Critser, Marion Nestle, Eric Schlosser and even Michael Fumento all appear to argue that obesity levels rose at the same time as the production and marketing of fast and convenience foods entered a new aggressive and sophisticated phase. This period, from the 1970s onwards, has also been a time of rapid economic and industrial deregulation in many Western countries. Of course, the argument that conclusively links rampant capitalism with the 'obesity epidemic' has not yet been made nor even seriously attempted. However, as speculative as this argument might currently be, it would seem a much more promising approach than lumping together every factor that might – or might not – be contributing and calling it 'Westernization' or 'modernization'.

The second problem with 'obesity epidemic' thinking that *The Hungry Gene* highlights relates to the value of science. Without exception, all of the books discussed in this chapter finish with the authors offering some potential solutions to the current crisis. However, having spent all but two chapters discussing the biomedical science of obesity, Shell's concluding chapter devotes only one paragraph to the future significance of this work. In it she considers the prospects that this research will lead to effective obesity treatments without the harmful side effects of previous drugs. She does not appear to be overly hopeful that this will happen. She writes:

> There are other such drugs in the pipeline. One or another of these preparations may one day mitigate the symptoms of obesity, and the diseases linked to it. But this is not at all certain. Nor is any weight loss drug likely to permanently alter human physiology or brain chemistry. To be effective against

obesity, drug treatment must be continuous, and administered under a watchful eye. Given the scope of the obesity pandemic this is not a particularly hopeful – or realistic – prospect.

(Shell 2002: 221)

She might also have recalled here her observation from earlier in the book that, at the time of writing, the genetic mutation, which it is claimed leads to obesity, had been discovered in only about a dozen people, mostly from developing countries. Simply put, her opening claim that the new sciences of obesity would revolutionize our understanding of human body weight, a claim stated plainly in the book's full title, comes to nothing. While *The Hungry Gene: The Science of Fat and the Future of Thin* starts out as yet another 'science will save us' story, it concludes as a passionate attack directed at 'Big Food'. In the end, she sees the 'obesity epidemic's' future cure stemming from 'moral outrage' (Shell 2002: 235) at what these companies do. Meanwhile, the science of genes, evolution and prenatal hormones are left far behind.

When science doesn't matter

The word 'science' and the claim that one's argument is 'scientific' *does* sell books and lend commentators an air of credibility. However, all of the authors discussed in this chapter start with scientific arguments and end up making moral and ideological ones. The science that they spend so much time collecting and dissecting leads them nowhere or, more precisely, it appears to make no difference to the direction in which they were already heading. The same scientific ideas, whether they are about television viewing, genetics or the amount of exercise people should do, are continually used to argue directly opposing points of view.

Some readers may see these as radical or counter-intuitive propositions. On the contrary, we would contend that the resolution of issues of scientific, social, cultural, political and economic significance very often, perhaps usually, depend on the relative power of the various stakeholders, as well as the moral and ideological arguments they are able to marshal. This does not mean that science is never important. There are some domains of life where scientific knowledge is crucial and where it is probably right that scientists have the final word. Overweight and obesity do not constitute one of these domains. The ideas upon which current debate rests – that excessive fatness is bad for one's health and that fatness is caused by too much food and/or not enough exercise – are millennia old. And although scientists – whether they study genes, ask children to carry pedometers around with them all day or ask people to tell them how much they ate in the last week – may, out of force of habit, call for 'more research' in the final paragraph of their research papers, none of this will make much difference to the future of fat or thin. Even though obesity scientists constantly claim that we need to understand why we are getting fatter in order to stop it from continuing, this is also a mistaken view. The reason why the 'obesity epidemic' has come about could not be less important. The future will be decided along moral and ideological – that is, political – grounds. Economic power will also be crucial. The fact that genetic and pharmacological solutions are attracting by far the most investment – not to mention that some, like Ellen Ruppel Shell, see genetics as bringing a previously lacking scientific credibility and glamour to obesity studies – is simply more proof that the answer to the 'obesity epidemic's' 'why?' question is completely immaterial and will probably never be known.

It is right and proper that matters of public concern be resolved on moral and ideological grounds and in the next chapter we offer some explicitly moral and ideological reasons for distrusting the idea of an 'obesity epidemic'. However, within the 'obesity science for the people' literature, as well as mainstream science, there is a tendency among authors to write as if a sober assessment of the available scientific evidence preceded the conclusions they came to. This is disingenuous. As this chapter shows, the state of science makes little if any difference to the conclusions people come to. This is true in part because, as we have argued throughout this book, scientific certainty about the things 'obesity epidemic' commentators write about is so elusive – science has not delivered the 'truth' about human body weight. But it is also true because moral and ideological questions are often simply more important than scientific ones.

8   Feminism and the 'obesity epidemic'

So far in this book we have provided a critique of the ways in which obesity has been talked about in the mass-media, the scientific literature and other popular publications. In each case, we have seen how people take for granted the proposition that 'overweight and obesity' are definable, recognizable, universally understandable, measurable 'real' objects. We have described how the ideology of the 'obesity epidemic' has been constructed, and how its central arguments have been marshalled and disseminated by journalists, scientists and other commentators.

While many writers have argued that the 'obesity epidemic' should be attributed to the nature of contemporary society, few stop to think about how the concept itself has come to be understood. Rarely do these researchers and writers reflect on the consequences of the ways overweight and obesity are talked about. Instead, there often seems a moral righteousness, if not zeal, about the way obese and overweight individuals are pursued as unable to 'care for themselves' and thus in need of expert help. The evangelical metaphors here are intended: like evangelical missionaries, alternative ways of thinking are ignored and evidence that challenges strongly held positions is either ignored or attacked.

In Chapter 1, ideology was described as providing 'tools' for understanding the world. In using ideology in this way, we acknowledge that all our ways of making sense of the world, our beliefs and values are ideological. In this sense, if we are to challenge the 'obesity epidemic' as an ideological construction we need to demonstrate that there are other ways of thinking about health, the body and weight. If we want to challenge this ideology, it is also not sufficient to argue that it is powerful and pervasive as so are all dominant ideologies by definition. What we need to argue is that the focus on obesity and overweight, the construction of the 'obesity epidemic' needs to be challenged because of its effects on the lives of individuals and social groups: effects that are not as positive and health promoting as proponents of the 'obesity epidemic' would have us believe. In this and the next chapter we will look to two broad areas of research and writing to do this: feminist writings on the body and contemporary sociological analyses of health.

The exploited body of patriarchy

It is generally agreed that second wave feminism has led the way, in the English-language literature, in challenging notions of the body that simply take it to be a biological object to be studied in the context of the medical and biological sciences. Feminists were originally suspicious of the body as a focus of resistance because of its apparently unassailable association with those 'natural' biological attributes (e.g. reproduction, physical weakness in comparison to men) that were assumed to be at the heart of women's oppression. Instead, they chose to take unequal and oppressive social and labour relations as their main object of concern. However, it soon became evident that the oppression of women reached deeply into their personal and daily lives and that the body was a major site on which culture was made manifest and through which patriarchal violence and exploitation was visited.

In 1968 Charlotte Bunch wrote: 'There is no private domain of a person's life that is not political and there is no political issue that is not ultimately personal. The old barriers have fallen' (quoted in Bordo 1993: 17). As Bordo argues, this heralded a new way of thinking about the body. 'What', she asks, 'after all, is more personal than the life of the body? . . . for women, culture's grip on the body is a constant intimate fact of everyday life' (Bordo 1993: 17).

Following this premise, feminists began to examine how patriarchal power relations shaped the way the female body should look, dress, move and with what consequences for what women could be and do. Feminists were interested in how expectations about feminine behaviour kept women in their place and set about raising the consciousness of women about how women's bodies were controlled and exploited in the contexts of domestic life, work, law, medicine and health.

At the centre of many feminist concerns about the body, in the 1960s and 1970s, was the exploitation and oppression deriving from the constraints imposed on women by social expectations of femininity associated with female attractiveness. As Andrea Dworkin wrote at the time:

> Standards of beauty describe in precise terms the relationship that an individual will have to her own body. They describe her motility, spontaneity, posture, gait, the uses to which she can put her body. They define precisely the dimensions of her physical freedom . . . In our culture, not one part of a woman's body is left untouched, unaltered. No feature or extremity is spared the art, or pain, of improvement. . . . From head to toe, every feature of a woman's face, every section of her body, is subject to modification, alteration. This alteration is an ongoing repetitive process. It is vital to the economy, the major substance of male-female differentiation, the most immediate physical and psychological reality of being a woman. From the age of 11 or 12 until she dies, a woman will spend a large part of her time and money, and energy on binding, plucking, painting and deodorizing herself.
>
> (Dworkin 1974 quoted in Bordo 1993: 21)

Central to contemporary feminist understanding of the body is the idea that what it means to be female is shaped by and in historical relations of power. What counts as femininity is not fixed but changes over time and in the context of different social, economic and political circumstances. This includes notions of female beauty including the shape and size of the body. In relation to themes developed in this book, the argument is that female attractiveness has not been, and is not everywhere, defined in terms of a thin body shape. Nor in terms of contemporary notions of feminine beauty is the ideal fixed, rather as Naomi Wolf suggests the yardstick keeps changing. For example, the average size of the female fashion model today is 23 per cent less than that of the average US woman, compared to 8 per cent less than a generation ago (Wolf 1990) and from the 1950s to the present, the body sizes of Miss America Pageant winners have decreased significantly (Spitzer et al. 1999).

The slender body

Feminist concerns with cultural expectations about the shape and size of the body gained focus in 1980s when feminist psychotherapists such as Susan Orbach (1988) and Kim Chernin (1981) drew attention to the increasing incidence of young women with clinical manifestations of 'eating disorders' such as 'compulsive eating', 'anorexia' and 'bulimia'. Contrary to the prevailing thinking in psychiatry at the time, they argued that this phenomenon could not be explained simply by individual pathologies but by the social and cultural context in which young women lived, contexts that were 'disabling' for women. They argued that it was no coincidence that these 'disorders' primarily affected women, and that this must have something to do with what it means to be female in contemporary Western society. Writing about 'compulsive eating', in *Fat is a Feminist Issue*, Susan Orbach argues the case:

> A feminist perspective to the problem of women's compulsive eating is essential if we are to move on from the ineffective blame the victim approach and the unsatisfactory adjustment model of treatment. While psychoanalysis gives us the tools to discover the deepest sources of emotional distress, feminism insists that those painful experiences derive from a social context in which female babies are born, within which they develop to become adult women. The fact that compulsive eating is overwhelmingly a woman's problem suggests that it has something to do with the experience of being female in our society. Feminism argues that being fat represents an attempt to break free of society's stereotypes. Getting fat can thus be understood as a definite and purposeful act; it is a directed, conscious or unconscious, challenge to sex-role stereotyping and culturally defined experience of womanhood.
>
> (Orbach 1988: 18)

While this may seem somewhat of an oversimplification of the issue and not everyone would agree with the psychoanalytic direction of this interpretation, feminist psychotherapists were able to capture public attention because of the increasing concern over the numbers of women who were engaging in practices that were at the least damaging to their health and at worst life-threatening. In addition, their arguments were not only concerned with 'disordered eating', but were directed to all women. They argued it was the feminine condition that lay at the root of women's alienation from their bodies and this was shared by women throughout the Western world. The themes emerging from their writing became the basis for much of the feminist work on the body that followed. These themes are exemplified in the following quote from Orbach:

Since women are taught to see themselves from the outside as candidates for men, they become prey to the huge fashion and diet industries that first set up ideal images and then exhort women to meet them. The message is loud and clear – the woman's body is not her own. The woman's body is not satisfactory as it is. It must be thin, free of 'unwanted hair', deodorized, perfumed and clothed. It must conform to an ideal physical type. Family and school socialization teaches girls to groom themselves properly. Furthermore, the job is never-ending, for the images change from year to year. In the early 1960s, the only way to feel acceptable was to be skinny and flat chested with long straight hair. The first of these was achieved by near starvation, the second, by binding one's breasts with an ace bandage and the third by ironing one's hair. Then in the early 1970s, the look was curly hair and full breasts. Just as styles in clothes change seasonally, so women's bodies are expected to change to fit these fashions. Long and skinny one year, petite and demure the next, women are continually manipulated by images of proper womanhood, which are extremely powerful because they are represented as the only reality. To ignore them means to risk being an outcast.

(Orbach 1988: 20–1)

Both Orbach's and Chernin's analyses have much to say about 'how women's bodies become damaged in patriarchal society' (Shilling 1993: 66). Shilling (1993) points out, however, that they also start from an essentialized notion of the female body. For Orbach, thin is healthy and fat is pathological: women engage in compulsive eating and ignore the physiological cues governing hunger because of the way they treat food as a solution to other problems; problems that are associated with women's social oppression. For Chernin, fat is natural and beautiful and women only desire to become thin because of unrealistic social expectations. Despite these reservations, Orbach and Chernin brought the relationship between social expectations of femininity and body issues to public attention.

The prevalence of 'eating disorders' among women continues to be a matter of public concern. This concern continues to provide a platform for feminist work that challenges mainstream ideas about the body, shape and weight, including those associated with the 'obesity epidemic'. Such work reminds of the dangers of messages and other social practices that tell women (and increasingly men) that their bodies are inadequate, unattractive and they need to engage in a process of self-surveillance and body disciplining if they are to be regarded as worthy people.

The textually mediated body

The psychotherapeutic and radical feminist approaches, discussed above, pointed the way to an understanding of the body as a social, rather than simply biological, phenomenon within patriarchal social relations. Neither of these approaches, however, provided an explanation of how and why women take up oppressive ways of being. A number of questions still had to be addressed: What were the processes by which women took up or even resisted messages about the body? Were these messages taken up by all women in the same way? Were women simply 'cultural dupes' of the media?

In the 1980s feminists looked to popular culture, and academic writing about it, in order to understand how femininity and masculinity were constructed and how some meanings about gender/sexuality had more power, more appeal than others. They used the tools of deconstruction and discourse analysis to examine the ways meanings about femininity and masculinity were produced in and through the social practices (or texts) of everyday language, media texts, school instruction and so on. They looked to psychoanalytic and other social theories to explain why individuals might take up some meanings in making sense of the world and themselves rather than others.

Dorothy Smith an influential feminist writing in the 1980s exemplifies this position:

> Certainly in our time to address femininity is to address the textual discourse vested in women's magazines and television, advertisements, the appearance of cosmetic counters, fashion displays, and to a lesser extent books. These are constituents of the social relations they organize. Discourse also involves the talk women do in relation to such texts, the work of producing oneself to realize the textual images, the skills involved in going shopping, making and choosing clothes, making decisions about colours, styles, make-up and the ways in which these become a matter of interest among men.
>
> (Smith 1988: 41)

Discourse not only provides the resources to understand what it means to be feminine and how to achieve it, as Smith points out, it also structures or creates a desire to be a particular kind of woman and to engage in the practices that will achieve this. The images promoted as desirable through women's magazines, health and fitness magazines, fashion models, television and movie stars are of young, beautiful and thin women. Other images are limited 'if not entirely repressed from representation' (Gamman 2000: 65).

Writing on the basis of her experience in the media industry, Cyndi Tebbel (2000) describes how this process of regulation works in a context where 'the cosmetics, fashion and diet industries, the mass-media and the burgeoning business of cosmetic surgery' all profit from the message that women can never be 'too thin or too young'. She describes, for example, the responses to her choice of Emme Aronson, a US size 16 model, for the cover of a Body Image Issue of *New Woman* magazine (Australia). Despite more positive mail for the issue than any other topic and good sales figures, a multinational cosmetics company pulled its advertising from the magazine and the management requested she 'stop promoting "unhealthy issues"'. She also describes how the American magazine *Mode*, launched specifically to cater for women size 14 and above, began featuring slimmer models after its first few issues.

There are few images in the popular media that match the bodies of most women. As women compare themselves to the images in advertising, magazines, on television and film and when they try on clothes made for youthful slim bodies in retail stores, they are always imperfect. There are few heterosexual women who escape the 'cult of slenderness'.

The irony is that most women 'know' how they are being positioned by the media (Oliver 2001; Oliver and Lalik 2000). So why then do they (and so many 'feminists') not resist these messages? The answer should be obvious. It is not only that the meanings about feminine heterosexual attractiveness and how to attain it are pervasive, but also that the risks of not paying heed to these messages are high. These include being socially marginalized, undesired and undesirable. Moreover, the media is not the only source of this 'knowledge' but it is also in the exchanges between mothers (and fathers) and daughters, between friends and strangers, in school textbooks and physical and health education curriculum. The sources of knowledge about which bodies are valued and which are not are also evident in the texts produced around the 'obesity epidemic'. Following Foucault, Bartky (1990: 74) argues that 'the disciplinary power that inscribes femininity is everywhere and it is nowhere; the disciplinarian is everyone and yet no one in particular'. She uses the example of

> women regarded as overweight who report that they are often admonished to diet, sometimes by people they hardly know. These intrusions are often softened by reference to the natural prettiness just waiting to emerge: 'People always said that I had a beautiful face and "if you'd only lose weight you'd be really beautiful"' (Millman 1980: 80). Here, 'people' – friends and casual acquaintances alike – act to enforce prevailing standards of body size.
>
> (Bartky 1990: 74–5)

The argument then is that women internalize these strictures, they come to discipline themselves, to regulate their behaviour so as not to offend social norms. As pointed out earlier, this includes the practices of monitoring the shape and weight of the body and attending to the balance of food in/energy expended in exercise. For large women however, it also means evaluations of their bodies that may lead to shame and to the avoidance of potentially embarrassing situations for themselves and as they see it, for others.

In pointing to ideals of the female body as socially constructed, feminists also offer ways of understanding how people come to know and accept these ideals and how to achieve them. Although some early analyses made relatively simple connections between media messages and women's anxieties about their bodies, as the feminist work in the area of the media and cultural studies developed, a more sophisticated understanding of how individuals negotiate media messages emerged. These understandings saw individuals making different readings of the media, sometimes taking up and sometimes resisting the meanings and values promoted by television and print-media, in ways that were contingent on their biographies and investments in particular ways of being. Despite considerable evidence, however, that women could deconstruct and challenge the media texts, there has been little evidence that this helps in changing their actual practices or anxieties about their bodies. In other words, although women are able to recognize how texts produce particular ideals of femininity, this does not prevent them from wanting to be like these ideals, and from buying products and engaging in particular forms of body practices, such as dieting, that promise to deliver these ideals.

The worked body

The early feminist literature on 'slenderness', was primarily concerned with women's relationship with food. As the fitness industry gathered momentum and traditional social constraints on women's participation in physical activity were relaxed, the desirable female body began to take on a more toned shape. For some feminists this demonstrated that social ideals of femininity had changed to liberate women from restrictive social norms, because the display of muscular strength was no longer unacceptable. Indeed, over the last thirty to forty years, opportunities for women's participation in sport and other forms of physical activity tradition-ally associated with men have been radically expanded, a point that should at least lead us to question the simplistic idea, constantly repeated in the popular and scientific literatures, that Western societies have become exercise 'phobic'. However in terms of women's appearance, these changes have not been quite so liberating as one might expect. As health came to take on more positive conno-tations rather than freedom from illness, 'good health' came to be associated with personal choices in terms of lifestyle behaviours. As Howell and Ingham (2001: 33) point out, 'nowhere was this relationship between self-improvement and lifestyle more commonly articulated than on [sic] the exercise and fitness market-place'. For women, then, health and physical attractiveness were conflated in the appearance of the body; social norms not only required a thin body but also evidence of a worked body.

With the fitness boom, feminists began to examine the ways in which exercise regimes, promoted through gyms, televisions shows and videos, contributed to the creation of new ideas and images of femininity. For some feminists, aerobics and other forms of exercise regimes promoted a cult of the 'worked-on' slender body. Now women had not only to watch what they ate but also were expected to build exercise into their lives. 'Being in shape' sets up a further set of imperatives, where any evidence of 'flab' or 'softness' had to be eradicated. In these contexts, over-weight becomes unacceptable and obesity nigh on obscene. The feminist literature on exercise is replete with quotes from women who are unhappy with all or 'problem' parts of their bodies, and who engage in ongoing and often unsuccessful attempts to achieve the ideal of the slim toned body. The following quote from Penny is just one of many, but it is typical of the self-hate and drive to exercise that characterizes many women's relationships with their bodies:

> Ultimately, I do exercise for weight reasons. . . . I hate my legs and my bum and my arms, because they are really horrible and fat. . . . I was happier when I lost weight at the beginning of the year. I go to the gym everyday . . . I wouldn't want to stop. I want the class to be hard. I want to come out of the class and feel that I've worked [out] and burned fat. If I was really thin I don't think that I would go at all.
>
> (quoted in Maguire and Mansfield 1998: 129)

Penny's comments can be read in the context of the popular messages about the body identified in MacNeill's (1998) analysis of workout videos. MacNeill argues that, although these videos claim to be promoting a holistic notion of health, they have created a 'mass mediated weight-loss club' that 'tends to target female participants specifically to promote "the workout" as method of weight reduction' (MacNeill 1998: 175). A need to work on the body is created through the disparagement of women's bodies, suggestions that they will be 'unloved' if not fit and toned, and messages that 'less size is better' and 'less size is healthier'.

Women's (and increasingly men's) dissatisfaction with their bodies means that they are particularly vulnerable to suggestions that their bodies can be changed and there are products to do this. Feminists working with postmodernist theories of the body, point to the ways the body has become constituted as though it is malleable or plastic, that is, it can be remade, transformed, corrected through cosmetic surgery, organ transplants and through technologies of bodywork. Bordo (2003: 246–7), for example, points out that 'we are constantly told that we can "choose" our own bodies'. She quotes *Fit* magazine: 'Create a masterpiece, sculpt your body into a work of art ... You visualize what you want to look like and then create that form' and from an advertisement for Evian water: 'The proper diet, the right amount of exercise and you can have, pretty much any body you desire'.

Bordo goes on to demonstrate that this is an empty promise, since not everyone can have the body they desire. Moreover the 'perfect body' promoted by advertisements is a body that denies or makes invisible social, cultural and individual differences. However, what happens in these advertisements is not only the promotion of a particular homogenized and universalized body but also the notion that it is only a matter of choice, that we can determine our own bodies. This is a message that for those whose bodies do not measure up allows further feelings of shame and guilt, but also allows for the public disapproval and condemnation of those who appear to have not made the 'appropriate' choices to ensure a socially acceptable body shape. As we have seen, the idea that a 'healthy body weight' is a simple matter of people making 'simple' and 'correct' choices is also widespread in the scientific obesity literature.

Alternative ways of approaching the issue

Most of the feminist and related work on weight and obesity discussed so far has been directed at the ways women have negotiated social and cultural ideals of femininity associated with the appearance of the body. More recently a number of writers, writing from feminist and/or 'queer' positions, have more directly addressed social constructions of fatness, and challenged the oppressive and discriminatory practices associated with these constructions. Some of these writers have addressed the issue by providing a 'voice' for those who see themselves, or are defined by society, as 'fat': that is, to document the experience of being a large woman in a society that regards fatness as not only ugly but also equates it with stupidity, illness, sloth, self-indulgence and moral weakness (e.g. Carryer 1997). Others have taken a more radical route, challenging the social self-righteousness about the badness of fat, celebrating fatness and publicly confronting prejudices and discrimination.

The embodied experience of largeness

If, as has been argued above, 'the tyranny of slenderness' requires women to take responsibility for and discipline their bodies to ensure that they meet the social requirements of femininity, what happens when women do not meet these ideals? So far in this chapter we have talked about the general anxiety associated with the cultural ideals of the slim body and the consequent monitoring of food and exercise behaviours, but we have not discussed the experiences of those women who do become large/fat by society's demanding standards. As Hartley (2001) and others (Bartky 1988; Carryer 1997; Davies 1998) point out, in this context women with large bodies are stigmatized in ways that profoundly effect their personal and public lives. In the first instance, they are blamed for exceeding the boundaries of their bodies, they are said to have 'let themselves go', which suggests that they have no self-control. Fatness is seen as the result of self-indulgence, as a rejection of the strictures of a society that expects self-denial and the repression of desire. In addition, from a medical perspective the fat woman is blamed for 'causing her own fat' as she is unable to manage her own body and therefore able to be subjected to the control of others, such as doctors and other health professionals.

What needs to be said here is that although few feminists would deny oppressive and discriminatory practices experienced by fat men, it is social expectations around femininity that shape the stigmatization of women and the ways they internalize these. The argument goes back to Chernin and others who argue that women's subordination requires that their power be contained, that they take up smaller amounts of physical space in society than men. This is not a requirement of men, large bodies can be powerful bodies, and appropriately masculine. The hostility with which large female bodies are regarded is thus, in part, attributed to the way they pose a fundamental challenge to men's power. Hartley explains how this works in the following quote:

> In 'capitulating to desire' fat women are seen as . . . breaking the rules, and culture's immediate reaction is to punish them. Bordo sees this ostensible rebellion as the source of society's hostility toward fat women: 'the obese – particularly those who claim to be happy although overweight – are perceived as not playing by the rules at all. If the rest of us are struggling to be acceptable and 'normal' we cannot allow them to get away with it; they must be put in their place, be humiliated and defeated' (Bordo 1993: 203).
>
> (Hartley 2001: 66)

Such persistent messages of disgust and abhorrence are difficult to resist. Bartky argues that women who perceive themselves to be fat internalize social expectations and perceptions and experience feelings of shame. They punish themselves for their 'failure to conform' and shun both public and personal scrutiny. She quotes examples of such stories from Marcia Millman's study of the lives of the overweight to demonstrate the degree to which this influences women's lives:

> I feel so clumsy and huge. I felt that I would knock over the furniture, bump into things, tip over chairs, not fit into VW's, especially when people were

trying to crowd into the back seat. I felt like I was taking over the whole room . . . I felt disgusting and I felt like a slob. In the summer I feel hot and sweaty and I knew people saw my sweat as evidence that I was too fat.

I feel so terrible with the way I look that I cut off connection with my body. I operate from the neck up. I do not look in mirrors. I do not want to spend time buying clothes. I do not want to spend time with make-up because it is painful for me to look at myself.

(Bartky 1990: 76)

In an other example, Carryer (1997: 105) describes how the participants in her research have spent their lives 'battling their unruly bodies which stubbornly resist a much sought after conformity' to the slim idea of contemporary feminine attractiveness. She points to how the medicalization of obesity has allowed particular treatments to be sanctioned that are, in the main, not successful as permanent or long-term solutions, but cause suffering and may even be dangerous. The most common and enduring of these has been reduction dieting together with the various pharmaceutical and other agents in vogue to assist in this process. These have included the rainbow pill (a combination of the sodium derivatives of the barbiturates amobarbital and secobarbital in a blue and red capsule) through the 1940s to the 1970s, jaw wiring and gastric bypass operations and phen phen/Redux (a popular weight reduction pill in the late 1990s banned by the FDA because it was linked with deaths from cardiac arrest). She points out that the prescription of reduction diets has persisted despite research that suggests overeating is not a characteristic of large people.

Carryer (1997: 105) describes how the women in her study, despite having been 'vigorous and determined dieters' have 'watched their bodies grow larger'. In a singularly unsympathetic counter argument, Michael Fumento's *The Fat of the Land*, discussed in the previous chapter, urges that people who fail at dieting just keep trying, arguing that we would never stop trying to cure a drug addict just because previous attempts had been unsuccessful. However, drawing on research that suggests bodies adapt to weight loss diets by conserving fat and slowing metabolism, Carryer suggests that this increase in body weight is as much part of their dieting as it is of other factors:

Many of the participants have lost and regained over 50 kgs in the course of several serious and protracted reduction diets under the auspices of 'Weight Watchers', 'Jenny Craig' or 'Diet Clinic' or other variations. Those who have not utilised formal dieting venues have used informal methods with the same varying degrees of short term success. These women have demonstrated enormous determination in enduring prolonged food deprivation requiring constant planning, special shopping, individual food preparation and considerable difficulty in social settings. Simultaneously, embodied largeness has been a persistent feature of their daily existence.

(Carryer 1997: 105)

Like the women in Millman's study, Carryer describes the many situations in which the women in her study endured pain and discomfort or withdrew from social and recreational participation to avoid humiliation. She describes how they are in a state of constant vigilance in anticipation of situations in which they will be exposed to ridicule.

She concludes her article by describing how she has searched for signs of resistance from her participants to the ways their bodies are positioned by dominant social discourses. She describes how one woman is constructing a work of fiction about embodied largeness, and how she herself offers some resistance through conducting and writing about her research, but her final paragraph makes clear the damage done by a society and all of those who continue to stigmatize largeness:

> Most of us [involved in the study] have with trepidation but growing conviction, relinquished the dieting and regaining cycle in favour of rediscovering the use of healthy food for the simple sustenance of hunger. Accordingly we have relinquished the one apparent hope for slenderness. Within feminist writing there has been a tendency to talk of working towards acceptance of fatness. At the point of nearing completion of this research project I can only argue that for participants in the project 'fat acceptance' seems a remote dream.
>
> (Carryer 1997: 108)

Reconfigurations of fatness

The dominant ideologies associated with obesity allow practices that marginalize a large group of people and set up situations where they can be pathologized, discriminated against, mistreated and abused. Despite the challenge that taking on such deeply embedded ideas in the social psyche presents, there are those, feminists and others, who have protested and rebelled, often loudly and in a very confrontational fashion, against oppressive discourses about fatness. This resistance has taken many forms: through theoretical and academic work aimed at 'reconfiguring fatness'; the formation of activist and support groups such as the National Association to Advance Fat Acceptance (NAAFA); and through performance, parody and confrontation. The Web has proved an important site for mobilizing resistance and sharing information, support and humour.

In one example, the possibility of changing the way society makes sense of fatness is taken up in an anthology of papers, *Out of Bounds: Fatness and Transgression*, edited by Braziel and LeBesco (2001). The central question that organizes the collection is 'how to reconceptualise and reconfigure corpulence' (Braziel and LeBesco 2001: 1). In relation to this they ask, what other ways of thinking about and viewing fatness are available other than the dominant American (Western) popular view of fatness; how can the fat body be made more 'visible and present' rather than being hidden away as 'unsightly'; how can fat bodies be defined differently from the ways they are defined in medical, psychological and economic discourses?

As a starting point, the anthology begins with a paper entitled 'Fat beauty' in which Richard Klein (2001) challenges the universality of thinness as a marker of beauty and instead argues that the 'taste' for fatness or for thinness changes with changing social, cultural and political contexts. Klein argues that throughout history there have been times when fat has been a marker of beauty and erotic desire and there have been other moments when thin has had its day. Implicit in his argument is that there is an inherent deficiency, a lack of generosity and indeed a certain vulgarity in those who prefer chic (thinness, angularity) and cannot recognize and appreciate the beauty of the rounded form. He begins with the examples of the tiny Stone Age Venuses found in caves in Europe. He argues that these are more than fertility fetishes: that some at least represented ideals of female beauty in times when 'famine lurked as a constant menace' (Klein 2001: 22). In particular, he describes the Balzi Rossi Venus who 'has the flattest stomach, a flat expanse of firmed-up waist stretching between the ballooning boobs on top and the rest. This woman is not pregnant'.

His argument is that there is not one unitary notion of beauty but that at different times, different degrees of fatness and thinness, of muscularity and solidity, have been judged as desirable. For the Greeks, it was desirable to be neither too thin nor too fat. Statues of Aphrodite by modern standards would deem her to be too fat. On the other hand, the asceticism of early Christianity prized the thin body, which exemplified self-denial and a retreat from the pleasures of the material world. In the seventeenth century, Ruben's nudes celebrated abundance:

> These women are cornucopia, with bodies that swell and plump. The graces hold and squeeze each other's arms, as if they cannot get enough of the exuberant fleshy beauty. Ruben was attracted by the twist and sweep, by the large arc of a hip, and 'the shining expanse of . . . stomach' (Clarke 1956: 144). He loves the comprehensiveness of these bodies, the way they sweep the eye around with arcs and twists, intriguing roles and blushing dimples. The roundness of these fat women inspires in the onlooker an enormously powerful desire to embrace them, to be embraced in their enclosing perfumed thicket of flesh.
>
> (Klein 2001: 31)

Klein's use of 'excessive' language to describe the beauty of fat challenges the readers' predisposition for restraint, for ascetic image of scarcity when describing the body. Klein's argument is confrontational in that it offers the possibility of celebrating a form of embodiment that is elsewhere in the mainstream popular and scientific literature constantly described in derogatory terms. He challenges aesthetic norms, which many of us have internalized (whether we admit to this or not), and use to judge our own and others' bodies.

The theme of reconfiguring fatness is taken up in other papers in the anthology. These draw on feminist, postmodernist and queer theory to analyse fatness, to make visible representations of fatness in the media, the ways fat people have constructed themselves and been constructed by others, how fatness and fat people have been subversive of social and sexual mores. As Kathleen LeBesco creatively argues in the following quote, the aim is to construct fatness as political in its subversion of dominant ideals:

> Aesthetically, fat is the antithesis of the beauty ideal of the day: tight, lean, and toned. Viewed then both as unhealthy and unattractive, fat people are

widely represented in popular cultures and in interpersonal interactions as revolting – they are agents of abhorrence and disgust. But if we think of *revolting* in terms of over-throwing authority, rebelling, protesting and rejecting, then corpulence carries a whole new weight as a subversive cultural practice that calls into question received notions about health, beauty and nature. We can recognize fat as a condition not simply aesthetic or medical but *political*.

(LeBesco 2001: 75 emphasis in original)

Drawing on the work of Judith Butler and Elizabeth Grosz, she wants to create ways of talking about bodies that avoid, indeed 'undermine' the notion of one ideal, and instead provide 'a defiant affirmation of multiplicity, a field of differences, or other kinds of bodies and subjectivities' (Grosz 1994, quoted in LeBesco 2001: 78). While her own work is primarily theoretical she encourages an interaction between theory and activism where 'fat activists plan events that focus less on official policy and more on the repositioning of fat in the cultural imaginary', where fat activists engage in performances that present 'a fatness that is not the victim of bad genes or its own lack of will' (LeBesco 2001: 83). She points to examples such as NAAFA, Roseanne Barr (who in 1999 hosted the 'Large and Luscious Beauty Contest') and 'individuals from varied socio-political, economic, and educational backgrounds who are all invested in projects of fat resignification' (LeBesco 2001: 84).

The social prejudices against fat are so deeply embedded and so naturalized, however, that confrontation, through language, through imagery and performance, often requires enormous amounts of courage. When the desire for so many fat people is to be invisible, it means becoming very visible, drawing attention to fat bodies, producing discomfort and risking shame. In addition, as LeBesco points out confrontation through performance is a complicated process because performers have little control on how their performances and their bodies are interpreted.

The people most difficult to challenge are often those who believe that they have the 'best interests' of fat people at heart, such as doctors, educators, health workers and health promoters. But these are the very people, as Samantha Murray points out, who through their pathologizing of fatness, are most likely to contribute to the ongoing stigmatization of the fat body. In a courageous act, Murray presented a paper to doctors at a menopause conference in Australia, which used her own experience to directly confront her audience with the consequences of their medical assumptions about fatness. In their stead, she proposed alternative ways of 'knowing' fatness that are not about objectifying fat bodies and characterizing them as diseased. Her paper begins with her describing how she feels she is 'seen' and 'known' though the clinical gaze:

I stand before you now, and I can feel you all 'knowing' my body. You see my fatness, and co-extensive with it, you perceive its indisputable deviation from practices of health and care of the body. I am aware that here, in this space, in fact in most spaces, my body is a quintessential symbol of pathology. When you witness me now: seeing my dimpled thighs, my soft bulges and fatty rolls, you believe you know me. The visible marker of my fatness is laden with knowledges of who I am. Looking at me now, you must ask your-self what you know about my body, and therefore, about me? What does my fat body signal? The visible markers of my fatness, my wide hips, protruding belly, vast thighs, all signal a 'knowingness' (Sedgwick 1993: 222) of pathology and disease. You read my fat as symptomatic of overeating, lack of exercise, poor nutrition. You see me as a high-risk candidate for diabetes, gall bladder disease, hypertension and heart attack. At a deeper level, you may see a lazy woman without willpower, a sedentary being, with questionable hygiene. You see a woman who will not help herself, a woman out of control, a woman of unmanaged desires and gluttonous obsessions.

(Murray 2003: 2)

She ends by challenging her audience to 'see' and 'know' her body differently:

I have tried to fill in the gap between the way you *see* my body and the way I *live* it. My body to you is a time bomb, ticking towards disease, deteriora-tion, death. Medicine has an irrefutable role in reinforcing and reinscribing the fat body, producing and reproducing popular understandings of fatness as symbolic of pathology and disease. There is a gap between the medical, clin-ical representation of fatness (which asks me to be ashamed of my flesh and to seek to transform it), and the way I want to take up my fatness and live it. . . . My body is not diseased, it is not pathological, it is not out of control. I am posing new body knowledges: there are pleasures and joys I *know* of my flesh that fall outside your pathologising, objectifying gaze. There is more to this fat flesh than disease, morbidity statistics and obesity epidemics. There is another way of *seeing* fatness, and another way of *living* fat, outside of the miseries of the constant readings of fat flesh as pathological and abhorrent. I'm not suggesting we take a view of fatness that is utopian. Rather, I am trying to *displace* the ways in which our society thinks about fat, and the way medicine urges society to *see* and *read* fat bodies.

(Murray 2003: 11, emphasis in original)

Samantha Murray represents an increasing presence of activism around fatness in all areas of social life. The Internet has provided a way to international activism and support. Websites vary from individual sites to large multilevel, well-organized sites such as NAAFA, which have information, offer support, organize campaigns against discriminatory legislation, offensive advertising and media depictions and so on.

The idea that people might agitate for the rights of large people presents an interesting juxtaposition with the scientific and popular literature. Michael Fumento, for example, sees fat activists as extraordinarily irresponsible and comes very close to accusing them of mass-murder. But it is also noticeable that obesity scientists very rarely acknowledge that their work feeds into cultural contexts where body weight is understood and talked about in particular ways. That people are constantly bombarded by a wide variety of messages and ideas about health, happiness and beauty is also not factored into the research agenda scientists embark upon nor the recommendations they make. Instead, they posit that one goal, the reduction of human body weight, is paramount.

In the context of this book, feminists and fat theorists and activists provide another way of 'seeing' and understanding the obesity epidemic. They draw attention to the ethical, personal and social consequences of the relentless pursuit of those regarded as overweight or obese and begin to explain why this might be so. In the next chapter we continue to explore other ways of 'seeing' and to further examine the consequences of the 'obesity epidemic' ideology for individuals and social groups.

9 Interrogating expert knowledge
Risk and the ethics of body weight

Our argument to this point has been that the 'obesity epidemic' is much more than a 'natural phenomenon' that can adequately be described and explained by science. Instead, we argue that the 'obesity epidemic' is, as much as anything else, a social idea (or an ideology), constructed at the intersection of scientific knowledge and a complex of culturally-based beliefs, values and ideals. As such, it seems useful to explore what it is sociologists have to say about the 'obesity epidemic', to help understand why the 'obesity epidemic' has come to such prominence as a health issue in the face of considerable scientific uncertainty, and with what consequences for individuals and for society. Like the feminist work in the previous chapter, sociologists (and those working in history, cultural studies and so on) provide alternative ways of talking and thinking about overweight and obesity from those offered by the sciences and the popular media. Perhaps most importantly, they provide an understanding of the 'obesity epidemic' as a social and cultural phenomenon, rather than as one explained in terms of population trends or individual behaviours.

Most contemporary sociologists would argue that an important role of sociology is to demonstrate that there is no one way of seeing and knowing the world. They would argue that sociological work (and the work now done under the rubric of cultural studies) should be concerned with identifying how some ways of seeing and talking about the world become taken for granted as 'truths' or the *only* ways of seeing and knowing, and others are made invisible or silenced. They point out that this is not the case because the dominant or most popular ways of seeing are indeed 'true', but because they are associated with power. This is part of the argument that we have been developing in this book: that the historical credibility given to the sciences and the translation of their messages into popular currency in the media and 'popular science' books (see Chapter 7) provides powerful means to convince of the 'truth' of their messages about body weight and health. Part of that power is also associated with our apparent desire as a society for certainty. We seem to want, and perhaps need, certain knowledge that we can use to guide our actions and our relationships. C. Wright Mills (2000) and others since (Berger 1967), have argued for the role of sociologists in helping to develop a 'sociological imagination': that is, bringing a lens to our everyday lives so that we question what we take for granted, the assumptions that we have about the world and how it works. This involves 'making the familiar strange' (Tinning 2004: 233): recognising that knowledge is uncertain and that experts are fallible. Such an approach is not only about being critical of particular positions, but also about providing alternative ways of thinking (Fox 1998). This is a position that often generates resistance because it 'troubles' long-held beliefs and the investments we have in those beliefs. How disturbing this can be has been evident to us in the strong emotional responses from our physical education students and colleagues when we raise questions about the 'obesity epidemic'.

Sociologists do not question from a vacuum. Their work contributes to an understanding of the relationships between individuals and society and how political, economic, cultural forces impact on individual lives. They identify how and why particular forms of knowledge and values (ideologies) are taken up and with what effects on the lives of individuals. They ask questions such as: How does a particular phenomenon come into being? What are the social, cultural, political and economic circumstances that have shaped it? What authority is being drawn on and what silenced? Whose interests are being served and with what consequences?

There are two main areas of sociology that are pertinent to this task in relation to the 'obesity epidemic'. The first is the area of sociology interested in understanding the body as a social phenomenon, and the second is interested in social inequalities in relation to health. The first of these takes up the work described in Chapter 8 to investigate how values and beliefs about what bodies 'matter' are not universal or fixed, but have changed over time and are different for different cultures. The second looks to social contexts to understand patterns of health and illness and helps to challenge the widespread position that health, and in this case overweight and obesity, are simply the outcome of poor lifestyle choices.

Uncertain knowledge and risk

As has been established in earlier chapters, one of the reasons the issue of overweight and obesity has come to prominence is through the argument that it is a major 'risk factor' in a number of 'lifestyle' diseases. From an epidemiological perspective, 'risk factors' are those host (e.g. sex, gender, age behavioural patterns, presence of co-existing disease, genetic background etc.) and/or environmental factors that increase the likelihood that a category of individual will develop a particular condition or disease (Shim 2002). In this sense, a risk factor presents a 'threat' to the health of the individual.

The apparent proliferation of 'risks', both in terms of health risks and other threats to society (such as terrorism and environmental degradation) is one of the main themes of current sociological writing. On a global scale, contemporary Western democracies have been characterized in contemporary sociology as 'risk societies' (Beck 1992; Giddens 1991). Risk societies are those in which social, political, economic and individual risks or threats, produced as a consequence of industrialized societies, increasingly escape the control of governments and institutions. At the same time, the knowledge about how to address such risks is increasingly uncertain and characterized by debate and conflicts. While there is little evidence that the contemporary world is any more dangerous than in the past, Beck suggests that contemporary societies are characterized by a profound anxiety about risks: risks for which there are no ready solutions (Hubbard 2003). The important point here is that risks are not actual events. Instead, particular phenomena are constructed as 'threats', and some are brought to public attention (usually via some form of electronic media) as being more threatening than others:

> Risk is something which has not happened yet, which frightens people in the present and therefore they might take action against it. Risk is not a cata-strophe; if catastrophe happens it is a fact, an event. Risk is about possibility, a future possibility . . .
>
> (Interview with Ulrich Beck by Boyne, cited in Hubbard 2003: 51)

The issue of global warming is a good example. It is a threat that may or may not be realized. Contrary knowledge about the 'risk' is made publicly available through the mass-media. This uncertainty provides spaces for those who have the power to make policy or direct resources to support those experts who provide opinion and research to justify their actions. Through the support of governments and other powerful agencies certain positions become legitimized over others. The role of the expert in a risk society, therefore, is to claim knowledge, expertise and an ability to control that which seems to be out of control. By managing uncer-tainty, the expert becomes central to the construction of a sense of control over the risks we live with.

In public health, the management of uncertainty about health risks is accom-plished by the quantification of risk through population studies, which calculate the likelihood of a phenomenon. Citing Hacking, Lupton (1995: 78) describes risk, in this sense, as depending 'on a belief in law-like mathematical regularities in the population, itself dependent upon the collection of data and its tabula-tion'. Epidemiology and biomedical research becomes the source of 'expert' knowledge in this context, and population studies the only source of valid know-ledge about public health. These identify 'risk factors' that effect populations as well as identifying 'populations at risk'. However, as those who research 'risk' in the area of health point out, risks are socially constructed and 'risk perceptions depend less on the nature of the hazard than on political, social, and cultural contexts' (Nelkin 2003: viii). As Nelkin suggests in the quote below, current constructions of risk use expert interpretations to anticipate future heath issues for individuals, while ignoring contextual factors.

> For years, risk assessments were based on technical assumptions. Risks were technically manageable: identification and measurement of risk were sufficient basis for public decisions . . . Most recently, attention has focused on inherent risks – often called predispositions. The anticipation of illness, of future risks, has become a preoccupation of our time (Lock 2001). This anticipatory notion of risk in asymptomatic people – the interpretations of the expert become more important than the perceptions of the person. It has also depoliticized risk, diverting attention toward individual predispositions and away from the social and institutional factors that contribute to risk (Tesh 1988).
>
> (Nelkin 2003: viii)

Fundamental to such notions of risks is that by so naming the risk it can be managed – that is, uncertainty can be reduced – and by understanding the lines of causality, one can act rationally to avoid it. Lupton (1995) points to the way in which health promotion 'risks' are managed by setting targets for the reduction of mortality or morbidity in particular populations (most at risk from a disease). Once the risk factors have been identified, the assumption is that targets can be reached 'if only the correct advice is taken' (Lupton 1995: 81). If targets are not met, then individuals can be blamed for not acting 'responsibly' on the information provided. For example, if targets for the reduction of overweight and obesity are not reached then responsibility can be attributed to individuals who do not engage in recommended and 'responsible' eating and exercise behaviour. This begs the question of the appropriateness of the targets in the first place, as well as the relevance of the health 'prescriptions' to the people targeted as being 'at risk'.

We have argued above that, within a 'risk society', 'experts' have an important role in managing uncertainty through their claim to knowledge and the ability to control that which seems to be out of control. Within the context of health, experts purport to manage the uncertainty of illness and death through the identification of risk factors – that is, factors that are deemed to be largely avoidable through the actions of individuals. There are a multitude of health issues that could be identified for public notice – why then do overweight and obesity gain such prominence? Why not bad backs or arthritis which also effect large numbers of the population and which could arguably also be associated with physical activity? Why overweight and obesity, which as we, in this book, together with many others (e.g. Blair and Brodney 1999; Hall and Stewart 1989; Jutel 2000; Knapp 1983; Savage and Scott 1998), have suggested has a more tenuous, and certainly complex and contradictory relationship, with health – particularly, at the level of the individual? Part of the explanation might lie in the set of activities that come into play once a health risk has been designated as such and the investment that key players (such as, epidemiologists, health researchers and health educators as well as the various beneficiaries in terms of consumer products) then have in maintaining a particular risk as one of prime importance.

The identification of risk factors is no simple matter when there are no straightforward links such as those between infectious agents and disease. In Chapter 5, Bruce Ross explains in detail how epidemiology works to provide statistical information to predict risks. His chapter examines the evidence for an 'obesity epidemic' by closely interrogating the key terms and measurements. He makes the case for regarding this evidence as 'uncertain' and for being sceptical about 'obesity epidemic' claims. From a sociological viewpoint, further grounds for uncertainty can be brought into play, when causal relationships are no longer based on reasonably straightforward environmental factors, such as water quality or the absence or presence of a disease agent, but on complex human factors, which occur in social contexts.

Frohlich and her colleagues (Frohlich et al. 2001) suggest that epidemiologists have been more concerned with getting the methodology right than with theorizing the complexities of the relationships between social and individual factors and disease outcomes. Their paper suggests we consider explanations that go beyond attributions that link material/structural factors such as income, education and housing to health inequalities. Instead, they suggest we consider 'the conditions that result from one's income, that is the psychosocial and physical factors that arise from one's income level' (Frohlich *et al.* 2001: 780). The epidemiological research examined earlier in this book in relation to overweight and obesity rarely goes beyond the most simplistic individual level risk factor research. Where it does begin to look at the relationship between social class, gender and race, it takes these as unproblematic social determinants: that is, decontextualized 'objective' variables like cigarette smoking in the case of lung cancer. There is no recognition that social class, race, gender and so on are social constructs, conventions for categorizing people, which represent complex sets of social relations and practices (Frohlich *et al.* 2001). By using such terms uncritically, certain truths and stereotypes are established about particular groups of people. Such stereotypes, in turn, allow interventions that target all people in that social category as though it is their membership of the category itself that puts them at 'risk' of the disease. In the following quote, Shim explains the logic behind the ways such associations, produced through epidemiological research, become validated and legitimated:

> Since risk factors *are* statistically associated with disease incidence, this kind of epidemiological research seemingly enables the prediction of future probability and distribution of health and illness based on demographic (and related behavioural) classifications of individuals and groups. At the same time, such work obscures considerable uncertainty over exactly how such inequalities are produced, that is, what exactly about race, class, sex/gender contributes to chronic disease. Epidemiological techniques and knowledge thereby help to construct an intelligible, orderly and seemingly certain story about the unequal distribution of health and chronic illness.
>
> (Shim 2002: 136, emphasis in original)

Epidemiological work is only part of the equation, however, in the identification, recognition and promotion of particular versions of health knowledge. As Garrety (1997, 1998) points out in her detailed investigation of 'the cholesterol controversy', the process of identifying causal relationships between lifestyle behaviours – in her example eating high-fat foods – and disease outcomes is a complex process shaped by social, political, economic and cultural forces. She demonstrates how pressure on scientists and policy makers from politicians, medical research lobbyists and consumer advocates 'to "do something" about CHD and other chronic diseases ... outweighed concerns regarding the lack of definitive evidence' (Garrety 1997: 222). For example, despite considerable evidence that lowering cholesterol in the diet had no discernible effect on reducing coronary heart disease, the US government endorsed policies and programmes that sought to reduce the intake of saturated fat and cholesterol for all Americans over the age of two years.

Her summary statement provides a salutary message for an assessment of the ways the information about overweight and obesity has been managed, and how policies and programmes have been generated in the face of considerable uncertainty about the nature of the 'problem', the factors contributing to the problem and explanations about why obesity has come to such prominence. Discussing the processes by which government policy on cholesterol was arrived at, she concludes:

Thus, the interface between science and policy in the cholesterol arena was shaped by complex and shifting distributions of power and legitimacy. Lay people, politicians, and commercial interests were able to modify the power and legitimacy of scientists. Despite scientific uncertainty, many scientists, food producers, and lay people simply decided that dietary change was desirable. They shaped scientific knowledge to support their policies and overpowered the voices of dissenters.

(Garrety 1997: 418)

As Garrety argues, once there is a commitment by government to a particular course of action, and policies and programmes are in place, then debate is difficult to sustain. Certainty is maintained by allowing some experts to speak and be heard and those proposing other points of view to be silenced and/or ignored.

In the cases of overweight and obesity, a similar process has taken place. In other chapters we have challenged the certainty of the biomedical claims concerning the 'obesity epidemic'. A socio-cultural perspective helps to explain why, despite the fact that some experts acknowledge that considerable uncertainty exists, obesity has come to such prominence as a health 'risk'. In the first instance, the quest for certainty privileges those 'risks' that are most readily quantifiable. As Jutel (2000: 284) suggests: 'The focus on weight in contemporary health care is buttressed upon a desire to quantify wellness and to locate health in a model of precise normalcy'. She proposes that contemporary policy documents '[i]n the campaign for weight loss . . . reproduce and institutionalise many moral beliefs about the body'. In keeping with our argument, she also suggests that 'as other enterprises rely on the "truths" produced in these documents, there is a reproduction ad infinitum of beliefs that individuals should reduce weight if they are large and should monitor their weight vigilantly if they are not' (Jutel 2001: 286–7).

Given the significance placed on body size and weight, in contemporary Western (and increasingly with globalization, other societies in the non-Western world), it is no surprise that a purported increase in the average weight of populations becomes a cause for concern. In addition, the way the 'obesity epidemic' is constructed emphasizes a statistical trend towards overweight and obesity where it will effect an increasing percentage of the population every year – obviously a catastrophe of major proportions that must be avoided at all cost. It is inevitable, then, that government agencies and private funding bodies, in their quest for solutions and for certainty, will support, resource and listen to those who claim to reduce the risk.

Once overweight and obesity were named as risk factors for chronic diseases such as heart disease and diabetes, and then diseases in their own right, they became objects that could be quantified, and generated epidemiological analyses that sought to understand their distribution and determinants. This research has been used to provide statistical evidence of its widespread occurrence and has generated dramatic graphs to suggest that, as a threat to social well-being, it has been growing exponentially. In other words, it has been constructed as a disease of *epidemic* proportions.

The term epidemic has traditionally been used for infectious diseases. In a risk society it is increasingly being used to characterize any health threat that needs to attract media attention and research resources (for example, an epidemic of mental illness among children). This characterization of obesity (really obesity and overweight although often the word 'obesity' is used as though it can stand for both) as a disease of epidemic proportions provides a context for the creation of a widespread anxiety, a moral panic, which calls a new set of imperatives into play.

> The risks which are selected by a society as requiring attention may therefore have no relation to 'real' danger but are culturally identified as important. . . . The imperative to do something, to remove the source of a health risk, however tenuous, impels action.
>
> (Lupton 1995: 80)

In the case of obesity, the use of the word 'epidemic' provides further impetus for urgent action. Epidemics of infectious diseases such as the plague, cholera and more recently AIDS are dramatic in their intensity. Responses to such diseases usually involve the stigmatization and avoidance of those who are believed to be carriers. 'Epidemics', as Lindenbaum (2001: 363) points out, also have major repercussions for institutions, cultures and societies: 'The Black Death [for example] is said to have contributed to the emergence of nation states, the rise of mercantile economies and the religious movements that led to the Reformation'.

Using the term 'epidemic' in relation to increases in rates of 'obesity' thus metaphorically evokes the high levels of emotion associated with infectious disease epidemics and legitimates the same kinds and levels of intervention and public response. Characterizing obesity firstly as a disease and then one of epidemic proportions requires the immediate mobilization of resources to bring about change. With infectious epidemics there is a sense that all are at risk if they come into contact with the organism. In the context of the 'obesity epidemic' this is translated into a sense that anyone might 'catch it', that people who are overweight or obese have already succumbed and are thereby dangerous 'carriers' to be avoided. This permits their stigmatization and permits actions to be taken because of the 'danger' to themselves and to society. For example, it permits the identification of disease by doctors on the basis of appearance (Carryer 1997; Murray 2003), and the prescription of additional exercise for children who are perceived to be overweight by their teachers (Leahy and Harrison 2003).

The argument then is that the current panic around obesity and overweight is a constructed phenomenon associated with particular political, economic and cultural conditions, rather than a 'natural' and universal phenomenon caused by the inappropriate and perverse behaviour of individuals. That construction, however, is not harmless but has effects for individuals and for groups; it allows an intervention in people's lives that most people in the same society would not tolerate.

A social theory of the body: obesity as a social construction

So far in this chapter we have demonstrated the process by which knowledge about obesity is managed and how it has been constituted as a disease of epidemic proportions. However, we have only partially answered the question: why obesity rather than other pressing health problems? In previous chapters of the book we have challenged the certainty of claims about obesity and overweight and their relationship to health. As we have pointed out, some of this uncertainty has to do with the ways in which definitions of obesity and overweight rely on shifting norms and forms of measurement. In addressing the question 'why obesity?' and 'why now?', we will take this challenge a few steps further to attempt to 'make strange' the notion of obesity as a representation of something real: that is, a 'natural' and universal phenomenon caused by the perverse behaviour of individuals. To do so we will draw on recent sociological writing about the body.

The first step in this process is to reject the notion of the body as simply or only a natural or biophysiological phenomenon, knowable through the biophysical sciences. Sociologists argue that the body is much more than that – it is a social entity on which social beliefs, social values and social practices are inscribed. Such inscriptions can literally range from the tribal markings and tattoos of both historical and contemporary 'tribes', to the ways in which particular imperatives about how heavy or light bodies should be, to how people should walk, sit and generally comport themselves. While tattoos may seem to be obvious markings of culture, obvious on the body's surface, other cultural imperatives about how bodies should be are more deeply 'written into' bodies. For example, social expectations about how bodies should move and look require years of work and years of using bodies in particular ways. Frigga Haug (1983: 127) in the memory work project described in *Female Sexualization*, provides many examples of how women's experience of their bodies is a 'thoroughly social preoccupation'. She describes how expressions like 'don't stick your tummy out', 'pull your tummy in', 'stand up straight' and 'you have to strengthen your tummy muscles' work to instil particular standards of being a woman. These are standards associated with a particular moral attitude and sense of responsibility appropriate to being a good person/woman:

> The theme addressed [by these phrases], or rather the problem being manufactured here is not, as it may first appear *having* a tummy: to have a tummy is equated instead with a negative deportment of the body. The term 'attitude' should be understood here in both of its senses; as an attitude of the body, and as a personal attitude of mind. Having a tummy becomes an immoral act. It is an expression of bad character – for having a tummy is a sign of having let oneself go.
>
> (Haug 1983: 127, emphasis in original)

The kinds of bodies that are valued are not the same for all times and for all cultures. There is no *one* neutral, non-historical, norm or standard body. Instead, as described in the previous chapter, particular kinds of bodies, particular shapes and sizes, particular comportments of the body, are valued over others in specific social and cultural contexts. Although 'beauty' has been celebrated, particularly for women, as part of their 'exchange' value, in most societies, in contemporary Western societies the size, shape and appearance of the body have taken on new meanings. The outward appearance of the body in such societies has become a form of physical capital not only for women: it has become a marker of an individual's self-identity and value as a person. How people see and evaluate themselves and others has become associated with the shape, size and appearance of their bodies as these compare to social and cultural ideals.

A number of sociologists have described the contemporary body as a 'project' whereby individuals are 'conscious of and actively concerned about the management, maintenance and appearance of their bodies' (Shilling 1993: 5). Shilling suggests that in times of risk and uncertainty the body has become a site over which individuals can feel that they have some control:

> Perhaps the most common example of the body as a project can be found in the unprecedented amount of attention given to the personal construction of healthy bodies. In a time when our health is threatened increasingly by *global* dangers, we are exhorted ever more to take *individual* responsibility for our bodies by engaging in strict self-care regimes ... Self-care regimes require individuals to take on board the notion that the body is a project whose interiors and exteriors can be monitored, nurtured and maintained as fully functioning. These regimes promote an image of the body as an island of security in a global system characterized by multiple and inescapable risks (Beck 1992).
>
> (Shilling 1993: 5, emphasis in original)

The body's appearance is taken to be evidence of the *care* taken of the body, that is, the time, effort and money invested in creating particular kinds of bodies. Such an investment has an exchange value in the contexts of work, leisure, relationships and so on. The shape and size of one's body influences whether one gets a job, is regarded as a capable participant in active leisure activities or a desirable sexual partner. There is a profound moral and class dimension to the assumptions underpinning this relationship between bodily appearance and individual worth. The assumption that the body is malleable and indicative of a choice of lifestyle is associated with a set of moral virtues about how a life should be lived. According to Bourdieu (1986), the care of the body as an end in itself is very much a middle-class value, associated with those who have the money and the desire to spend time working on the body. The more affluent members of society are also more likely to believe that they have more control over their own health: control that can be exercised by choosing an appropriate lifestyle. As the group most influential in setting social values around health, it is these values that are promoted as the appropriate values for all in relation to health and the body.

These values, however, are not necessarily shared by all. According to Bourdieu, for the working class, or those less affluent, the body is not an end in itself, but a means to an end. The body is regarded as a useful and necessary 'machine' that needs to be maintained to meet other priorities in life, such as being able to fulfil family responsibilities through paid work or work in the home, go on a holiday, enjoy life. In this context, devoting time to exercise to maintain the body's appearance or to insure against health risks in the future are not likely to be priorities. Physical activity is more likely to be about present pleasures and exercise taken up for health reasons once personal and immediate risks have been identified. These class differences are illustrated in the results of a study conducted in Australia on the 'cultural tastes' of people from different occupational backgrounds. Bodily practices such as weight control through dieting and exercise were more likely to be associated with the wealthy and with women than with manual or skilled workers. As the authors report:

> practices of weight control are different and differently valued across the social spectrum. Weight-dieters are richer than most, and they are neither old nor young, being concentrated between 25 and 59. Employers score very highly indeed, followed by managers supervisors and – because of the gendering of this diet – sales and clerical workers. Manual workers and skilled workers score very low, probably because weight reduction diets are perceived as feminine.
>
> (Bennett *et al.* 1999: 123)

Walking as a form of physical activity was most widely shared across all social categories – gender, age, social class and income. Membership of health and sports organizations, however, was more indicative of 'the standard profile of that proportion of the population who exercises' (Bennett *et al.* 1999: 127):

> There are two significantly low figures, for those whose country of birth is not Australian, and for Aborigines. Otherwise the scores conform to a familiar pattern: membership of health and sporting organizations declines, but not sharply with age; it is fairly constant across all classes, but professionals are significantly above the mean (26.8% against a mean of 20.7%); men outnumber women by a ratio of 23% to 18.8%; memberships is highest among the tertiary-educated and among the two highest income groups; and provincial cities ... score significantly higher than other locations.
>
> (Bennett *et al.* 1999: 127)

If we understand bodies as socially constructed, and the kinds of bodies that are valued at particular times and cultures as not fixed, then it is possible to make an argument that the current focus on obesity and overweight is as much to do with a social and cultural response to particular kinds of bodies as it has to do with health. As argued in the previous chapter, the aesthetics of the body have been able to encompass a wide range of body shapes at different times in history. What kinds of bodies are taken to be aesthetically pleasing and/or sexually attractive seem to be very much associated with social, cultural and economic forces operating at different times.

Thus, from a sociological point of view the values associated with particular kinds of bodies have changed over time. For the purposes of this book what is important here are that:

1   notions of beauty and in particular socially valued body shapes and sizes are not fixed;
2   the shapes and forms of the body that are currently valued are generally thinner and more indicative of work on the body than has been the case in earlier years; and
3   the aesthetics of the body are inseparable from particular imperatives about care of the body to maintain health.

This begins to explain the current preoccupation with body weight and obesity, but is not in itself a sufficient explanation.

The medicalization of obesity and its effects

In Chapter 8, we described how the aesthetics of the fat body have changed through history and, from Klein's (2001) point of view, are likely to change again if food scarcity becomes widespread. That discussion was conducted in the context of challenging readers to see fatness in ways other than those so powerfully mandated by contemporary Western society. What we have argued above is that the body per se has taken on particular importance in how people make judgements about their own worth and the worth of others. This alone suggests bodies that matter are those that meet social ideals – these are normal bodies and others deviate from the norm. Concerns with 'fatness', however, have gone beyond the purview of morality and aesthetics and in the twentieth century became the focus of biosciences and medicine. With this eventuality, fat people have come under further scrutiny and the righteousness and the stridency of lay judgements have been bolstered by health discourses of risk. In the following section of this chapter we will map the medicalization of fatness and the consequences of this for individuals in societies where overweight and obesity have become the focus of public health.

In the sociological literature, 'medicalization' has been described as 'the process by which certain behaviours or conditions are defined as medical problems (rather than, for example, moral or legal problems), and medical intervention becomes the focus of remedy and social control' (Chang and Christakis 2002: 152). Once a condition is defined as a medical problem it changes from being 'wilful and sinful, or even criminal' (Chang and Christakis 2002: 152) and subject to punishment to a condition of illness requiring therapy. Although this seems to take some of the responsibility from the individual, it is the individual body that is taken to be 'diseased', and thus becomes the focus of diagnosis and intervention.

The medicalization of obesity

As we argued above and in Chapter 8, how fatness is regarded varies between historical eras and across cultures. Sobal (1995) claims that some people in the past and the majority of people currently living in 'traditional' cultures consider fatness to be a sign of health and wealth (Sobal 1995). In many traditional societies, fat was valued as an indicator of wealth, since only the wealthy could afford the food and the leisure necessary to acquire fat. With agricultural and industrial revolutions assuring more regular food supplies, 'thinness became valued and associated with membership in high social status groups, with a rising emphasis on the value of slimness by the 1920s (Levenstein 1988)' (Sobal 1995: 68). With the increasing social value associated with thinness, fatness became increasingly constituted as morally bad, with fat people stigmatized as being weak and lacking will-power.

> Thus fat had shifted from being evaluated as good and healthy in traditional societies to being seen as being bad, sinful and ugly. This provided the basis

for the moral model of fatness, which suggests that fat people are responsible for their condition and should be punished as a means of social control for being fat.

(Sobal 1995: 69)

Such a position provided a context for the social stigmatization of fat people and overt discrimination in education, rental housing, employment and other areas of life, which continues today (Herndon 2002; Sobal 1995). It was not until the 1950s, however, that fatness was regarded as a serious social problem, and one which required widespread medical intervention.

The conditions under which obesity could be medicalized began even earlier than this. Medicalization requires the capacity to measure, standardize and associate particular norms with health outcomes. In relation to overweight and obesity it requires a shift from the observable dimensions of 'fat', to an interest in the measurable phenomenon of weight. According to Jutel, this shift occurred in the late nineteenth century, when an interest in weight from a scientific point of view developed out of the desire to quantify wellness and to define standards against which normalcy and deviance could be compared. Such standards were developed through the measurement of the body sizes of 'vast populations' (Jutel 2000: 284). As well as providing indicators of health and longevity, these standards were used 'to identify racial groups and to confirm the superiority of the white man':

> This desire to capture the average man (sic) as well as the deviant, in measurement and proportion, led to the emergence of a new disease concept by the early 20th century. Being overweight became a 'clinical' condition carrying with it a corresponding set of rules for diagnosis, treatment and prognosis. It might seem surprising to think of being overweight as a new clinical entity. Previous concern with body size, however, was based not on weight or measure but rather on fatness, an important distinction.
>
> (Jutel 2000: 285)

The assessment of the normalcy of particular body weight was made possible early in the twentieth century through the invention of affordable scales for doctors' surgeries, and the development of height–weight charts by insurance companies. The height–weight scales were initially designed to provide insurance companies with the means to assess the financial risk of insuring overweight people but were taken up with enthusiasm by the medical community. These scales and tables allowed normality to be captured in a formula, which could be brought to bear to confirm aesthetic and moral judgments about body shape and size.

The medicalization of obesity was given further impetus in the 1950s with the shift of focus from infectious diseases and undernourishment to diseases of affluence or 'lifestyle' diseases such as cardiovascular disease, cancer and diabetes. The medicalization of obesity as a process did not occur by chance, but was a process which gained momentum 'as medical people and their allies made increasingly frequent, powerful and persuasive claims that they should exercise social control over fatness in contemporary society' (Sobal 1995: 69). Sobal describes how the medicalization of obesity took place through the popularization of the term 'obesity' (rather than the more moralistic and derogatory terms 'fat' and 'corpulent'); the definition of obesity as a disease through its listing in the *International Classifications of Diseases*; the formation of specific medical societies; the application of medical treatments including surgery; the development of specialist clinics; and through strategies such as staking claims in medical journals and making statements to the mass-media.

He points to two roles for individuals in this process: crusaders and experts. Crusaders 'work to expand the jurisdiction of the medical model of obesity, by seeking attention for the problem, mobilize resources to support medical claims, publicly and privately press medical claims and work to counter opposing claims made under other models' (Sobal 1995: 79). 'Experts', on the other hand, are called on as authorities to support claims that obesity can only be dealt with in ways designated by science and clinical practice and to refute counter claims that challenge this position. They are responsible for the construction of certainty within the medical community in the face of a high degree of divergent information and uncertain knowledge. Medical textbooks are one important source of such certainty. Chang and Christakis (2002: 154) in their content analysis of the various editions of a major medical textbook in the US, from the 1920s to 2000, describe how the conceptualization of obesity, 'a presumably unambiguous and cohesive object of knowledge', was transformed over that period 'quite independently of definitive experimental evidence'.

In each of the editions of the medical textbook the fundamental definition of obesity as resulting from 'a simple excess of calorie intake over expenditure' did not change. Obesity was thus defined in terms of 'a basic input/output model of mechanical/economic function and efficiency' (Chang and Christakis 2002: 154). Between the first edition in 1927 and the twenty-first in 2000, the obese person, however, was transformed from a 'societal parasite' who eats far more than they require, to a 'societal victim' of modern consumer society with its abundance of rich foods and/or a victim of their genetics. In the latest edition, there were also references to the discrimination likely to be experienced by people with 'severe obesity' and the difficulties of weight loss. The conceptualization of obesity and the obese person was thus as much a product of the social and cultural contexts in which the editions were written as it was based on 'scientific evidence'. Like Bouchard and others quoted in earlier chapters, however, reconceptualizations of obesity were provided in the textbook without qualification; new truths about obesity were made available to each generation of medical students who used the texts without acknowledgement of the ways in which this knowledge varied from that which had come before, nor of the uncertain knowledge on which such certain statements were made.

Why does it matter?

From what has been said so far, it is possible to take up a comfortable position where one could say: 'so the scientific knowledge about obesity is a little uncertain and we haven't always been so adverse to fat bodies, but in the end isn't it preferable to alert people to the dangers of being fat. It can't do any harm.'

It all seems so straightforward, and this is the power of ideology. Certain beliefs and values are constructed as 'truths', and challenges to such beliefs are disparaged as overly analytical, critical, misguided or just 'sour grapes'. What we have argued above, however, is that particular sets of beliefs and values have come into play to influence the way people in Western societies think about the body's appearance, and, in particular, come to conclusions about the body in relation to its weight and shape. Medical labels have come into common parlance to give credibility to the aesthetic and moral evaluations – that is, moral judgements are now bolstered by assumptions about the kinds of health practices that individuals engage in, that they have put themselves at risk and, furthermore, they are a cost to the nation that could be prevented. Ideologies constructed around the 'obesity epidemic' are far from harmless, however: they allow individuals to be evaluated as 'bad' and/or 'sick' people; they allow institutional interventions and practices that are damaging to the people these practices affect; they cause widespread anxiety, which is in itself unhealthy; and they influence the relationships and practices within families in ways we would also argue are detrimental to the well-being of parents and children and their relationships with each other.

Particular regimes of truth or, for the purposes of this book, 'ideologies' provide resources for the ways in which bodies can be understood and therefore provide guidance for how social institutions such as medicine, the law and education can govern and regulate bodies through their particular practices. For example, Davies points out how categorization of bodies through the standards set by height–weight tables, and more recently BMI and body fat indexes, serve to normalize particular bodies and make others 'deviant' or 'improper bodies'. As she and we have argued, this not only ignores the validity of such standards, but also ignores the effects of such categorizations in terms of the 'real-life effects' and social implications for those whose bodies are labelled as 'overweight'.

> A person perceived to be the bearer of 'excess' weight is considered to be the owner of a 'weight problem' because the categorisation of 'overweight' comes with an entire wealth of meanings about the 'overweight' body and about what it is to be an 'overweight' person.
>
> (Davies 1998: 142)

Being defined as 'overweight' means that a whole range of institutions, and individuals associated with those institutions, are provided with the right and indeed the responsibility to identity people so categorized, or people who might be 'at risk' of such categorizations, and to regulate their behaviours. For example, doctors in Australia are being charged with the responsibility to 'diagnose' overweight or clients at risk of overweight and counsel them about their risk and suggest weight management treatment (this whether or not there is any other medical indication of risk). This may seem common sense. But from the point of view of those who may be targeted by this practice, it is far from being so straightforward. Such medical practices are neither valid – diagnosing an individuals' health risk on the basis of population statistics – nor sensitive to their effects on the individual being so categorized. As Davies (1998: 149) suggests, 'in such a social climate it is difficult to conceive of person who is "overweight" finding it possible to speak about being in good health'.

The ideology of the 'obesity epidemic' allows us – the public, health workers, teachers – to construct those who are overweight as lazy and morally wanting. The discourse of overweight carries with it certain meanings of overweight bodies – that is, they are 'out of control, undisciplined, deviant, and dangerously unhealthy' (Davies 1998: 142). It gives permission on a daily basis for ridicule and harassment and the right to publicly monitor the body shape of others. It stimulates a constant self-surveillance and helps to produce a lifestyle that Atrens (2000: 2) describes as 'riddled with needless anxiety and conspicuously short of fun'.

Perhaps as intended by those who promote the 'obesity epidemic' through the media and through health promotions and health education programmes and policies, it has generated a widespread anxiety about the body's shape and weight. Social policy and health strategies thus target individuals' behaviours as though all were at risk. The preoccupations of the affluent with the body's appearance are visited on the wider population, through a simple fear of fat. In Chapter 8 the consequences of such anxieties for women were demonstrated – the preoccupation with the energy value and fat content of food, yo-yo dieting and, at its extremes, anorexia and bulimia. The message of the 'obesity epidemic' goes beyond women, although women are likely to be most responsive to its message. The message is that anyone could get fat, everyone is at risk of falling outside the norm and that the risk begins very early in life. This message has been very successful. Shilling (1993) and others (Burrows *et al.* 2002) point to studies where children as young as nine demonstrate a knowledge of the discourse of obesity and express a fear of being fat.

With the identification of obesity as a social problem, blame for the problem has been variously attributed to social, cultural and personal factors. For example, writers cited in earlier chapters have variously laid blame on the fast food industry, technology and changes in family values. While the identification of forces outside the individual has a place to play in understanding why the weight of populations has increased, such an analysis does not examine how the material conditions of people's lives influence the kinds of 'choices' they are able to exercise and the kinds of priorities they construct that make sense in the contexts of their circumstances.

In the context of the biomedical and public health discourses, which construct obesity as a disease of epidemic proportions and a social problem, responsibility is not attributed to social factors or structural constraints but to individuals (or groups of individuals as social categories) and their inappropriate lifestyle choices. What is then required are interventions that will change individual behaviour such as health promotion campaigns and weight control programmes which emphasize the responsibility of the individual in making appropriate choices. As Davies (1998: 147) points out 'the unacknowledged assumption is that if people are given the ability and knowledge they will make "rationale" choices about their own health care'. In this context not to lose weight 'can only be understood as nonsensical; even irrational', not to comply is 'a dereliction of duty in the care of the self' (Davies 1998: 148).

In Chapter 6 we suggested that in the epidemiological data there is a relationship between socio-economic status and overweight and obesity that is generally ignored. While these data are important starting points, as Frohlich *et al.* (2001)

and Shim (2002) point out, it is important that such information be theorized in ways that take into account the complexity of social and cultural factors. In the first instance, in wanting to point to relationships between social groups and health outcomes, it is important not to fall into the same trap of taking for granted simple relationships between what are essentially social constructs (such as, 'race' and 'socio-economic status') and patterns of health and illness. In looking for 'causation' what is currently missing, according to Frohlich *et al.* (2001), are explanations and strategies based on:

> a discussion between agency (the ability for people to deploy a range of causal powers), practices (the activities that make and transform the world we live in) and social structure (the rules and resources in society). Without such an understanding, factors associated with people's disease experiences within a context tend to be denuded of social meaning.
>
> (Frohlich *et al.* 2001: 781)

Despite these obvious limitations, those working in the context of public health draw on large-scale epidemiological studies to develop policy and strategies to change the 'lifestyle choices' of individuals. This 'knowledge' about populations is used to develop health promotion programmes and health education strategies. In the process what seems to happen is that the message becomes simplified particularly when strategies involve mass-media campaigns. What is essentially uncertain knowledge, based on complex relationships between contextual determinants of health, is simplified and applied to all people to define how they should live. Health promotion strategies locate the responsibility with all individuals to monitor their behaviours and those of others in keeping with desired health outcomes. In doing so, the specific social, cultural and material conditions of people's lives are ignored. Programmes such as 'Life. Be In It' and 'Active Australia' are two such examples in Australia. As Fullagar (2001) points out, the strategies that are often employed in these programmes assume that individuals are free to make decisions and choices in relation to health – for example, in relation to what they eat and how they engage in physical activity. This means that people who do not exercise their 'freedom' to choose in ways that are productive to health, can be categorized and stigmatized as lazy, undisciplined, lacking in will-power or just downright 'bad' (they are like Norm, the 'couch potato', in the Australian 'Life. Be In It' campaign). It is such individuals who then become targeted as in need of regulation so that they might be brought to act appropriately.

What is rarely acknowledged is that priorities in people's lives are not always organized in situations where they are free to 'choose' active leisure or 'healthy' planned eating. Long hours of work, obligations to family and other social relationships, lack of discretionary income and poor transport and facilities all contribute to the ways in which people set priorities and make decisions. But it also goes beyond this: such moral imperatives change the ways in which people think about themselves and their everyday practices, they become the 'thought'/ 'body' police of themselves and others. Physical activity has to be purposive: it becomes exercise rather than play. Certain forms of physical activity are valued over others because of their capacity to expend energy (or to shape the body in specific ways). These imperatives and the practices they create persist despite the lack of evidence that imposing such ways of seeing on people has any effect other than to raise levels of anxiety and guilt.

Childhood obesity

A word needs to be said specifically on childhood obesity. Children have been targeted as a group particularly 'at risk', not so much for their present health but in anticipation of health issues to come. The epidemiological data that suggest children who are overweight and obese are more likely to be overweight and obese adults have provided a rationale for health promotion programmes and interventions focused on children and those who are deemed to be responsible for their weight and the behaviours, which are believed to affect it. The imperatives to change 'lifestyle' behaviours thus fall to parents (particularly mothers) and schools. Institutions and individuals dealing with children are co-opted into identifying children 'at risk' and into monitoring and regulating children's behaviours to prevent and to treat overweight and obesity. The expectations that individuals will take responsibility for their own health, with respect to children, is handed over to parents. If children show signs of being overweight then parents are blamed and assumptions are made about the quality of their parenting. Such an approach draws on particular ideas about parenting that again ignore the social contexts of children's and families' lives and find it easier to hold mothers responsible. As described in Chapter 2, the media has particularly revelled in the opportunities provided by the so-called epidemic of childhood obesity to dramatize the situation and to blame to parents and schools.

In relation to schools and other institutions concerned with the care of children, the panic generated around childhood obesity has produced a range of policies and practices that permit the surveillance of children's weight and the regulation of their behaviours if they are deemed to be a risk. The House of Commons report, *Tackling Obesity in England*, for example, recommends the following: 'Practice nurses, dieticians and school nurses can also play a valuable role in identifying patients with weight problems and in providing advice and support on weight control, and lifestyle change in a more relaxed environment' (National Audit Office 2001: 2).

In schools, the panic associated with the perceived increase in childhood obesity provides a rationale for practices that identify (often publicly) children who are perceived to be overweight and obese and create programmes specifically designed to address 'their' problem. One perennial example is the public weighing of children and young people in physical and health education classes. The following quote from field notes Burns collected in an Australian primary school is suggestive of some of the problems with this practice:

> In no other test were the differences more noticeable than in the simple weighing of the children. The boys seemed indifferent, with the odd self-conscious body-hugging from both the skinny and the really chubby, while most eagerly bounced on and sent the machine's arm swinging. The girls moved up in tight groups, and while one stepped on the others gathered to

read the result even before the tester. Heads turned, eyes rolled, and of the large range of mostly pre-pubescent shapes, it was sometimes the most trim and athletic youngster who asked for the result. 'My god, I *knew* I was getting fat!' 'Help!! I'll have to go on a diet!' 'I *can't* be that much!'

(Burns 1993: 78, emphasis in original)

In the name of 'protecting' children from obesity, policies and practices are emerging that seem to be completely counter to the emotional well-being of children and damaging to the relationships between parents and their children. For example, Leahy and Harrison (2003) write about health programmes, such as the 'Primary Fightback Healthy Eating and Physical Activity' resource for teachers, which, on one hand, contain imperatives to promote body acceptance and develop self-esteem and, on the other, pronounce on escalating obesity rates and create an idea of all children as being 'at risk'. They also describe the phenomenon of 'fat laps' (so called by both teachers and students) where primary school students who have been identified as being overweight – and at risk of obesity – are taken out at lunchtimes and made to run around the oval to help them lose weight. In another example, teachers were encouraged to engage in 'lunch box surveillance' and to award points for particular foods – 5 points for a piece of fruit, 5 points for wholemeal bread, 0 points for lollies or a lunch order. These examples may seem mere aberrations, however, in North America 'weight report cards' are being used to 'battle obesity' by encouraging parents to take action (Chomitz et al. 2003).

In the UK, there are proposals to extend the school day to enable pupils to engage in an extra two hours of physical activity (Wright and Burrows 2004). The benefits of these extended hours are explained by Barry Gardiner, the Labour MP who is championing the plan, in the following quote. His assumptions about young people's lives clearly draw on the constructions of the problem of childhood overweight and obesity fuelled by the research critiqued in other chapters in this book, together with popular ideas of young people as 'trouble':

Isn't it better to have children still in school at four o'clock either playing or learning than at home watching television, eating crisps and doing nothing more strenuous than reaching for the remote control, or hanging around the streets causing trouble.

(quoted in Campbell 2002)

One of the consequences when ideologies become widely accepted is that other ways of thinking and doing are closed off. For example, the prevention of obesity in children has become one of the main rationales for physical education in primary schools in many Western countries (Wright and Burrows 2004). Resources for both research and intervention programmes are diverted to solve the problems of overweight and obesity despite, as demonstrated in earlier chapters, the lack of evidence of the efficacy of such programmes. Physical activity comes to have value in schools and in wider society only insofar as it helps to 'burn energy'. Such an approach is in danger of taking the pleasure out of physical activity and even further marginalizing those forms of physical activity that are not demonstrably 'fat burning'.

A sociological perspective is no more a neutral perspective than any other perspective discussed in this book. What is does provide, however, is what might be called an ethical engagement with the ideology of the 'obesity epidemic' that takes account of its social and emotional costs and examines the extent to which the evangelism associated with the 'obesity epidemic' is motivated by self-interest, aesthetic sensibilities, an unquestioning belief in the efficacy of science and a more generalized pessimism about young people. Such an approach points in particular to the limitations of simply blaming individuals for engaging in behaviours that are judged by 'expert authority' to put them 'at risk' of ill health, and points to the importance of taking into account the material conditions of people's lives in shaping their priorities and how they make sense of their lives and those of their children.

On a positive note, a sociological perspective, in this case a postmodern perspective, can also propose an alternative way of working with people to improve their health, one which proposes an ethical engagement with others:

> Such a response would entail at least: an emphasis which would act very locally, as opposed to more indiscriminate or totalising interventions; programs which enable people to make active decisions about the lives they lead; a celebration of diversity in the target population, rather than a perspective which sees individuals as deviates from some norm of behaviour; involvements which take advantage of spaces in routines and lives to explore new possibilities for activities and identity; and programs which do not detract from the humanity of those who are clients, for example, by an overblown emphasis on 'being healthy' as opposed to 'becoming this or that'.
>
> (Fox 1998: 20)

10 Beyond body weight

In the final weeks of writing this book an international 'obesity epidemic' conference was held at an Australian university. Although obesity conferences have become commonplace, this one was a little different in that it sought to educate obesity scientists in the art of lobbying government officials. Despite the publicity that the 'obesity epidemic' has generated, there are those who believe that governments are still not treating the matter with the seriousness it deserves.

At this stage it is not completely clear what the scientific community would have governments do, particularly in light of uncertainty about what is actually causing the 'obesity epidemic'. Nonetheless, among the suggestions we have read in the scientific literature have been changing building codes and urban planning practices in order to force people to exercise more; higher taxes on 'unhealthy' foods; bans on advertising for 'junk food' during children's television periods; compulsory fitness training and testing in schools; the development of national fitness benchmarks against which all children can be measured; teacher monitoring of the contents of children's lunch boxes; the placement of 'healthy diet' posters and messages by parents around the home; and even higher taxes on those citizens who do not achieve a certain amount of weekly exercise. In this context, it may not be altogether surprising if governmental response continues to lag behind the demands of obesity science.

However, there is perhaps a more straightforward reason why governments, to this point, have not sprung into action. It may actually be the case that not everyone is quite so convinced that overweight and obesity is the 'drop everything' problem we have been told it is. Despite the insistence of parts of the scientific community that overweight or obesity are states of disease, perhaps other people can see that it is quite possible to be healthy, happy and large. Perhaps, even without the benefit of a scientific education, people sense that the pathways that lead from overweight and obesity to premature death are extremely indirect, that daily exercise does not ensure good health and that food should be enjoyed, not agonized over. Perhaps they look around the world and see that the health of Western nations is comparatively good, probably improving, and that wholesale changes to the way we live are simply not warranted. Perhaps they see that, given the health challenges that currently face different parts of the world, describing entire Western populations as 'sick' seems a bit of a stretch. Perhaps they have come to the understanding that what Dubos (1971) called the mirage of perfect health is just that, a mirage, and that lives are lived in the context of

188 Beyond body weight

a range of competing priorities, such as cultural tradition, interpersonal relationships, physical pleasure and economic resources. While the case for making overweight and obesity our number one health concern may seem obvious to obesity scientists, perhaps outside in the wider world life is seen as more complex and more prone to compromise.

At the same time, it is clear that some sections of the general public have taken up the idea of an 'obesity epidemic' with some enthusiasm. This should come as no surprise, since the more affluent sections of Western countries have been paying close attention to the changing directives of medical science for over a century. As a result, it is not difficult to see the current panic around overweight and obesity generating even more ways for people to spend money on their own and their children's fitness and for these to be presented as a 'healthy' and 'responsible' use of resources. Either because or despite of these measures (we will have no way of telling), at some point in the future, overweight and obesity levels will begin to level out among more affluent groups. If the history of health is any guide, at this point we will probably hear the first declarations of victory in the 'war on obesity' as middle-class anxieties begin to drift elsewhere. Social disparities in disease incidence and life expectancy will probably remain largely unchanged and the issue of fatness will do as it has done many times before: disappear for a time only to re-emerge at a later historical moment for new moral and ideological reasons. Meanwhile, how the measures currently being proposed by obesity science will affect the extremely high rates of diabetes and heart disease among groups such as indigenous Australians (Hoy et al. 1999) is, to say the least, unclear.

Whether or not obesity science still believes in the myth of the 'body as machine' will also be an important determinant of how people think about body weight in the future. In *The Myths We Live By*, the English philosopher Mary Midgley writes:

> Myths are not lies. Nor are they detached stories. They are imaginative patterns, networks of powerful symbols that suggest particular ways of interpreting the world. They shape its meaning. For instance, machine imagery, which began to pervade our thought in the seventeenth century, is still potent today. We still often tend to see ourselves, and the living things around us, as pieces of clockwork: items of a kind that we ourselves could make, and might decide to remake if it suits us better.
>
> (Midgley 2003: 1)

To describe an idea as a myth is not the same thing as saying that the idea is bad. The idea of the body as a machine has been extraordinarily productive in the fields of anatomy, physiology and medicine. As Jonathan Miller (2000) argues, the invention of particular machines has been fundamental to the expansion of human imagination generally and to our understanding of the human body in particular. Prior to the invention of the hydraulic pump, for example, the idea that the heart might work in a similar way was literally unthinkable.

But while myths are not essentially bad, they also have a tendency to be overextended by people who use them. So while it may be useful to think of the body as a machine, it is a myth; the body is not a machine. As Midgley goes on to say, ideas such as that of the machine are quite properly used by scientists, but they are not just passive pieces of apparatus like thermostats. They have their own influence. They are living parts of powerful myths – imaginative patterns that we all take for granted – ongoing dramas inside which we live our lives. These patterns shape the mental maps that we refer to when we want to place something . . . They are the matrix of thought, the background that shapes our mental habits. They decide what we think important and what we ignore. They provide tools with which we organise the mass of incoming data. When they are bad they can do a great deal of harm by distorting our selection and slanting our thinking. That is why we need to watch them so carefully.

(Midgley 2003: 3–4)

We have had a long time to watch the 'body as machine' model shape the study of human body weight. Our argument in this book has been that it has failed to produce useful ways of thinking and shows no sign of doing so in the future. This is important because, in its efforts to appear mechanistically scientific, the science of obesity has failed to see its own moral and ideological biases. The moral and ideological dimensions of the 'obesity epidemic' are not just an understandable consequence of the fact that flesh-and-blood people, with their pre-existing prejudices, do the research. The problem is deeper than this. It is that the actual subject matter, the body weight of human beings, does not actually lend itself easily to scientific analysis. Treated as a 'science', the study of body weight produces only more questions and uncertainty, which are then obscured with more unhelpful generalizations and calls for more research. Is it any wonder that rather than producing solutions to the alleged problem of 'Western lifestyles', the science of obesity is increasingly concerned with hypothetical prehistoric evolutionary scenarios, genetics and the search for more effective obesity pills? Outside the rarified realm of genetic manipulation, it is difficult to see how the present knowledge base of obesity science has moved us beyond the advice of seventeeth-century English dramatist John Dryden (1631–1700):

> Better to hunt in fields, for health unbought,
> Than fee the doctor for a nauseous drought.
> The wise, for cure, on exercise depend;
> God never made his work, for man to mend.
>   (*Oxford Dictionary of Quotations* 1977: 192)

Indeed, given the present-day tendency of scientists and other commentators to blame the 'obesity epidemic' on the (alleged) disappearance of hard manual labour and the fact that Western people are no longer forced to hunt for their food, Dryden's words could scarcely be more contemporary or more representative of *current* scientific thinking.

It need not be this way, but for the last 100 years the scientific approach has not been able to accommodate a sophisticated understanding of the different ways people choose and are forced to live. It is for this reason, not governmental ignorance and inertia, that the world outside of obesity science does not always respond in the way medical science would wish. We would also suggest that the credibility of obesity science is not helped when many of its most prominent names predict that the entire population of the US or Australia or the UK will be overweight or obese by 2025 or 2050. Predictions about the state of the world at some distant point in the future, based on current rates of change, have rarely turned out to be accurate in the past, and we suspect that many people either ignore or simply discount such predictions.

Two potential new courses of action are open to those who are interested in body weight and health. One of these is unlikely to be welcomed by the medical and scientific communities despite, we would argue, enjoying a good deal of scientific support. This would be simply to 'get over' body weight altogether. Not only have the solutions offered by obesity science in the past (and still prosecuted today) not worked, but also a renewed all-out 'war on obesity' will have other unforeseen consequences for how people relate to each other and feel about themselves, which may be both unhealthy and plainly unethical. The issue of how their proposed solutions will affect people socially and psychologically is rarely even acknowledged, let alone addressed, in obesity science.

The other course of action would be to leave the model of 'body as machine' behind, just as disciplines as disparate as sociology and theoretical physics have done, and to begin to see and experience the world as others see and experience it. Science is an important element in our lives but it is not the source of all truths and the fact that people do not think as scientifically as scientists is, on balance, a good thing. In the case of obesity science, scientists themselves do not think as scientifically as they might imagine themselves to do. The trouble is, many scientists will interpret this point as a criticism when, in fact, the ability to think beyond science is a great untapped resource. For people who really do want to do something about the body weight of Western populations, the difficult, complex and, above all, highly political work of influencing government policy and people's beliefs and behaviours lies ahead, since few in obesity science have tackled it in the past. However, we see no prospect for success without a thorough engagement with issues such as economic disadvantage, the workings of capitalism, increasingly deregulated labour markets and the imperative for companies, particularly, but not only, those that sell food, to be profitable. This would mean the fields of science, medicine and health developing and articulating positions that are overtly moral and ideological, a project which would mean changing the very nature of science itself.

References

Abernethy, P., Macdonald, D. and Bramich, K. (1997) 'Undergraduate subject relevance: a human movement studies case study', *ACHPER Healthy Lifestyles Journal* 44, 4: 5–10.

Allchin, W. H. (1906) 'The dietetic treatment of obesity', *The Practitioner* 76: 514–26.

Anderssen, R. E. (2000) 'The spread of the childhood obesity epidemic', *Canadian Medical Association Journal* 163, 11: 1461–2.

Anderssen, N., Jacobs, D. R., Sidney, S., Bild, D. E., Sternfeld, B. *et al.* (1996) 'Change and secular trends in physical activity patterns in young adults: a seven-year longitudinal follow-up in the Coronary Artery Risk Development in Young Adults Study', *American Journal of Epidemiology* 143, 4: 351–62.

Angier, N. (2000) 'Who is fat? It depends on culture', *New York Times*, 7 November (Section F): 1.

Anonymous (1993) 'Methods for voluntary weight loss and control. NIH Technology Assessment Conference Panel', *Annals of Internal Medicine* 119, 7 (Pt 2): 764–70.

Arnold, P. J. (1965–6) 'Physical education and the needs of society', *Physical Education Yearbook*: 13–20.

Astrup, A. (2001) 'The role of dietary fat in the prevention and treatment of obesity. Efficacy and safety of low-fat diets', *International Journal of Obesity and Related Metabolic Disorders* 25, 1(Suppl.): S46–50.

Atkins, R. C. (2000) *Dr Atkins Age Defying Diet Revolution*, Milsons Point: Random House Australia.

Atrens, D. (1988) *Don't Diet*, Sydney: Bantam.

Atrens, D. (2000) *The Power of Pleasure: Why Indulgence is Good For You, and Other Palatable Truths*, Sydney: Duffy & Snellgrove.

Australian Association for Exercise and Sports Science Newsletter (1999) 'Roundtable – the BMI. Just how useful is it?', 4: 1–3.

Ayers, W. M. (1958) 'Changing attitudes toward overweight and reducing', *Journal of the American Dietetic Association* 34 (January): 23–9.

Ballor, D. L. and Keesey, R. E. (1991) 'A meta-analysis of the factors affecting exercise-induced changes in body mass, fat mass and fat-free mass in males and females', *International Journal of Obesity* 15, 11: 717–26.

Bartky, S. L. (1988) 'Foucault, femininity and the modernization of patriarchal power', in I. Diamond and L. Quinby (eds) *Feminism and Foucault*, Boston, MA: Northeastern University Press.

Bartky, S. L. (1990) *Femininity and Domination: Studies in the Phenomenology of Oppression*, London: Routledge.

Bauman, A. and Owen, N. (1999) 'Physical activity of adult Australians: epidemiological evidence and potential strategies for health gain', *Journal of Science and Medicine in Sport* 2, 1: 30–41.

Baur, L. A. (2001) 'Obesity: definitely a growing concern', *Medical Journal of Australia* 174, 11: 553–4.

Beaglehole, R., Bonita, R. and Kjellström, T. (2002) *Basic Epidemiology*, Geneva: World Health Organization.

Beck, U. (1992) *Risk Society*, London: Sage.

Beebe, R. (2002) 'Size matters: understanding morbid obesity and its associated complications', *Journal of Emergency Medical Services* 27, 1: 22–8.

Bell, F. M. (1914) 'The "why" of obesity', *New York Medical Journal* 99: 731–3.

Bennett, T., Emmison, M. and Frow, J. (1999) *Accounting for Tastes: Australian Everyday Cultures*, Cambridge: Cambridge University Press.

Berger, P. (1967) *Invitation to Sociology: A Humanist Perspective*, New York: Anchor Books.

Bernal, J. D. (1929) *The World, the Flesh and the Devil*, London: Jonathan Cape.

Biddle, S. J., Gorely, T., Marshall, S. J., Murdey, I. and Cameron, N. (2004) 'Physical activity and sedentary behaviours in youth: issues and controversies', *Journal of the Royal Society of Health* 124, 1: 29–33.

Blair, S. N. and Brodney, S. (1999) 'Effects of physical inactivity and obesity on morbidity and mortality: current evidence and research issues', *Medicine and Science in Sports and Exercise* 31, 11 (Suppl.): S646–62.

Blair, S. N. and Connelly, J. C. (1996) 'How much physical activity should we do? The case for moderate amounts and intensities of physical activity', *Research Quarterly for Exercise and Sport* 67, 2: 193–205.

Blair, S. N., Kohl, H. W., Gordon, N. F. and Paffenbarger, R. S. (1992) 'How much physical activity is good for health?', *Annual Review of Public Health* 13: 99–126.

Blundell, J. E. and King, N. A. (1999) 'Physical activity and regulation of food intake: current evidence', *Medicine and Science in Sports and Exercise* 31, 11 (Suppl.): S573–83.

Booth, M. L., Chey, T., Wake, M., Norton, K., Hesketh, K. *et al.* (2003) 'Change in the prevalence of overweight and obesity among young Australians, 1969–1997', *American Journal of Clinical Nutrition* 77, 1: 29–36.

Booth, M. L., Macaskill, P., Lazarus, R. and Baur, L. A. (1999) 'Sociodemographic distribution of measures of body fatness among children and adolescents in New South Wales, Australia', *International Journal of Obesity* 23, 5: 456–62.

Booth, M. L., Okely, A. D., Chey, T., Bauman, A. E. and Macaskill, P. (2002) 'Epidemiology of physical activity participation among New South Wales school students', *Australian and New Zealand Journal of Public Health* 26, 4: 371–4.

Bordo, S. (1993) *Unbearable Weight: Feminism, Western Culture and the Body*, Berkeley: University of California Press.

Bordo, S. (2003) *Unbearable Weight: Feminism, Western Culture and the Body*, 10th edition, Berkeley: University of California Press.

Boreham, C. and Riddoch, C. (2003) 'Physical activity and health through the lifespan', in J. McKenna and C. Riddoch (eds) *Perspectives on Health and Exercise*, Basingstoke: Palgrave.

Bouchard, C. (2000) *Physical Activity and Obesity*, Champaign, IL: Human Kinetics.

Bouchard, C. and Blair, S. N. (1999) 'Introductory comments for the consensus on physical activity and obesity', *Medicine and Science in Sports and Exercise* 31, 11 (Suppl.): S498–501.

Bourdieu, P. (1986) *Distinction: A Social Critique of the Judgement of Taste*, London: Routledge and Kegan Paul.

Bradfield, R. B., Paulos, J. and Grossman, L. (1971) 'Energy expenditure and heart rate of obese high school girls', *American Journal of Clinical Nutrition* 24, 12: 1482–8.

Bradford Hill, A. (1977) *A Short Textbook of Medical Statistics*, London: Hodder and Stoughton.

Bravata, D. M., Sanders, L., Huang, J., Krumholz, H. M., Olkin, I. *et al.* (2003) 'Efficacy and safety of low-carbohydrate diets: a systematic review', *Journal of the American Medical Association* 289, 14: 1837–50.

Bray, G. A. (1979) *Obesity. Disease-a-month,* Chicago, IL: Year Book Medical Publishers.

Bray, G. A. (1990) 'Obesity: historical development of scientific and cultural ideas', *International Journal of Obesity* 14, 11: 909–26.

Bray, G. A. (2000) 'Overweight, mortality, and morbidity', in C. Bouchard (ed.) *Physical activity and obesity,* Champaign, IL: Human Kinetics.

Bray, G. A. (2003) 'Evaluation of obesity; Who are the obese?' *Postgraduate Medicine* 114, 6: 19–27, 38.

Bray, G. A. and Popkin, B. M. (1998) 'Dietary fat intake does affect obesity!', *American Journal of Clinical Nutrition* 68, 6: 1157–73.

Bray, G. A., Lovejoy, J. C., Smith, S. R., DeLany, J. P., Lefevre, M. *et al.* (2002) 'The influence of different fats and fatty acids on obesity, insulin resistance and inflammation', *Journal of Nutrition* 132, 9: 2488–91.

Braziel, J. E. and LeBesco, K. (eds) (2001) *Bodies out of Bounds: Fatness and Transgression,* Berkeley: University of California Press.

British Heart Foundation (2000) *Couch Kids: The Growing Epidemic – Looking at Physical Activity in Children in the UK,* British Heart Foundation.

British Heart Foundation (2004) Prevalence of obesity, latest available data, all available countries. Online. Available at: www.heartstats.org/search.asp (accessed 29 January, 2004).

Brochu, M., Poehlman, E. T. and Ades, P. A. (2000) 'Obesity, body fat distribution, and coronary artery disease', *Journal of Cardiopulmonary Rehabilitation* 20, 2: 96–108.

Brodney, S., Blair, S. N. and Lee, C. D. (2000) 'Is it possible to be overweight or obese and fit and healthy?', in C. Bouchard (ed.) *Physical Activity and Obesity,* Champaign, IL: Human Kinetics.

Brown, P. J. and Konner, M. (1987) 'An anthropological perspective on obesity', *Annals of the New York Academy of Sciences* 499: 29–46.

Brown, W. (2001) 'Couch potato: no quick fix', *Sport Health* 19, 1: 9–10.

Brownell, K. D. and Horgen, K. B. (2004) *Food Fight: The Inside Story of the Food Industry, America's Obesity Crisis, and What We Can Do About It,* Chicago, IL: Contemporary Books.

Brownell, K. D. and Stunkard, A. J. (1989) 'Physical activity in the development and control of obesity', in J. E. Stunkard (ed.) *Obesity,* New York: W. B. Saunders.

Bruch, H. (1940) 'Obesity in childhood: physiologic and psychologic aspects of the food intake of obese children', *American Journal of Diseases of Children* 59: 739–81.

Bruch, H. (1941) 'Obesity in childhood and personality development', *American Journal of Orthopsychiatry* 11: 467–75.

Bruch, H. (1944) 'Dietary treatment of obesity in childhood', *Journal of the American Dietetic Association* 20: 361–4.

Bruch, H. and Touraine, G. (1940) 'Obesity in childhood: V. The family frame of obese children', *Psychosomatic Medicine* 2, 2: 141–206.

Bryant, J. (2000) 'Britain learns lesson over schools sport', *The Times,* 6 April: 37.

Bullen, B. A., Reed, R. B. and Mayer, J. (1964) 'Physical activity of obese and nonobese adolescent girls appraised by motion picture sampling', *American Journal of Clinical Nutrition* 14: 211–23.

Burns, R. (1993) 'Health fitness and female subjectivity: what is happening to school health and physical education', in L. Yates (ed.) *Feminism and Education,* Melbourne: La Trobe University Press.

Burrows, L., Wright, J. and Jungersen-Smith, J. (2002) '"Measure your belly": New Zealand children's constructions of health and fitness', *Journal of Teaching in Physical Education* 22, 1: 29–38.

Burstyn, P. G. (1990) *Physiology for Sportspeople. A Serious User's Guide to the Body*, Manchester: Manchester University Press.

Burt, R. (1995) *The Male Dancer: Bodies, Spectacle, Sexualities*, London: Routledge.

Cahnman, W. J. (1968) 'The stigma of obesity', *Sociological Quarterly* 9: 283–99.

Cameron, A. J., Welborn, T. A., Zimmet, P. Z., Dunstan, D. W., Owen, N. et al. (2003) 'Overweight and obesity in Australia: the 1999–2000 Australian Diabetes, Obesity and Lifestyle Study (AusDiab)', *Medical Journal of Australia* 1789, 9: 427–32.

Cameron, D. and Jones, I. G. (1983) 'John Snow, the Broad Street pump and modern epidemiology', *International Journal of Epidemiology* 12, 4: 393–6.

Campbell, D. (2000) 'Schools rear crop of couch potatoes', *Observer*, 27 February: 6.

Campbell, D. (2002) 'British school day could rise to 10 hours', *Observer*. Online. Available at: www.observer.co.uk (accessed 5 April 2003).

Campos, P. (2003) 'Big fat lie', *Weekend Australian*, 11–12 January: 13, 16.

Carryer, J. (1997) 'The embodied experience of largeness: A feminist exploration', in V. Grace and M. de Ras (eds) *Bodily Boundaries, Sexualised Genders and Medical Discourses*, Palmerston North, NZ: Dunmore Press.

Chakravarthy, M. V. and Booth, F. W. (2003) 'Inactivity and inaction: we can't afford either', *Archives of Pediatrics and Adolescent Medicine* 157, 8: 731–2.

Chandler, T. J. L. (1996) 'The structuring of manliness and the development of rugby football at the public schools and Oxbridge, 1830–1880', in T. J. L. Chandler and J. Nauright (eds) *Making Men: Rugby and Masculine Identity*, London: Frank Cass.

Chang, V. W. and Christakis, N. A. (2002) 'Medical modelling of obesity: a transition from action to experience in a 20th century American medical textbook', *Sociology of Health and Illness* 24, 2: 151–77.

Chernin, K. (1981) *Womansize: The Tyranny of Slenderness*, London: The Women's Press.

Chomitz, V. R., Collins, F., Kim, J., Kramer, E. and McGowan, R. (2003) 'Promoting healthy weight among elementary school children via a health report card approach', *Archives of Pediatrics and Adolescent Medicine* 157, 8: 765–72.

Chrisler, J. C. (1996) 'Politics of women's weight', *Feminism and Psychology* 6, 2: 181–4.

Colditz, G. A. (1999) 'Economic costs of obesity and inactivity', *Medicine and Science in Sports and Exercise* 31, 11 (Suppl.): S663–7.

Colditz, G. A. and Mariani, A. (2000) 'The cost of obesity and sedentarism in the United States', in C. Bouchard (ed.) *Physical Activity and Obesity*, Champaign, IL: Human Kinetics.

Coleman, P. (1998) 'I'll take the health benefits of exercise without the risks please', *The Lancet* 352, 9126: 492.

Conway, D. (2003) 'Aussie sport is in crisis', *Geelong Advertiser*, 4 December: 1, 54.

Cooke, R. (2003) 'Fat attack: the big issue', *Observer*, 9 March: 25.

Cornwall, E. E. (1916) 'The treatment of obesity by a rational diet', *Boston Medical and Surgical Journal* 175, 17: 601–2.

Corrigan, P. (2000) 'Lottery lunacy and schools for scandal', *Independent*, 12 March: 19.

Cowley, G. (2000) 'Generation XXL', *Newsweek*, 3 July: 40–4.

Crace, J. (2000) 'Literacy 2, sport 0', *Guardian Education*, 29 February: 4.

Craig, P. E. (1955) 'Obesity: a practical guide to its treatment based on a controlled study of 821 consecutive cases', *Medical Times* 83: 156–64.

Crawford, D. A., Jeffery, R. W. and French, S. A. (1999) 'Television viewing, physical inactivity and obesity', *International Journal of Obesity and Related Metabolic Disorders* 23, 4: 437–40.

Critser, G. (2000) 'Let them eat fat', *Harper's Magazine*, March: 41–7.

Critser, G. (2003) *Fat Land: How Americans Became the Fattest People in the World*, London: Penguin Books.

Crosset, T. (1990) 'Masculinity, sexuality, and the development of early modern sport', in M. A. Messner and D. F. Sabo (eds) *Sport, Men, and the Gender Order: Critical Feminist Perspectives*, Champaign, IL: Human Kinetics.

Crouch, B. (2002) 'Parent and child fitness bond broken. We're too busy to be role models', *Sunday Mail*, 14 April: 17.

Daily Telegraph (2003) 'TV "can make you fit not fat"', 10 December: 21.

Damcott, C. M., Sack, P. and Shuldiner, A. R. (2003) 'The genetics of obesity', *Endocrinology and Metabolism Clinics of North America* 32, 4: 761–86.

Darwin, E. (1968) *A Plan for the Conduct of Female Education in Boarding Schools*, New York: Johnson Reprint Corp.

Davies, D. (1998) 'Health and the discourse of weight control', in A. Petersen and C. Waddell (eds) *Health Matters: A Sociology of Illness, Prevention and Care*, Buckingham: Open University Press.

Deckelbaum, R. J. and Williams, C. L. (2001) 'Childhood obesity: the health issue', *Obesity Research* 9, 4 (Suppl.): 239S–43S.

de Garine, I. and Pollock, N. J. (eds) (1995) *Social Aspects of Obesity*, Luxembourg: Gordon and Breach.

Dennison, B. A., Erb, T. A. and Jenkins, P. L. (2002) 'Television viewing and television in bedroom associated with overweight risk among low-income preschool children', *Pediatrics* 109, 6: 1028–35.

Dennison, B. A., Russo, T. J., Burdick, P. A. and Jenkins, P. L. (2004) 'An intervention to reduce television viewing by preschool children', *Archives of Pediatrics and Adolescent Medicine* 158, 2: 170–6.

Dietz, W. H. (2001) 'The obesity epidemic in young children: reduce television viewing and promote playing', *British Medical Journal* 322, 7282: 313–14.

Dietz, W. H. (2002) 'Foreword', in W. Burniat, T. Cole, I. Lissau and E. Poskitt (eds) *Child and Adolescent Obesity: Causes and Consequences, Prevention and Management*, Cambridge: Cambridge University Press.

Dietz, W. H. and Gortmaker, S. L. (1985) 'Do we fatten our children at the television set? Obesity and television viewing in children and adolescents', *Pediatrics* 75, 5: 807–12.

Dietz, W. H., Bandini, L. G., Morelli, J. A., Peers, K. F. and Ching, P. L. (1994) 'Effect of sedentary activities on resting metabolic rate', *American Journal of Clinical Nutrition* 59, 3: 556–9.

Dinger, M. K. (1998) 'Physical activity: how much is enough?', *Parks and Recreation* 33, 8: 26–30, 32.

Dionne, I. and Tremblay, A. (2000) 'Human energy and nutrient balance', in C. Bouchard (ed.) *Physical Activity and Obesity*, Champaign, IL: Human Kinetics.

DiPietro, L. (1999) 'Physical activity in the prevention of obesity: current evidence and research issues', *Medicine and Science in Sports and Exercise* 31, 11 (Suppl.): S542–6.

Doll, R. and Hill, A. (1964) 'Mortality in relation to smoking: Ten years' observations of British doctors', *British Medical Journal* 1: 1399–1410 and 1460–7.

Donnelly, J. E., Jacobsen, D. J., Jakicic, J. M. and Whatley, J. E. (1994) 'Very low calorie diet with concurrent versus delayed and sequential exercise', *International Journal of Obesity and Related Metabolic Disorders* 18, 7: 469–75.

Dubbert, P. M., Carithers, T., Sumner, A. E., Barbour, K. A., Clark, B. L. et al. (2002) 'Obesity, physical inactivity, and risk of cardiovascular disease', *American Journal of the Medical Sciences* 324, 3: 116–26.

Dubos, R. J. (1971) *Mirage of Health: Utopias, Progress, and Biological Change*, New York: Harper and Row.

Durant, R. H., Baranowski, T., Johnson, M. and Thompson, W. O. (1994) 'The relationship among television watching physical activity, and body composition of young children', *Pediatrics* 94, 4 (Pt 1): 449–55.

Durnin, J. V., Lonergan, M. E., Good, J. and Ewan, A. (1974) 'A cross-sectional nutritional and anthropometric study, with an interval of 7 years, on 611 young adolescent schoolchildren', *British Journal of Nutrition* 32, 1: 169–79.

Eaton, S. B., Konner, M. and Shostak, M. (1988) 'Stone agers in the fast lane: chronic degenerative diseases in evolutionary perspective', *American Journal of Medicine* 84, 4: 739–49.

Ebbeling, C. B., Pawlak, D. B. and Ludwig, D. S. (2002) 'Childhood obesity: public-health crisis, common sense cure', *The Lancet* 360, 9331: 473–82.

Eberstadt, M. (2001) 'Home-alone America', *Policy Review*. Online. Available at: www.policyreview.org/jun01/eberstadt.html (accessed 28 February 2004).

Eberstadt, M. (2003) 'The child-fat problem', *Policy Review*, February and March: 3–19.

Edelstein, S. L. and Barrett-Connor, E. (1993) 'Relation between body size and bone mineral density in elderly men and women', *American Journal of Epidemiology* 138, 3: 160–9.

Ehrenreich, B. (2002) *Nickel and Dimed: Undercover in Low-Wage USA*, London: Granta Books.

Engel, M. (2002) 'Land of the fat', *Guardian*, 2 May: 2.

Ennis, C. D. (1999) 'Creating a culturally relevant curriculum for disengaged girls', *Sport, Education and Society* 4, 1: 31–49.

Epstein, L. H. and Goldfield, G. S. (1999) 'Physical activity in the treatment of childhood overweight and obesity: current evidence and research issues, *Medicine and Science in Sports and Exercise* 31, 11 (Suppl.): S553–9.

Evans, A. (2001) 'Stopping Australian getting fatter and slacker? It will be no mean feet!', *Sport Health* 19, 1: 15–16.

Evans, J. and Clarke, G. (1988) 'Changing the face of physical education', in J. Evans (ed.) *Teaching, Teachers, and Control in Physical Education*, Barcombe, Lewes: Falmer.

Ezzati, M., Lopez, A. D., Rodgers, A., Vander Hoorn, S. and Murray, C. J. L. (2002) 'Selected major risk factors and global and regional burden of disease', *The Lancet* 360, 9343: 1347–60.

Ezzati, M., Vander Hoorn, S., Rodgers, A., Lopez, A. D., Mathers, C. D. *et al.* and Comparative Risk Assessment Collaborating Group (2003) 'Estimates of global and regional potential health gains from reducing multiple major risk factors', *The Lancet* 362, 9380: 271.

Fentem, P. H. (1994) 'Benefits of exercise in health and disease', *British Medical Journal* 308, 6939: 1291–5.

Field, A. E., Austin, S. B., Taylor, C. B., Malspeis, S., Rosner, B. *et al.* (2003) 'Relation between dieting and weight change among preadolescents and adolescents', *Pediatrics* 112, 4: 900–6.

Fisher, J. O., Johnson, R. K., Lindquist, C., Birch, L. L. and Goran, M. I. (2000) 'Influence of body composition on the accuracy of reported energy intake in children', *Obesity Research* 8, 8: 597–603.

Fitzgerald, F. T. (1981) 'The problem of obesity', *Annual Review of Medicine* 32: 221–31.

Flegal, K. M. (1999) 'The obesity epidemic in children and adults: current evidence and research issues', *Medicine and Science in Sports and Exercise* 31, 11 (Suppl.): S509–14.

Flegal, K. M., Carroll, M. D., Ogden, C. L. and Johnson, C. L. (2002) 'Prevalence and trends in obesity among US adults, 1999–2000', *Journal of the American Medical Association* 288, 14: 1772–3.

Fogelholm, M., Nuutinen, O., Pasanen, M., Myöhänen, E. and Säätelä, T. (1999) 'Parent-child relationship of physical activity patterns and obesity', *International Journal of Obesity and Related Metabolic Disorders* 23, 12: 1262–8.

Foreyt, J. and Goodrick, K. (1995) 'The ultimate triumph of obesity', *The Lancet* 346, 8968: 134–5.

Fox, N. J. (1998) 'Postmodernism and "health"', in A. Petersen and C. Waddell (eds) *Health Matters: A Sociology of Illness, Prevention and Care*, Sydney: Allen & Unwin.

Fox, S. (2003) 'Children weighing more than 140 kg treated at hospital', *Fairfax New Zealand Limited*. Online. Available at: www.stuff.co.nz/stuff/0,2106,2746069a7144,00.html (accessed 8 December 2003).

Frank, A. (1993) 'Futility and avoidance: medical professionals in the treatment of obesity', *Journal of the American Medical Association* 269, 16: 2132–3.

Franzen, J. (2002) *How to be Alone*, London: Fourth Estate.

French, S. A., Story, M. and Jeffery, R. W. (2001) 'Environmental influences on eating and physical activity', *Annual Review of Public Health* 22: 309–35.

Friedman, J. M. (2003) 'A war on obesity, not the obese', *Science* 299, 5608: 856–8.

Frohlich, K. L., Corin, E. and Potvin, L. (2001) 'A theoretical proposal for the relationship between context and disease', *Sociology of Health and Illness* 23, 6: 776–97.

Fullagar, S. (2001) 'Governing the healthy body: discourses of leisure and lifestyle within Australian health policy', *Health* 6, 1: 68–94.

Fuller, S. (1997) *Science*, Buckingham: Open University Press.

Fumento, M. (1990) *The Myth of Heterosexual AIDS: How a Tragedy Has Been Distorted by the Media and Partisan Politics*, New York: Basic Books.

Fumento, M. (1997a) *The Fat of the Land: The Obesity Epidemic and How Overweight Americans Can Help Themselves*, New York: Viking.

Fumento, M. (1997b) *Polluted Science: The EPA's campaign to Expand Clean Air Regulations*, Washington, DC: AEI Press.

Fumento, M. (2003) *BioEvolution: How Biotechnology is Changing Our World*, San Francisco, CA: Encounter Books.

Gaesser, G. A. (1998) 'Thinness and weight loss: beneficial or detrimental to longevity', *Medicine and Science in Sports and Exercise* 31, 8: 1118–28.

Gaesser, G. A. (2002) *Big Fat Lies: The Truth About Your Weight and Your Health*, Carlsbad, CA: Gurze Books.

Gamman, L. (2000) 'Visual seduction and perverse compliance', in S. Bruzzi and P. Church Gibson (eds) *Fashion Cultures: Theories, Explanations and Analysis*, London and New York: Routledge.

Garrety, K. (1997) 'Negotiating dietary knowledge inside and outside laboratories: the cholesterol controversy', unpublished Ph.D. thesis, Sydney: The University of New South Wales.

Garrety, K. (1998) 'Science, policy and controversy over the cholesterol arena', *Symbolic Interaction* 21, 4: 401–24.

Garrow, J. S. (1978) *Energy Balance and Obesity in Man*, Oxford: Elsevier/North-Holland Biomedical Press.

Garrow, J. S. (1992) 'Treatment of obesity', *The Lancet* 340, 8816: 409–13.

Germov, J. and Williams, L. (1996) 'The epidemic of dieting women: the need for a sociological approach to food and nutrition', *Appetite* 27, 2: 97–108.

Giddens, A. (1991) *Modernity and Self-Identity: Self Society in the Late Modern Age*, Cambridge: Polity Press.

Gilman, S. L. (2004) *Fat Boys: A Slim Book*, Lincoln: University of Nebraska Press.

Goldstein, M. S. (1992) *The Health Movement: Promoting Fitness in America*, New York: Twayne Publishers.

Goodbody, J. (2000) '£150m bid to get couch potatoes into school gym', *The Times*, 6 April: 10.

Goran, M. I., Reynolds, K. D. and Lindquist, C. H. (1999) 'Role of physical activity in the prevention of obesity in children', *International Journal of Obesity and Related Metabolic Disorders* 23, 3 (Suppl.): S18–33.

Gortmaker, S. L., Must, A., Sobol, A. M., Peterson, K., Colditz, G. A. *et al.* (1996) 'Television viewing as a cause of increasing obesity among children in the United States, 1986–1990', *Archives of Pediatrics and Adolescent Medicine* 150, 4: 356–62.

Gortmaker, S. L., Peterson, K., Wiecha, J., Sobol, A. M., Dixit, S. *et al.* (1999) 'Reducing obesity via a school-based interdisciplinary intervention among youth: Planet Health', *Archives of Pediatrics and Adolescent Medicine* 153, 4: 409–18.

Gould, S. J. (1981) *The Mismeasure of Man*, Harmondsworth: Penguin.

Gould, S. J. (1996) *Life's Grandeur: The Spread of Excellence from Plato to Darwin*, London: Jonathan Cape.

Green, B. and Bigum, C. (1993) 'Aliens in the classroom', *Australian Journal of Education* 37, 2: 119–41.

Green, K. (1998) 'Philosophies, ideologies and the practice of physical education', *Sport, Education and Society* 3, 2: 125–43.

Greenberg, B. S., Eastin, M., Hofschire, L., Lachlan, K. and Brownell, K. D. (2003) 'Portrayals of overweight and obese individuals on commercial television', *American Journal of Public Health* 93, 8: 1342–8.

Griffiths, S. (2002) 'Heading for the top?', *Sunday Times*, 10 March: 10.

Griffiths, S. and Wallace, J. (1998) *Consuming Passions: Food in the Age of Anxiety*, Manchester: Manchester University Press.

Grund, A., Krause, H., Siewers, M., Rieckert, H. and Müller, M. J. (2001) 'Is TV viewing an index of physical activity and fitness in overweight and normal weight children?', *Public Health Nutrition* 4, 6: 1245–51.

Grundy, S. M., Blackburn, G., Higgins, M., Lauer, R., Perri, M. G. *et al.*(1999) 'Physical activity in the prevention and treatment of obesity and its comorbidities', *Medicine and Science in Sports and Exercise* 31, 11 (Suppl.): S502–8.

Guerzoni, E. (1996) 'Getting physical', *Sport Health* 14, 4: 10–11.

Gutman, J. (1916) 'The treatment of obesity: some cardinal principles in the dietetics of obesity', *New York Medical Journal* 103: 161–4.

Hall, A. and Stewart, R. (1989) 'Obesity: time for sanity and humanity', *New Zealand Medical Journal* 102, 864: 134–6.

Hanley, A. J., Harris, S. B., Gittelsohn, J., Wolever, T. M., Saksvig, B. *et al.*(2000) 'Overweight among children and adolescents in a Native Canadian community: prevalence and associated factors', *American Journal of Clinical Nutrition* 71, 3: 693–700.

Hannan, E. (2003) 'Chewing the fat', *The Age*, 31 May: 8.

Hardman, A. E. and Stensel, D. J. (2003) *Physical Activity and Health: The Evidence Explained*, London: Routledge.

Hartley, C. (2001) 'Letting ourselves go: Making room for the fat body in feminist scholarship', in J. E. Braziel and K. LeBesco (eds) *Bodies out of Bounds: Fatness and Transgression*, Berkeley: University of California Press.

Hatziandreu, E. I., Koplan, J. P., Weinstein, M. C., Caspersen, C. J. and Warner, K. E. (1988) 'A cost-effectiveness analysis of exercise as a health promotion activity', *American Journal of Public Health* 78, 11: 1417–21.

Haug, F. (1983) *Female Sexualization*, London: Verso.

Heini, A. F. and Weinsier, R. L. (1997) 'Divergent trends in obesity and fat intake patterns: the American paradox', *American Journal of Medicine* 102, 3: 259–64.

Hernández, B., Gortmaker, S. L., Colditz, G. A., Petersen, K. E., Laird, N. M. *et al.* (1999) 'Association of obesity with physical activity, television programs and other forms of video viewing among children in Mexico City', *International Journal of Obesity* 23, 8: 845–54.

Herndon, A. (2002) 'Disparate but disabled: Fat embodiment and disability studies', *NWSA Journal* 14, 3: 120.

Hesse-Biber, S. J. (1996) *Am I Thin Enough Yet?: The Cult of Thinness and the Commercialization of Identity*, New York: Oxford University Publishers.

Heymsfield, S. B., Casper, K., Hearn, J. and Guy, D. (1989) 'Rate of weight loss during underfeeding: relation to level of physical activity', *Metabolism: Clinical and Experimental* 38, 3: 215–23.

Hill, A. (2002) 'Warning: Too tubby tots face lifetime of obesity', *Observer*, 7 April: 9.

Hill, J. O. and Melanson, E. L. (1999) 'Overview of the determinants of overweight and obesity: current evidence and research issues', *Medicine and Science in Sports and Exercise* 31, 11 (Suppl.): S515–21.

Hill, J. O. and Peters, J. C. (1998) 'Environmental contributions to the obesity epidemic', *Science* 280, 5368: 1371–4.

Hoberman, J. (1995) 'Toward a theory of Olympic Internationalism, *Journal of Sport History* 22, 1: 1–37.

Hollis, J. F., Carmody, T. P., Connor, S. L., Fey, S. G. and Matarazzo, J. D. (1986) 'The nutrition attitude survey: associations with dietary habits, psychological and physical well-being, and coronary risk factors', *Health Psychology* 5, 4: 359–74.

Hope, D. (2002) 'Premier's obesity solution "rubbish"', *The Australian*, 23 September: 3.

Hopple, C. and Graham, G. (1995) 'What children think, feel, and know about physical fitness testing', *Journal of Teaching in Physical Education* 14, 4: 408–17.

Howell, J. and Ingham, A. (2001) 'From social problem to personal issue: the language of lifestyle', *Cultural Studies* 15, 2: 326–51.

Hoy, W., Kelly, A., Jacups, S., McKendry, K., Baker, P. *et al.* (1999) 'Stemming the tide: reducing cardiovascular disease and renal failure in Australian Aborigines', *Australian and New Zealand Journal of Medicine* 29, 3: 480–3.

Hoyten, W. J. (1906) 'Thyroid gland in obesity', *British Medical Journal* 2: 197–8.

Hu, F. B., Li, T. Y., Colditz, G. A., Willett, W. C. and Manson, J. E. (2003) 'Television watching and other sedentary behaviors in relation to risk of obesity and type 2 diabetes mellitus in women', *Journal of the American Medical Association* 289, 14: 1785–91.

Hubbard, P. (2003) 'Fear and loathing in the multiplex: everyday anxiety in the post-industrial city', *Capital & Class* Summer, 80: 51.

Hurrell, B. (2003) 'Young talent crisis has hit', *Adelaide Advertiser*, 4 December: 104.

Hurry, J. B. (1917) 'Obesity and its vicious circles', *The Practitioner* 99: 164–82.

Janz, K. (2002) 'Physical activity and bone development during childhood and adolescence. Implications for the prevention of osteoporosis', *Minerva Pediatrica* 54, 2: 93–104.

Jarrett, R. J. (1986) 'Is there an ideal body weight?', *British Medical Journal* 293, 6545: 493–5.

Jebb, S. A. and Moore, M. S. (1999) 'Contribution of a sedentary lifestyle and inactivity to the etiology of overweight and obesity: current evidence and research issues', *Medicine and Science in Sports and Exercise* 31, 11 (Suppl.): S502–8.

Jeffcote, W. (1998) 'Obesity is a disease: food for thought', *The Lancet* 351, 9106: 903–4.

Johnson, A. (2001) 'Weight of a nation', *Marie Claire*, March: 233–5.

Johnson, M. L., Burke, B. S. and Mayer, J. (1956) 'Relative importance of inactivity and overeating in the energy balance of obese high school girls', *American Journal of Clinical Nutrition* 4: 37–44.

Jones, S. (1999) *Almost Like a Whale: The Origin of Species Updated*, London: Doubleday.

Judd, J. (2000) 'Sports colleges "useless to most pupils"', *Independent* 6 April: 3.

Jutel, A. (2000) 'Does size really matter? Weight and values in public health', *Perspectives in Biology and Medicine* 44, 2: 283–96.

Kabat, G. C. and Wynder, E. L. (1992) 'Body mass index and lung cancer risk', *American Journal of Epidemiology* 135, 7: 769–74.

Kahn, H. S., Tatham, L. M. and Heath, C. W. J. (1997) 'Contrasting factors associated with abdominal and peripheral weight gain among adult women', *International Journal of Obesity & Related Metabolic Disorders* 21, 10: 903–11.

Katz, D. L. (2003) 'Pandemic obesity and the contagion of nutritional nonsense', *Public Health Reviews* 31, 1: 33–44.

Kazis, K. and Iglesias, E. (2003) 'The female athlete triad', *Adolescent Medicine State of the Art Reviews* 14, 1: 87–95.

Kelly, J. (2003) 'Experts warn of an obesity crisis', *Herald-Sun*, 12 September: 1, 9.

Keys, A. (1980) 'Overweight, obesity, coronary heart disease and mortality', *Nutrition Reviews* 38: 297–307.

Kirk, D. (1996) 'The crisis in school physical education: an argument against the tide', *ACHPER Healthy Lifestyles Journal* 43, 4: 25–7.

Kirk, D. (1998) *Schooling Bodies: School Practice and Public Discourse, 1880–1950*, London: Leicestershire University Press.

Klein, R. (1996) *Eat Fat*, London: Picador.

Klein, R. (2001) 'Fat beauty', in J. E. Braziel and K. LeBesco (eds) *Bodies out of Bounds: Fatness and Transgression*, Berkeley: University of California Press.

Klein, S. (1999) 'The war against obesity: attacking a new front', *American Journal of Clinical Nutrition* 69, 6: 1061–3.

Klein, S. (2004) 'The national obesity crisis: a call for action', *Gastroenterology* 126, 1: 6.

Klesges, R. C., Hanson, C. L., Eck, L. H. and Durff, A. C. (1988) 'Accuracy of self-reports of food intake in obese and normal-weight individuals: effects of parental obesity on reports of children's dietary intake', *American Journal of Clinical Nutrition* 48, 5: 1252–6.

Knapp, T. R. (1983) 'A methodological critique of the "ideal weight" concept', *Journal of the American Medical Association* 250, 4: 506–10.

Krieger, N. (1994) 'Epidemiology and the web of causation: has anyone seen the spider?' *Social Science and Medicine* 39, 7: 887–903.

Kuhn, T. S. (1970) *The Structure of Scientific Revolutions*, Chicago, IL: University of Chicago Press.

Kunz, T. (2003) 'Fighting obesity in kids', *Chicago Daily Herald*, 23 September: 1.

Last, J. M. (1995) *A Dictionary of Epidemiology*, Oxford: Oxford University Press.

Leahy, D. and Harrison, L. (2003) 'Fat laps and fruit straps: childhood obesity, body image, surveillance and education', paper presented at the New Zealand Association for Research in Education/Australian Association for Research in Education Conference, Aukland, NZ, December.

LeBesco, K. (2001) 'Queering fat bodies/politics', in J. E. Braziel and K. LeBesco (eds) *Bodies out of Bounds: Fatness and Transgression*, Berkeley: University of California Press.

Lee, I. M. and Paffenbarger, R. S. (1996) 'How much physical activity is optimal for health? Methodological considerations', *Research Quarterly for Exercise and Sport* 67: 206–8.

Lee, I. M., Hsieh, C. C. and Paffenbarger, R. S. (1995) 'Exercise intensity and longevity in men. The Harvard Alumni Health Study', *Journal of the American Medical Association* 273, 15: 1179–84.

Le Fanu, J. (1987) *Eat Your Heart Out. The Fallacy of the Healthy Diet*, London: Papermac.

LeMura, L. M. and Maziekas, M. T. (2002) 'Factors that alter body fat, body mass, and fat-free mass in pediatric obesity', *Medicine and Science in Sports and Exercise* 34, 3: 487–96.

Leonard, W. R. and Robertson, M. L. (1997) 'Comparative primate energetics and hominid evolution', *American Journal of Physical Anthropology* 102, 2: 265–81.

Lewontin, R. (2000) *It Ain't Necessarily So: The Dream of the Human Genome and Other Illusions*, London: Granta Books.

Lindenbaum, S. (2001) 'Kuru, prions and human affairs: thinking about epidemics', *Annual Review of Anthropology* 30, 363–85.

Livingstone, M. B., Robson, P. J., Wallace, J. M. and McKinley, M. C. (2003) 'How active are we? Levels of routine physical activity in children and adults', *Proceedings of the Nutrition Society* 62, 3: 681–701.

Lockett, C. (2003) 'Carry that weight', *New Zealand Listener*, 29 November–5 December: 16–21.

Love, I. N. (1900) 'Thyroid in juvenile obesity: a clinical note', *Journal of the American Medical Association* 34: 975–6.

Lowry, R., Wechsler, H., Galuska, D. A., Fulton, J. E. and Kann, L. (2002) 'Television viewing and its associations with overweight, sedentary lifestyle, and insufficient consumption of fruits and vegetables among US high school students: differences by race, ethnicity, and gender', *Journal of School Health* 72, 10: 413–21.

Lupton, D. (1995) *The Imperative of Health: Public Health and the Regulated Body*, London: Sage.

McCullagh, C. (2003) 'Red light on cream donut', *Illawarra Mercury*, 28 October: 16.

McKay, J., Gore, J. M. and Kirk, D. (1990) 'Beyond the limits of technocratic physical education', *Quest* 42, 1: 52–76.

McKenna, J. and Riddoch, C. (eds) (2003) *Perspectives on Health and Exercise*, Basingstoke: Palgrave.

McKenzie, T. L., Feldman, H., Woods, S. E., Romero, K. A., Dahlstrom, V. *et al.* (1995) 'Children's activity levels and lesson context during third-grade physical education', *Research Quarterly for Exercise and Sport* 66, 3: 184–93.

McKenzie, T. L., Marshall, S. J., Sallis, J. F. and Conway, T. L. (2000) 'Student activity levels, lesson context, and teacher behavior during middle school physical education', *Research Quarterly for Exercise and Sport* 71, 3: 249–59.

McKeown, T. (1979) *The Role of Medicine: Dream, Mirage or Nemesis?*, Oxford: Blackwell.

McLaren, A. (1997) *The Trials of Masculinity: Policing Sexual Boundaries 1870–1930*, Chicago, IL: The University of Chicago Press.

McMichael, T. (2002) 'Not knowing what makes us tick has made us sick', *The Australian*, 17 September: 9.

MacNeill, M. (1998) 'Sex, lies and videotape: the political and cultural economies of celebrity fitness videos', in G. Rail (ed.) *Sport in Postmodern Times*, New York: SUNY Press.

Maes, H. H., Neale, M. C. and Eaves, L. J. (1997) 'Genetic and environmental factors in relative body weight and human adiposity', *Behavior Genetics* 27, 4: 325–51.

Magarey, A. M., Daniels, L. A. and Boulton, T. J. C. (2001) 'Prevalence of overweight and obesity in Australian children and adolescents: reassessment of 1985 and 1995 data against new standard international definitions', *Medical Journal of Australia* 174, 11: 561–4.

Maguire, J. and Mansfield, L. (1998) '"No-body's perfect": women, aerobics, and the body beautiful', *Sociology of Sport Journal* 15, 2: 109–37.

Mallam, K. M., Metcalf, B. S., Kirby, J., Voss, L. and Wilkin, T. J. (2003) 'Contribution of timetabled physical education to total physical activity in primary school children: cross sectional study', *British Medical Journal* 327, 7415: 592–3.

Mangan, J. A. (2000) 'Global fascism and the male body: ambitions, similarities and dissimilarities', in J. A. Mangan (ed.) *Superman Supreme: Fascist Body as Political Icon – Global Fascism*, London: Frank Cass.

Marshall, S. J., Biddle, S. J. H., Sallis, J. F., McKenzie, T. L. and Conway, T. L. (2002) 'Clustering of sedentary behaviours and physical activity among youth: a cross national study', *Pediatric Exercise Science* 14, 4: 401–17.

Martínez-González, M. A., Martínez, J. A., Hu, F. B., Gibney, M. J. and Kearney, J. (1999) 'Physical inactivity, sedentary lifestyle and obesity in the European Union', *International Journal of Obesity* 23: 1192–201.

Maxfield, E. and Konishi, F. (1966) 'Patterns of food intake and physical activity in obesity', *Journal of the American Dietetic Association* 49, 5: 406–408.

Mayer, J. (1953) 'Genetic, traumatic and environmental factors in the etiology of obesity', *Physiological Reviews* 33: 472–508.

Mayer, V. F. (1983a) 'The fat illusion', in L. Schoenfielder and B. Wieser (eds) *Shadow on a Tightrope*, San Francisco, CA: Spinsters/Aunt Lute.

Mayer, V. F. (1983b) 'The questions people ask', in L. Schoenfielder and B. Wieser (eds) *Shadow on a Tightrope*, San Francisco, CA: Spinsters/Aunt Lute.

Meek, J. (2003) 'Trillion dollar disease', *London Review of Books* 25, 15: 29–31.

Melby, C. L., Ho, R. C. and Hill, J. O. (2000) 'Assessment of human energy expenditure', in C. Bouchard (ed.) *Physical Activity and Obesity*, Champaign, IL: Human Kinetics.

Meloan, E. L. (1941) 'Excessive appetite: behavior symptom in maladjusted children', *Journal of Pediatrics* 19: 632–7.

Midgley, M. (2003) *The Myths We Live By*, London: Routledge.

Miller, J. (2000) *The Body in Question*, London: Pimlico.

Miller, L. (2003) '"Fat Land" by Greg Critser', *Salon*. Online. Available at: www.salon.com/books/review/2003/01/09/fat/print.html (accessed 18 January 2003).

Ministry of Health (2003) *Nutrition and the Burden of Disease: New Zealand 1997–2011* (Occasional Bulletin Number 7 No. 17). Wellington: Ministry of Health.

Montgomery, B. (1999) 'Our ancestors would barely recognise us. Australians are growing taller. And much, much fatter. The future is not a good look', *Weekend Australian*, 'Features' section, 8–9 May: 4–6.

Morange, M. (2002) *The Misunderstood Gene*, Cambridge, MA: Harvard University Press.

Morris, J. N. (1995) 'Obesity in Britain: lifestyle data do not support sloth hypothesis', *British Medical Journal* 311, 7019: 1568–9.

Morris, J. N. (1996) 'Exercise versus heart attack: questioning the consensus?', *Research Quarterly for Exercise and Sport* 67, 2: 216–20.

Morrison, S. (2003) 'Obesity a growing threat to our children', *Hamilton Spectator*, 14 August: 1.

Muecke, L., Simons-Morton, B., Huang, I. W. and Parcel, G. (1992) 'Is childhood obesity associated with high-fat foods and low physical activity?', *Journal of School Health* 62, 1: 19–23.

Murray, C. J. and Lopez, A. D. (2000) 'On the comparable quantification of health risks: lessons from the Global Burden of Disease Study', *Epidemiology* 10, 5: 594–605.

Murray, C. J., Gakidou, E. E. and Frenk, J. (1999) 'Health inequalities and social group differences: what should we measure?' *Bulletin of the World Health Organization* 77, 7: 537–43.

Murray, S. (2003) '(Un)becoming fat: pathologising the fat female body', paper presented to seventh Australasian Menopause Society Congress, Hobart, Tasmania, 14 November.

Must, A. (2003) 'Does overweight in childhood have an impact on adult health?', *Nutrition Reviews* 61, 4: 139.

Myers, R. J., Klesges, R. C., Eck, L. H., Hanson, C. L. and Klem, M. L. (1988) 'Accuracy of self-reports of food intake in obese and normal-weight individuals: effects of obesity on self-reports of dietary intake in adult females', *American Journal of Clinical Nutrition* 48, 5: 1248–51.

Nash, M. (2003) 'Obesity goes global', *Time*, 7 July: 56–7.

National Audit Office (2001) *Report of the Controller and Auditor General. HC 220 Session, 2000–2001: 15th February*, London: The Stationery Office.

Needham, K. (2002) 'Doctors' orders: get moving or risk cancer', *Sydney Morning Herald*, 26 June: 5.

Nelkin, D. (2003) 'Foreword: the social meanings of risk', in B. H. Harthorn and L. Oaks (eds) *Risk, Culture and Health Inequality: Shifting perceptions of danger and blame*, Westport, CT: Praeger.

Nestle, M. (2000) 'Obese? Food firms say "eat more"', *Deseret News*, 29 June: A19.

Nestle, M. (2002) *Food Politics: How the Food Industry Influences Nutrition and Health*, Berkeley: University of California Press.

Nestle, M. and Jacobson, M. F. (2000) 'Halting the obesity epidemic: a public health policy approach', *Public Health Reports* 115, 1: 12–24.

Neumark-Sztainer, D., Story, M., Hannan, P. J., Tharp, T. and Rex, J. (2003) 'Factors associated with changes in physical activity: a cohort study of inactive adolescent girls', *Archives of Pediatrics and Adolescent Medicine* 157, 8: 803–10.

Newburgh, L. H. and Johnston, M. W. (1930) 'The nature of obesity', *Journal of Clinical Investigation* 8: 197–213.

New York Times (2001a) 'Obesity alarm', 16 December: 2.

New York Times (2001b) 'U.S. warning of death toll from obesity', 14 December: 26.

Nicholl, J. P., Coleman, P. and Brazier, J. E. (1994) 'Health and healthcare costs and benefits of exercise', *Pharmacoeconomics* 5, 2: 109–22.

O'Connor, R. (1980) *Choosing for Health*, Philadelphia, PA: Saunders College.

Oliver, K. L. (2001) 'Images of the body from popular culture: engaging adolescent girls in critical inquiry', *Sport Education and Society* 6, 2: 143–64.

Oliver, K. L. and Lalik, R. (2000) *Bodily Knowledge: Learning about Equity and Justice with Adolescent Girls*, New York: Peter Lang.

Orbach, S. (1988) *Fat is a Feminist Issue*, London: Arrow Books.

Oxford Dictionary of Quotations, The (1977) Oxford: Oxford University Press.

Pangrazi, R. P., Corbin, C. B. and Welk, G. J. (1996) 'Physical activity for children and youth', *Journal of Physical Education, Recreation and Dance* 67, 4: 38–40, 42–3.

Panter-Brick, C. (2002) 'Sexual division of labor: energetic and evolutionary scenarios', *American Journal of Human Biology* 14, 5: 627–40.

Panter-Brick, C. (2003) 'The anthropology of physical activity', in J. McKenna and C. Riddoch (eds) *Perspectives on Health and Exercise*, Basingstoke: Palgrave.

Papanek, P. E. (2003) 'The female athlete triad: an emerging role for physical therapy', *Journal of Orthopaedic and Sports Physical Therapy* 33, 10: 594–614.

Park, R. J. (1988) 'How active were early populations?', in R. Malina and H. Eckert (eds) *Physical Activity in Early and Modern Populations*, Champaign, IL: Human Kinetics.

Parker, D. R., Lapane, K. L., Lasater, T. M. and Carleton, R. A. (1998) 'Short stature and cardiovascular disease among men and women from two southeastern New England communities', *International Journal of Epidemiology* 27, 6: 970–5.

Pate, R. R., Trost, S. G., Felton, G. M., Ward, D. S., Dowda, M. *et al.*(1997) 'Correlates of physical activity behaviour in rural youth', *Research Quarterly for Exercise and Sport* 68, 3: 241–8.

Patty, A. (2000) 'Poor diet, exercise put young at risk', *Daily Telegraph*, 2 August: 19.

Pearce, N. (1996) 'Traditional epidemiology, modern epidemiology, and public health', *American Journal of Public Health* 86, 5: 678–83.

Pennington, A. W. (1954) 'Treatment of obesity: developments of the past 150 years', *American Journal of Digestive Diseases* 21: 65–9.

Peters, J. C., Wyatt, H. R., Donahoo, W. T. and Hill, J. O. (2002) 'From instinct to intellect: the challenge of maintaining a healthy weight in the modern world', *Obesity Reviews* 3, 2: 69–74.

Petersen, L., Schnohr, P. and Sorensen, T. I. (2004) 'Longitudinal study of the long-term relation between physical activity and obesity in adults', *International Journal of Obesity and Related Metabolic Disorders* 28, 1: 105–12.

Pirani, C. (2002) 'A great weight of hope in one pill', *Weekend Australian*, 31 August–1 September: 21.

Pirozzo, S., Summerbell, C., Cameron, C. and Glasziou, P. (2003) 'Should we recommend low fat diets for obesity?', *Obesity Reviews* 4, 2: 83–90.

Pi-Sunyer, F. X. (1999) 'Comorbidities of overweight and obesity: current evidence and research issues', *Medicine and Science in Sports and Exercise* 31, 11 (Suppl.): S602–8.

Pi-Sunyer, F. X. (2002) 'The obesity epidemic: pathophysiology and consequences of obesity', *Obesity Research* 10, 2 (Suppl.): 97S–104S.

Pollock, C. L. (1992) 'Does exercise intensity matter?', *Physician and Sportsmedicine* 20, 12: 123–6.

Pollock, N. J. (1995) 'Social fattening patterns in the Pacific – the positive side of obesity. A Nauru case study', in I. de Garine and N. J. Pollock (eds) *Social Aspects of Obesity* 1, South Australia: Gordon and Breach.

Pool, R. (2001) *Fat: Fighting the Obesity Epidemic*, New York: Oxford University Press.

Powell, S. (2000) 'One in four Australian children is overweight. Slower, stiffer, heavier – they are the cotton-wool generation', *Weekend Australian*, 'Review' section, 27–28 May: 6–8.

Pratt, M., Macera, C. A. and Blanton, C. (1999) 'Levels of physical activity and inactivity in children and adults in the United States: current evidence and research issues', *Medicine and Science in Sports and Exercise* 31, 11 (Suppl.): S526–33.

Prentice, A. M. and Jebb, S. A. (1995) 'Obesity in Britain: gluttony or sloth?', *British Medical Journal* 311, 7002: 437–9.

Proctor, M. H., Moore, L. L., Gao, D., Cupples, L.A., Bradlee, M.L. *et al.* (2003) 'Television viewing and change in body fat from preschool to early adolescence: the Framingham Children's Study', *International Journal of Obesity and Related Metabolic Disorders* 27, 7: 827–33.

Pronger, B. (1995) 'Rendering the body: the implicit lessons of gross anatomy', *Quest* 47, 4: 427–46.

Radford, T. (2002) 'World health "threatened by obesity"', *Guardian*, 18 February: 8.

Raethel, S. (1996) 'Students caught out on sports' skill', *Sydney Morning Herald*, 17 January: 3.

Raethel, S. (1998) 'Students lack basic sporting abilities', *Sydney Morning Herald*, 14 February: 2.

Rehor, P. and Cottam, B. (2000) 'Physical activity levels of northern Tasmanian high school students', *ACHPER Healthy Lifestyles Journal* 47, 1: 14–17.

Rippe, J. M. and Hess, S. (1998) 'The role of physical activity in the prevention and management of obesity', *Journal of the American Dietitic Association* 98, 10 (Suppl. 2): S31–8.

Rissanen, A. and Fogelholm, M. (1999) 'Physical activity in the prevention and treatment of other morbid conditions and impairments associated with obesity: current evidence and research issues', *Medicine and Science in Sports and Exercise* 31, 11 (Suppl.): S635–45.

Robinson, T. (2003) 'Rest easy, couch potato, and blame it on your genes', *Virginian Pilot and the Ledger Star*, 19 January: C1.

Robinson, T. N. (1999) 'Reducing children's television viewing to prevent obesity: a randomized controlled trial', *Journal of the American Medical Association* 282, 16: 1561–7.

Robinson, T. N., Hammer, L. D., Killen, J. D., Kraemer, H. C., Wilson, D. M. *et al.* (1993) 'Does television viewing increase obesity and reduce physical activity? Cross-sectional and longitudinal analyses among adolescent girls', *Pediatrics* 91, 2: 273–80.

Roby, F. B. (1969) 'Physical activity: the prevention and control of obesity', *Physical Educator* 26, 4: 158–61.

Rogers, L. (1999) *Sexing the Brain*, London: Weidenfeld and Nicolson.

Rolland-Cachera, M. F. and Bellisle, F. (2002) 'Nutrition', in W. Burniat, T. Cole, I. Lissau and E. Poskitt (eds) *Child and Adolescent Obesity: Causes and Consequences, Prevention and Management*, Cambridge: Cambridge University Press.

Rush, E. C., Plank, L. D., Laulu, M. S. and Robinson, S. M. (1997) 'Predictions of the percentage of body fat from anthropometric measurements: comparison of New Zealand European and Polynesian women', *American Journal of Clinical Nutrition* 66: 2–7.

Russell, L. (1986) *Is Prevention Better than Cure?*, Washington, DC: Brookings Institution.

Safe, M. (2000) 'Nation wide', *The Australian*, 'The Australian Magazine' section, 30 September–1 October: 14–21.

Salbe, A. D. and Ravussin, E. (2000) 'The determinants of obesity', in C. Bouchard (ed.) *Physical Activity and Obesity*, Champaign, IL: Human Kinetics.

Salmon, J., Bauman, A., Crawford, D., Timperio, A. and Owen N. (2000) 'The association between television viewing and overweight among Australian adults participating in varying levels of leisure-time physical activity', *International Journal of Obesity and Related Metabolic Disorders* 24, 5: 600–6.

Saltin, B., Blomqvist, G., Mitchell, J. H., Johnson, R. L., Wildenthal, K. *et al.* (1968) 'Response to exercise after bed rest and after training', *Circulation* 28, 5 (Suppl. 7): VII, 1–78.

Saris, W. H. M., Blair, S. N., van Baak, M. A., Eaton, S. B., Davies, P. S. W. *et al.* (2003) 'How much physical activity is enough to prevent unhealthy weight gain? Outcome of the IASO 1st Stock Conference and consensus statement', *Obesity Reviews* 4, 2: 101–14.

Savage, M. P. and Scott, L. B. (1998) 'Physical activity and rural middle school adolescents', *Journal of Youth and Adolescence* 27, 2: 245–9.

Savill, T. D. (1893) 'Obesity treated by an exclusively nitrogenous diet and copious libations of warm water, with remarks on the excretion of uric acid by A. Haig', *The Lancet* 2: 133–4.

Schlosser, E. (2001) *Fast Food Nation: What the All-American Meal is Doing to the World*, London: Allen Lane.

Schoeller, D. A. (2003) 'But how much physical activity?', *American Journal of Clinical Nutrition* 78, 4: 669–70.

Schoenfelder, L. and Wieser, B. (eds) (1983) *Shadow on a Tightrope*, San Francisco, CA: Spinsters/Aunt Lute.

Schutz, Y. and Maffeis, C. (2002) 'Physical activity', in W. Burniat, T. Cole, I. Lissau and E. Poskitt (eds) *Child and Adolescent Obesity: Causes and Consequences, Prevention and Management*, Cambridge: Cambridge University Press.

Schwartz, H. (1986) *Never Satisfied: A Cultural History of Diets, Fantasies and Fat*, New York: The Free Press.

Schwartz, M. B. and Puhl, R. (2003) 'Childhood obesity: a societal problem to solve', *Obesity Reviews* 4, 1: 57–71.

Science News Letter (1952) 'Obesity is now no. 1 U.S. nutritional problem', 62, 27 December: 408.

Seidell, J. C. (2000) 'The current epidemic of obesity', in C. Bouchard (ed.) *Physical Activity and Obesity*, Champaign, IL: Human Kinetics.

Seidell, J. C., Hautvast, J. G. and Deurenberg P. (1989) 'Overweight: fat distribution and health risks. Epidemiological observations', *Infusionstherapie* 16, 6: 276–81.

Senn, N. (1887) 'Foreign correspondence', *Journal of the American Medical Association* 9: 347–51.

Sesso, H. D., Paffenbarger, R. S. and Lee, I. M. (2000) 'Physical activity and coronary heart disease in men: the Harvard Alumni Health Study', *Circulation* 102, 9: 975–80.

Sesso, H. D., Paffenbarger, R. S. and Lee, I. M. (2001) 'Alcohol consumption and risk of prostate cancer: the Harvard Alumni Health Study', *International Journal of Epidemiology* 30, 4: 749–55.

Shanahan, A. (2002) 'Why fat is a family issue', *Sunday Telegraph*, 15 September: 97.

Shannon, B., Peacock, J. and Brown, M. J. (1991) 'Body fatness, television viewing and calorie-intake of a sample of Pennsylvania sixth grade children', *Journal of Nutrition Education* 23: 262–8.

Sheehan, P. (2003) 'Reality bites – if you're fat, you're lazy too', *Sydney Morning Herald*, 13 January: 13.

Shell, E. R. (2002) *The Hungry Gene: The Science of Fat and the Future of Thin*, New York: Atlantic Monthly Press.

Shephard, R. J. (1989) *Body Composition in Biological Anthropology*, London: Cambridge University Press.

Shephard, R. J. (1994) 'Physical activity and reduction of health risks: how far are the benefits independent of fat loss?', *Journal of Sports Medicine and Physical Fitness* 34, 1: 91–8.

Shephard, R. J. (1997) 'What is the optimal type of physical activity to enhance health?', *British Journal of Sports Medicine* 31, 4: 277–84.

Shephard, R. J. (1999) 'How much physical activity is needed for good health?', *International Journal of Sports Medicine* 20, 1: 23–7.

Shepherd, R. and Stockley, L. (1987) 'Nutrition knowledge, attitudes and fat consumption', *Journal of American Dietetic Association* 87, 5: 615–19.

Shilling, C. (1993) *The Body and Social Theory*, London: Sage.

Shim, J. K. (2002) 'Understanding the routinised inclusion of race, socioeconomic status and sex in epidemiology: the utility of concepts from technoscience studies', *Sociology of Health and Illness* 24, 2: 129–50.

Siedentop, D. (1996) 'Valuing the physically active life: contemporary and future directions', *Quest* 48, 3: 266–74.

Simons-Morton, B. G., Taylor, W. C., Snider, S. A. and Huang, I. W. (1993) 'The physical activity of fifth-grade students during physical education classes', *American Journal of Public Health* 83, 2: 262–4.

Simons-Morton, B. G., Taylor, W. C., Snider, S. A., Huang, I. W. and Fulton, J. E. (1994) 'Observed levels of elementary and middle school children's physical activity during physical education classes', *Preventive Medicine* 23, 4: 437–41.

Skrabanek, P. (1992) 'The poverty of epidemiology', *Perspectives in Biology and Medicine* 35, 2: 182–5.

Slattery, M. L. (1996) 'How much physical activity do we need to maintain health and prevent disease? Different diseases – different mechanisms', *Research Quarterly for Exercise and Sport* 67, 2: 209–12.

Sleap, M., Warburton, P and Waring, M. (2000) 'Couch potato kids and lazy layabouts: the role of primary schools in relation to physical activity among children', in A. Williams (ed.) *Primary School Physical Education: Research Into Practice*, London: Routledge.

Smith, D. E. (1988) 'Femininity as discourse', in L. G. Roman and L. K. Christian-Smith (eds) *Becoming Feminine: The Politics of Popular Culture*, Lewes: Falmer Press.

Smith, W. D. (1974) *Stretching Their Bodies: The History of Physical Education*, Melbourne: Wren Publishing.

Sobal, J. (1995) 'The medicalization and demedicalization of obesity', in D. Maurer and J. Sobal (eds) *Eating Agendas: Food and Nutrition as Social Problems*, New York: Aldine de Gruyter.

Sobal, J. and Stunkard, A. J. (1989) 'Socioeconomic status and obesity: a review of the literature', *Psychological Bulletin* 105, 2: 260–75.

Spitzer, B. L., Henderson, K. A. and Zivian, M. T. (1999) 'Gender differences in population versus media body sizes: a comparison over four decades', *Sex Roles* 40, 7/8: 545–65.

Stacey, M. (1994) *Why Americans Love, Hate and Fear Food*, New York: Simon & Schuster.

Stearns, P. N. (1997) *Fat History: Bodies and Beauty in the Modern West*, New York: New York University Press.

Stehbens, W. E. (1992) 'Causality in medical science with particular reference to heart disease and atherosclerosis', *Perspectives in Biology and Medicine* 36, 1: 97–119.

Stice, E., Cameron, R. P., Killen, J. D., Hayward, C. and Taylor, C. B. (1999) 'Naturalistic weight-reduction efforts prospectively predict growth in relative weight and onset of obesity among female adolescents', *Journal of Consulting and Clinical Psychology* 67, 6: 967–74.

Strauss, R. S. and Pollack, H. A. (2001) 'Epidemic increase in childhood overweight, 1986–1998', *Journal of the American Medical Association* 286, 22: 2845–8.

Strauss, R. S. and Pollack, H. A. (2003) 'Social marginalization of overweight children', *Archives of Pediatrics and Adolescent Medicine* 157, 8: 746–52.

Stunkard, A. J. (1991) 'Genetic contributions to human obesity', *Research Publications – Association for Research in Nervous and Mental Disease* 69: 205–18.

Stunkard, A. J and Penick, S. B. (1979) 'Behavior modification in the treatment of obesity – the problem of maintaining weight loss', *Archives of General Psychiatry* 36, 7: 801–6.

Stunkard, A., d'Aquili, E., Fox, S. and Filion, R. D. L. (1972) 'Influence of social class on obesity and thinness in children', *Journal of the American Medical Association* 221, 6: 579–84.

Stunkard, A. J., Harris, J. R., Pedersen, N. L. and McClearn, G. E. (1990) 'The body-mass index of twins who have been reared apart', *New England Journal of Medicine* 322, 21: 1483–7.

Stunkard, A. J., La Fleur, W. R. and Wadden, T. A. (1998) 'Stigmatization of obesity in medieval times: Asia and Europe', *International Journal of Obesity and Related Metabolic Disorders* 22, 12: 1141–4.

Sunday Advertiser (2000) 'Aussie silver for obesity', 10 September: 7.

Sunnegardh, J., Bratteby, L. E., Hagman, U., Samuelson, G. and Sjolin, S. (1986) 'Physical activity in relation to energy intake and body fat in 8- and 13-year-old children in Sweden', *Acta Paediatrica Scandinavica* 75, 6: 955–63.

Swan, P. A. (1993) 'This is really important, you need to know this': hierarchies of subject knowledge within physical education teacher education and student intention, unpublished Ed.D. thesis, Geelong: Deakin University.

Sweeney, M. E., Hill, J. O., Heller, P. A., Baney, R. and DiGirolamo, M. (1993) 'Severe vs moderate energy restriction with and without exercise in the treatment of obesity: efficiency of weight loss', *American Journal of Clinical Nutrition* 57, 2: 127–34.

Swinburn, B. and Egger, G. (2002) 'Preventive strategies against weight gain and obesity', *Obesity Reviews* 3, 2: 289–301.

Swinburn, B. A., Ley, S. J., Carmichael, H. E. and Plank, L. D. (1999) 'Body size and composition in Polynesians', *International Journal of Obesity* 23: 1178–83.

Sydney Morning Herald (2001) 'Americans too well rounded to feel the pinch', 10 January: 7.

Tabakoff, J. (2002) 'Slam the brakes on fast food before health problems get any worse', *Sydney Morning Herald*, 13 August: 11.

Taras, H. L., Sallis, J. F., Patterson, T. L., Nader, P. R. and Nelson, J. A. (1989) 'Television's influence on children's diet and physical activity', *Journal of Developmental and Behavioral Pediatrics* 10, 4: 176–80.

Tebbel, C. (2000) *The Body Snatchers: How the Media Shapes Women*, Sydney: Finch Publishing.

Telama, R. and Yang, X. (2000) 'Decline of physical activity from youth to young adulthood in Finland', *Medicine and Science in Sports and Exercise* 32, 9: 1617–22.

Teutsch, D. (2002a) 'High blood pressure and only aged seven', *Sun-Herald*, 20 January: 10–11.

Teutsch, D. (2002b) 'Aussie kids can't jump . . . as far as they used to', *Sun-Herald*, 7 July: 10–11.

Thornhill, R. and Palmer, C. T. (2000) *A Natural History of Rape: Biological Bases for Sexual Coercion*, Cambridge, MA: MIT Press.

Tinning, R. (2004) 'Conclusion: ruminations on body knowledge and control and the spaces for hope and happening', in J. Evans, B. Davis and J. Wright (eds) *Body Knowledge and Control: Studies in the Sociology of Physical Education and Health*, London: Routledge, pp. 218–39.

Tinning, R. and Fitzclarence, L. (1992) 'Postmodern youth culture and the crisis in Australian secondary school physical education' *Quest* 44, 3: 287–304.

Tremblay, A., Cote, J. and LeBlanc, J. (1983) 'Diminished dietary thermogenesis in exercise-trained human subjects', *European Journal of Applied Physiology* 52: 1–4.

Trost, S. G., Pate, R. R., Dowda, M., Saunders, R., Ward, D. S. *et al.* (1996) 'Gender differences in physical activity and determinants of physical activity in rural fifth grade children', *Journal of School Health* 66, 4: 145–50.

Tucker, L. A. (1986) 'The relationship of television viewing to physical fitness and obesity', *Adolescence* 21, 84: 797–806.

Tverdal, A. (1986) 'Body mass index and incidence of tuberculosis', *European Journal of Respiratory Diseases* 69, 5: 355–62.

Twisk, J. W. R. (2001) 'Physical activity guidelines for children and adolescents: a critical review', *Sports Medicine* 31, 8: 617–27.

Vatten, L. J. and Kvinnsland, S. (1992) 'Prospective study of height, body mass index and risk of breast cancer', *Acta Oncologica* 31, 2: 195–200.

Viru, A. and Harro, M. (2003) 'Biological aspects of physical activity and health', in J. McKenna and C. Riddoch (eds) *Perspectives on Health and Exercise*, Basingstoke: Palgrave.

Vogel, S. (1999) *The Skinny on Fat: Our Obsession with Weight Control*, New York: W. H. Freeman and Company.

Wake, M., Hesketh, K. and Waters, E. (2003) 'Television, computer use and body mass index in Australian primary school children', *Journal of Paediatrics and Child Health* 39, 2: 130–4.

Waller, C. E., Du, S. and Popkin, B. M. (2003) 'Patterns of overweight, inactivity, and snacking in Chinese children' *Obesity Research* 11, 8: 957–61.

Wang, Y. (2001) 'Cross-national comparison of childhood obesity: the epidemic and the relationship between obesity and socioeconomic status', *International Journal of Epideimology* 30, 5: 1129–36.

Wannamethee, S. G., Shaper, A. G. and Walker, M. (1998) 'Changes in physical activity, mortality, and incidence of coronary heart disease in older men', *The Lancet* 351, 9116: 1603–8.

Waters, E. B. and Baur, L. A. (2003) 'Childhood obesity: modernity's scourge', *Medical Journal of Australia* 178, 9: 422–3.

Waxman, M. and Stunkard, A. J. (1980) 'Caloric intake and expenditure of obese boys', *Journal of Pediatrics* 96, 2: 187–93.

Weinsier, R. L., Hunter, G. R., Heini, A. F., Goran, M. I. and Sell, S. M. (1998) 'The etiology of obesity: relative contribution of metabolic factors, diet, and physical activity', *American Journal of Medicine* 105, 2: 145–50.

Weinstock, R. S., Dai, H. and Wadden, T. A. (1998) 'Diet and exercise in the treatment of obesity: effects of 3 interventions on insulin resistance', *Archives of Internal Medicine* 158, 22: 2477–83.

West, K. M. (1974) 'Culture, history and adiposity, or should Santa Clause reduce', *Obesity and Bariatric Medicine* 3, 2: 48–52.

Westerterp, K. R. (1999a) 'Assessment of physical activity level in relation to obesity: current evidence and research issues', *Medicine and Science in Sports and Exercise* 31, 11 (Suppl.): S522–5.

Westerterp, K. R. (1999b) 'Obesity and physical activity', *International Journal of Obesity and Related Metabolic Disorders* 23, 1 (Suppl.): 59–64.

Whitehead, R. G., Paul, A. A. and Cole, T. J. (1982) 'Trends in food energy intakes throughout childhood from one to 18 years', *Human Nutrition: Applied Nutrition* 36: 57–62.

Whitfield, K. E., Weidner, G., Clark, R. and Anderson, N. B. (2002) 'Sociodemographic diversity and behavioural medicine', *Journal of Consulting and Clinical Psychology* 70, 3: 463–81.

Willett, W. C. (1998) 'Is dietary fat a major determinant of body fat?', *American Journal of Clinical Nutrition* 67, 3 (Suppl.): 556S–62S.

Willett, W. C. and Leibel, R. L. (2002) 'Dietary fat is not a major determinant of body fat', *American Journal of Medicine* 113, 9B (Suppl.): 47S–59S.

Williams, A. S. and Roughan, P. (1986) 'Fat – again', The *Medical Journal of Australia*, 145, 9: 429–30.

Wilmore, J. H. (1983) 'Body composition in sport and exercise: directions for future research', *Medicine and Science in Sports and Exercise* 15, 1: 21–31.

Wing, R. R. (1999) 'Physical activity in the treatment of the adulthood overweight and obesity: current evidence and research issues', *Medicine and Science in Sports and Exercise* 31, 11 (Suppl.): S547–52.

Wolf, A. M., Gortmaker, S. L., Cheung, L., Gray, H. M., Herzog, D. B. *et al.* (1993) 'Activity, inactivity, and obesity: racial, ethnic, and age differences among schoolgirls', *American Journal of Public Health* 83, 11: 1625–7.

Wolf, N. (1990) *The Beauty Myth*, London: Chatto & Windus.

Wooley, S. C. and Wooley, O. W. (1984) 'Should obesity be treated at all?', in A. J. Stunkard and E. Stellar (eds) *Eating and Its Disorders*, New York: Raven Press.

World Health Organization (2000) *Obesity: Preventing and Managing the Global Epidemic* (WHO Technical Report Series 894). Geneva: World Health Organization.

World Health Organization (2004) *WHO Mortality Data Base*. Online. Available at: www3.who.int/whosis/menu.cfm?path=whosis,mort&language=english (accessed 10 February 2004).

Wright, J. and Burrows, L. (2004) '"Being healthy": the discursive construction of health in New Zealand children's responses to the National Education Monitoring Project', *Discourse* 25, 2: 211–30.

Wright Mills, C. (2000) [1959] *The Sociological Imagination*, Oxford: Oxford University Press.

Yelling, M., Penney, D. and Swaine, I. L. (2000) 'Physical activity in physical education', *European Journal of Physical Education* 5, 1: 45–66.

Young, K. (2001) 'War on obesity begins in infancy', *Ottawa Citizen*. Online. Available at: www.ottawacitizen.com/national/010307/5054309.html (accessed 10 March 2001).

Index

Note: page numbers in *italics* denote material in figures or tables